Robert A. Ortalda, Jr., CPA

How to Live Within Your Means and Still Finance Your Dreams

A FIRESIDE BOOK
PUBLISHED BY SIMON & SCHUSTER INC.
NEW YORK · LONDON · TORONTO · SYDNEY · TOKYO

FIRESIDE
Simon & Schuster Building
Rockefeller Center
1230 Avenue of the Americas
New York, New York 10020

First Fireside Edition, 1990
Published by arrangement with Doubleday, a division of
Bantam, Doubleday, Dell Publishing Group, Inc.

FIRESIDE and colophon are registered trademarks
of Simon & Schuster Inc.

Manufactured in the United States of America

10   9   8   7   6   5   4   3   2   1   Pbk.

Library of Congress Cataloging in Publication Data

Ortalda, Robert A.
    How to live within your means and still finance your dreams /
Robert A. Ortalda, Jr.—1st Fireside ed.
        p.   cm.
    "A Fireside book."
    1. Finance, Personal.   2. Debt.   I. Title.
HG179.O773   1990
332.024—dc20
                                                            89-23660
                                                            CIP

ISBN 0-671-69607-6 Pbk.

To Mary, Michelle and Michael, the sources of my Sanity, Financial and otherwise

Acknowledgments

I can't possibly thank all the people who helped make this book a reality. Here are some of the major players.

Mary, my wife and favorite Financial Sanity pal, who invented more of the system than even she knows, and who has been a Financial Sanity widow for more than three years as I have labored to bring this work to you, the reader.

Claire Ortalda, kid sister and the best editor in the whole damned world. Claire spent hours and days poring over every detail of this book—from initial conception to final draft—to make a very technical subject as readable as possible. Where this book is understandable and light, you are seeing Claire's work. Where it is ponderous, obscure or pedantic, you are seeing where I got in Claire's way.

Marcia Lanahan, who did a little bit of everything on this book, especially research, organization, transcription and manuscript typing. Without Marcia's sunny disposition and loyal assistance, I'd be a whole lot grouchier and the manuscript would still not be complete.

Robin Castagno, who first encouraged me to invent the Financial Sanity system and present it in workshops; Carol Orsborn, who conceived of the book project and showed me how to make it happen.

Linda Stradley, who inspired me to my first successful budget; Fred Monson, with whom I developed my first original analytical model; Jeanne Kolchak, who helped develop some of the original materials for the Financial Sanity Workshop; John Brockman and Katinka Matson; Les Pockell at Doubleday, for having faith in this book before a single chapter had been written; Casey Fuetsch, my editor at Doubleday; Vic Bull and Tom Petrie of Thunderware, Inc., who have been accommodating, understanding and supportive.

Volunteer editors Carol Costello and Dave Sylvester, whose valuable insights helped shape this book and whose appreciation and encouragement helped keep me going.

My parents, Jeanne and Bob Ortalda, who learned to let me challenge every Great Truth—even the ones they believed.

Many, many others who helped critique, name, promote and perfect the Financial Sanity system and this book. I thank you all.

Contents

xii Contents

xiv   Contents

xvi   Contents

Do we not live in dreams?
—*Alfred, Lord Tennyson*

There is nothing like dream to create the future.
—*Victor Hugo*

Introduction

We live in dreams. Our hopes, aspirations and goals get us up in the morning and—sometimes—keep us up at night.

Our dreams are romantic, lofty, sexy and boring. They are mundane, responsible and sensible. But more than anything else they are ours, and whether we are happy or satisfied with our lives depends, in great part, on whether we have dreams and whether we can make them happen.

This is, first and foremost, a book about dreams. The focus on money is incidental. Because people think that money is what's in the way of achieving their dreams, money becomes a dragon to slay along the road to fulfilling our hopes and aspirations.

This, then, is more than a book about money. True, every chapter is filled with details of what I believe is the best money management system ever published. But nowhere do I ask you to care about money for its own sake. Money is for making your dreams happen—nothing more and nothing less.

The Financial Sanity Workshop

The material in this book is based on a workshop I developed and have been teaching in the San Francisco Bay Area since 1985. The Financial Sanity Workshop (originally called the Personal Budgeting Workshop and, later, the Income/Outcome Seminar) focuses on making decisions—about debt, about spending, about what your priorities are—decisions not just about money, but about your life.

But even before you get to the decision-making "guts" of the program, the Financial Sanity system helps you answer three key questions:

- Where are you going?
- Where are you right now?
- How much financial power do you have to get you where you want to go?

Where Are You Going?

I'll have you delve into your hopes and dreams very early on in this book. After a short pep talk and an all-out attack on financial fallacies, I'll encourage you to romp among your fondest aspirations. Enjoy yourself. (We'll think about reality later.)

Whatever your dreams:

- buying a house
- reducing five-figure debt to zero
- going back to school
- quitting work to devote full time to raising children
- taking time off to write a novel
- starting a business
- building a dream house
- taking a trip to Nepal
- breaking out of a hated job

the Financial Sanity system can help you get there.

Where Are You Right Now?

After you've done some constructive fantasizing, we'll explore where you are now. I'll guide you through the rather traditional exercise of building your own Balance Sheet and calculating your Net Worth.

Although most of the techniques in the Financial Sanity system are new and radical, preparing the Balance Sheet is not. If you already know about putting a Balance Sheet together, skim through Chapters 4 and 5 quickly.

While the Balance Sheet is one measure of your financial health—describing what you own and owe at a single point in time—another important question is how much money is flowing in and out of your financial life each month. The Inflow-Outflow Information Sheet described in Chapter 6 is an elegantly efficient system for capturing that data on just one or two sheets of paper. After you've "put your filing cabinet on a diet" with the Balance Sheet and Inflow-Outflow worksheet, you'll be able to do the rest of your planning at the beach, if you want.

How Much Spending Power Do You Have?

The concept of Spending Power, which we tackle in Chapter 7, is much trickier, but it has the potential to teach you more about the dynamics of your personal finances than you could discover anywhere else. We will bring reality face-to-face with your dreams, allowing you to map out financially the wish list you developed earlier in the book.

At some point, you may be seized with the urge to revamp your entire personal accounting system. When that happens, feel free to jump to Appendix A, where I've included a number of helpful hints on keeping your books organized.

Decision-Making

In the Financial Sanity system, budgeting is not "financial dieting" but a *decision-making* process. It focuses not on accounting or self-discipline but rather on making decisions about your life and choosing specific plans to make them real.

We start with decisions about debt. You'll learn my step-by-step approach to deciding *how* and *when* you'll get rid of the unwanted debt in your life. By the time you're done, you'll be able to tell anyone who'll listen exactly when you'll have your credit cards (or any other debt) paid off.

Next, I introduce you to *funding,* which forms the most important and most enjoyably useful part of the Financial Sanity system. This revolutionary and sophisticated version of a very traditional and unsophisticated money management technique—the old practice of stuffing money in different labeled envelopes—has been expanded to provide financial peace to those of us whose lives are far more complicated than the lives of our grandparents or even our parents, who might have used this system in its earlier, simple form.

Funding is both the guts of the Financial Sanity system and its magic. It's the part that makes your dreams come true.

Through funding we put an end to the entire concept of saving. I don't believe in saving, and I'll try to turn you against it, too. If you can accept my rejection of this traditional and time-honored concept, you'll improve your grasp of financial reality several hundred percent.

Once you have developed the habits and skills to fund a vacation, you'll see that it is a short step to expand your funding program to include longer-range goals, such as your children's education and your retirement.

No book about budgeting would be complete without talking about balancing the budget. (You may want to buy a copy of this book for your congressman, with a bookmark in Chapter 20.) To make sure that your carefully laid budget plans aren't pure fantasy, this chapter also shows you how to monitor your actual performance.

The rest of this book covers some of the more advanced budgeting situations you may face. And you *will* face at least some of them. Financial planning in the eighties and nineties is a simple matter for very few of us.

I show you how to cope with bonuses and erratic income. You'll see how "Yellow-Pad Mini-Budgets" help you avoid spending "extra" money two or three times over.

We'll discuss in detail the planning issues involved in buying a first house—or a bigger one.

We cover techniques to make sure your dreams come true, including the "necessary dream" of attaining financial independence, either at retirement age or before. And I'll show you how to realize the kinds of dreams that are typically hard to plan for—and therefore often not attained.

And when you've dreamed and planned and funded your way through my system, you'll achieve another dream—a dream you may not even know you had, but one which most people share. That dream is to exercise, once and for all, mastery over your own money.

A Vision of Success

What does it feel like to master money?

First of all, mastering money doesn't feel like something—it feels like something gone. It feels like a burden taken off your shoulders, a mist removed from in front of your eyes, an ache taken out of your stomach.

I remember the chilling feeling of checking the mail for terrifying bills I might not be prepared to handle. I remember racing deposits to the bank, trying to beat checks I had written days ago. And I remember lying in bed at night, when the noise of the day had quieted enough for me to listen to my anxieties about money. Somehow, with the money mastery I've gained from my Financial Sanity system, I've had to learn to live without these little rushes of adrenaline.

Money has ceased to be a problem. It's just no longer a source of anxiety, a reason for disappointment. Anything my wife Mary and I want to do, we can do. Some things we have to wait for—but we always know how many months we have to wait. And sometimes it is just a question of adjusting priorities. We aren't inflexible. We make plans and change them—often—but always using the Financial Sanity system as our analytical and decision-making tool.

We're in charge. We're masters of our destinies. We're like kids playing house: anything we invent can come true. All we have to do is want it more than something else. It isn't magical, it just works.

I hope this book helps you develop the same relationship with money. Maybe you and I can start a little revolution—a very quiet revolution of people who neither show off our money nor complain about it, just use it as the tool it is for the far more important goal of realizing our dreams.

I wish you quiet, peaceful prosperity.

BOB ORTALDA
Redwood City, California

How to Live Within Your Means and Still Finance Your Dreams

Whatever the baby boom wants, the baby boom is going to get.
  —*Bickley Townsend*

It's hard to renounce materialism when materialism is renouncing you.
  —*James Kunen*

1

Baby Boomer Economics

When I developed the Financial Sanity system in 1985, I did it to help my friends, members of that vast, overanalyzed, much-marketed-to baby boom generation born within the fifteen years following World War II.

The Failure of Conventional Wisdom

Because I was a certified public accountant, my friends would ask me for advice: "We need a tax shelter," they would say. So, they would come in for an appointment. They would show me their $40,000 incomes and complain about their huge $7,000 tax bills. I would say: "You don't need a tax shelter. At $40,000 a year you really don't make enough to afford a tax shelter. Besides—you have no cash! The best you can do is try to save up enough to put a down payment on a house."

These friends were victims of misconception and myth. They heard so much about tax sheltering from their friends, from brokers, from the media, from everyone, that they assumed that that was what you did when you made a little money. So whenever my friends developed the initiative to put their financial house in order, they were likely to consult an investment or tax advisor rather than do what they should be doing—analyzing their goals and deciding how to meet them.

But it was the story of Tom and Jennifer that really opened my eyes to the failure of the investment-oriented community of financial planners to help the high-earning but free-spending baby boomers.

Tom and Jennifer made a handsome joint income. Convinced that they were "getting killed with taxes," they were determined to invest in a tax shelter. They consulted a certified financial planner I knew and a few days later, at their request, I checked with the financial planner to review what he had recommended.

"They're making good money, but they're spending everything they make. I put them into a mutual fund," he said. "They're going to send me $50 a month to invest."

I was shocked. "Fifty dollars a month?" I asked. "These people make $150,000 a year!"

"I know," said the financial planner, "but that's all they said they could afford."

I was disappointed and a little worried by all this. But the real revelation came a few months later when I checked on Tom and Jennifer: How did they like the financial planner? How was their investment program going?

They confessed: They hadn't kept up with the program. Cash flow was just too tight.

What was going on here? A working couple ought to be able to scrape by on $150,000 a year! What's $50 next to more than $10,000 in pretax monthly income? Five hundred dollars a month should have been easy for them—and they couldn't save $50.

I realized that there was something wrong with either the economics or the psychology of this generation—or with both. Why can't a young professional family live—and save—on $150,000? Why does everyone seem to have huge credit card debt?

Why are so many of my friends having a hard time buying a house? What use is the conventional wisdom on buying a house when real estate prices escalate so fast that you "lose" more than you save while you're trying to save up for a down payment?

Are we supposed to listen to Uncle George's investment advice? When he learned investing, mutual funds were exotic. We're offered GNMA funds, mortgage-backed securities, real estate and other limited partnerships, options, futures, commodities, single-premium life insurance . . .

With a six-figure income and five-figure credit card debt, are we supposed to consult budgeting systems designed for high-school students? Or, at the other extreme, heed financial planning books that don't even have a single chapter on budgeting?

Maybe we should read national magazines that cover money and finance. Their articles and ads seem to be aimed at people like us, but all they ever really talk about is investing. When is someone going to tell us how to manage our portfolios—of debt?

The plain and awful truth is that no one addresses the real needs of the young individual, couple or family that enjoys a reasonably adequate income but is still not out of the woods financially. What is supposed to be the most advertised-to, catered-to, targeted group in the country has been patently ignored on what may be its most vital issue.

What's behind this lack of informed guidance? Surely there is no organized conspiracy to rob baby boomers of prosperity. Conventional wisdom failed us simply because the financial environment changed while no one was looking.

Bait and Switch: A Generation Fooled

For decades and decades a happy, reliable pattern had occurred in the postwar American economy. People tended to make more money after working ten years or so. The American full-time worker could count on climbing the economic ladder with ever-increasing prosperity.

But the oldest of our generation were fooled. Hit by the double blow of inflation and a deluge of competition among ourselves, the first baby boomers actually experienced a decrease in real earnings in their second decade in the work force. This unforeseen and unnoticed phenomenon, coupled with a less thrifty attitude than that of prior generations, put us in debt and out of control.

By historical pattern, Americans had come to expect a significant increase in real income in the decade following what might be called our "entry-level" ages of 25 to 34. ("Real" increases are wage increases that have been adjusted for the loss of buying power due to inflation.)

The man who is 65* today experienced an average of 63 percent more buying power from the time he was 30 to the time he was 40.

Now let's look at what happened to people who are 55 today. First of all, they started off making more money at 30 than the generation ten

---

*Statistics for men's incomes are used because those for the entire population reflect too many variables, including changes in the status and participation of women in the workplace.

years older. Today's 55-year-olds earned 44 percent more at 30 than the group before them earned at 30.

And today's 55-year-olds also experienced a very comfortable 49 percent increase in real earnings from when they were 30 to when they were 40.

We have a nice pattern going here, don't we? Every decade, the younger workers make more than their predecessors had at the same age. And then, after working about ten years, they make about half again as much as they did when they were 30.

Now let's look at those people who are now about 45, the first baby boomers.

In the beginning, everything looked rosy. At 30 this group made 37 percent more than the group that came ten years earlier. Presumably these vanguard baby boomers had every reason to believe that, after inflation was taken into account, their earnings would go up about 50 percent by the time they were 40. After all, that's what had happened to the generations that preceded them.

But that's not what happened to the people who are now 45. On the average, after working ten years, this group wasn't making any more money than they were a decade earlier.

If you're not yourself a member of this age group, imagine the confusion these older baby boomers must have felt (and are, perhaps, still feeling). Keep in mind that no one knew their real earnings were going down. Paychecks were, after all, getting larger—but inflation was moving faster.

The other happy pattern of history—the general rise in incomes of 30-year-olds—was destined to reverse itself when people like me, who are now nearing forty, were 30. Instead of making about a third more than the men 10 years before us, we made 26 percent less.

In short, most people were unaware that real earnings were falling— and some still haven't figured it out. They think they're just somehow missing the financial management boat.

"Maybe Dad was right," they say.

Why Dad and Uncle Ralph Were Wrong

Dad and Uncle Ralph were probably saying: "Don't go running up a lot of debt. If you haven't got the cash for it, don't buy it."

"You've got some pretty fancy tastes for someone who's had a job for only six months," they would accuse. And they would warn ominously that it was none too soon to start putting aside cash for retirement.

So, while Dad and Uncle Ralph were more than happy to tell you everything they thought you needed to know about how to manage your money, you were likely to be rolling your eyes at the ceiling, crossing your arms, sighing and tapping your toe with characteristic patience.

Five or ten years later, Dad and Uncle Ralph were waiting for us to humbly admit that they were right again. But we weren't humble. Why? Because Dad and Uncle Ralph *weren't* right. They were wrong!

This whole scene took place in an environment of hyperinflation. The money Dad and Ralph saved was worth less than when they first entered it in their savings passbooks. On the other hand, *we* had learned the fine art of buying now—before the price goes up—and paying later, with cheaper dollars.

Dad and Uncle Ralph's advice was of no use to us. What we were learning "in the real world" was far more reliable. But what we were learning was about leverage and how to survive in an inflationary economy. What happens when inflation is gone? We are left with no skills, no guidance. Everything we know about economics is based on an inflationary model. Not only do we not have any noninflationary real-world experience, we don't have any credible advice from the old-timers, Dad and Ralph having been thoroughly discredited long ago.

Not that Dad and Uncle Ralph really had anything to say to us at this point. You see, they lived in one world, while we lived in ours.

Dad, Ralph and virtually everyone they played golf with already owned his own home. They had low-interest mortgages, with payments that couldn't cover our studio apartment rent. Their housing costs fixed, inflation hit them lightly and often did more to increase their salaries than it did to increase their costs of living.

Inflation did not hit us lightly at all. During inflationary spirals, it's better if you have things—houses, furniture, cars and so forth—already. We were new kids on the block and we didn't own much of anything already. We had to buy it all at new and higher prices. Inflation and a glut of graduating baby boomers on the job market dealt a nasty double blow that caused (inflation-adjusted) real entry-level wages to fall for the first time in postwar history.

And we entered an economically *complex* time—a time when the old, simple rules that Dad and Ralph had relied on would no longer work. We lived with the anxiety of not owning real estate while home prices escalated all around us. Other innovations added to the complexity, including the relatively new all-purpose credit cards, tax shelters, new kinds of investments and new kinds of debt. The low interest offered by still-regulated bank savings accounts became a cruel joke.

6   How to Live Within Your Means

Easy Money: The Credit Conspiracy

Fortunately, The Pusher was there to help us out of our bind. And, like any good dealer, this pusher got us hooked on free samples:

> Because of your excellent credit, you automatically qualify for the SilliBank NastyCard. Yes, because you ran up your last card to its limit in two months and have been making minimum payments ever since [meaning you won't pay off your balance for 5 years], we know you can handle credit wisely. That's why we're sending you this *new* card . . .

Or:

> Just sign the enclosed draft and we will send you a check for $2,000 right now. Spend it any way you like—take a vacation, buy a stereo, make home improvements [on the house you'll never be able to buy because you've buried yourself in consumer debt that will take you a decade to pay off]. . . .

You get the picture. We were willing to delude ourselves. After all, these banks had granite columns and marble floors. If they said it was all right to take their money, who were we to argue?

While the bait-and-switch phenomenon encouraged us to overspend, the new credit cards let us do it painlessly. Credit cards had became a way of life—our life. Giddy inflation encouraged other kinds of debt as both borrowers and banks got carried away with the prospect of high future incomes and low costs of funds from still-regulated bank accounts. And plastic was just one of the girders propping up our lifestyles.

Propping Up Our Lifestyles

The baby boom generation has employed a variety of tricks to mask—mostly from itself—the decline in real earning power. Frank Levy and Richard Michels of the Urban Institute have helped identify six key strategies we use (often unconsciously) to make up for the fact that our incomes are often woefully inadequate to support the lifestyle to which we have chosen to become accustomed:

- postponing marriage
- postponing children
- help from parents (especially for first-time home buyers)
- two-career couples
- smaller houses
- borrowing (instead of saving a little bit each month and building up the proverbial nest egg, the baby boomers have tended to overspend a little bit each month, establishing benchmark standards of living

that their incomes don't support, and building up a "portfolio of debt" that they now feel compelled to get rid of)

The implications of these dynamics frighten some observers. They worry that the baby boomers may not be able to withstand a recession, or that we will be financially unprepared for retirement. And, based solely on the performance of our generation to date, the doomsayers have the strength of evidence on their side.

I am more hopeful, however. I sense that the mood of the generation is shifting toward a new era characterized by more and more people resolving to get their individual acts together. As I observe baby boomers in the Financial Sanity Workshops and in my consulting practice, and as I track the mood of the larger population as reflected in the media, it seems that there is new emphasis on financial responsibility, on reducing debt. The free-spending yuppie has been declared dead by none other than the Madison Avenue flacks who conveniently promoted and characterized him. The sexy and expensive BMW is no longer de rigueur among the generation. The new trademarks are more pedestrian Hondas, minivans and little square jeeps. It all adds up to what I call "financial maturity."

But it's likely to take more than a mood swing to get an entire generation on firm financial footing—to convince the economically weary not to give up on unfulfilled dreams.

The Three Stages of Financial Maturity

In observing the way that baby boomers spend their money, I have identified three stages of financial maturity:

- *Adolescent*—spends tomorrow's earnings today.
  FUNDAMENTAL ATTITUDES: "Why can't I have it now?" "I deserve it." "Why wait?" "Things will work out somehow."
  DANGER: Easily plunged into disaster by unforeseen events. Building up debt that will prove to be a hardship later.
  CLASSIC EXAMPLES: The yuppie cliché; the federal government.
- *Young Adult*—spends today's earnings today and repays overspending from adolescent stage.
  FUNDAMENTAL ATTITUDES: "Gotta get out of debt—and stay out." "Still want to enjoy the present. Will work on the future later."
  DANGER: Financial condition still fragile. Poor planning may result in no progress.
  CLASSIC EXAMPLES: First-time home buyers; new parents.
- *Mature Adult*—finances tomorrow's spending today.
  FUNDAMENTAL ATTITUDE: "Be prepared."

DANGER: Too much fear and not enough planning, leading to oversaving. Or poor planning leading to undersaving.
CLASSIC EXAMPLE: Your parents.

You might want to notice where you are on this scale. Don't automatically assume that you're not in the Adolescent Stage—a great many people of our generation are. There isn't anything inherently immoral about this stage, but everyone has to give it up and bite the bullet sooner or later. As a generation, we just tend to stay at the Adolescent Stage longer, not so much by immature and irresponsible choice but by the failure of our apparently growing incomes to keep pace with our expectations and with galloping inflation.

This book takes its readers from the Adolescent Stage to the stage I'm calling Young Adult. This transformation involves two potentially wrenching adjustments:

• reversing a pattern of overspending
• paying off the debt generated by overspending in the past

This "double" adjustment is plenty to bite off. Beware of the impulse to leapfrog to the Mature Adult Stage. To immediately add retirement planning to your financial program might overburden it. The work you do (in the Young Adult Stage) to reduce debt and bring your spending and income into alignment is essentially "brush-clearing" that you need to do before you can start laying the foundations of your retirement-planning structure.

This book also moves you directly—almost automatically—from the Young Adult Stage to the Mature Adult Stage—when you're ready.

The Young Adult, as well as the Adolescent, experiences nagging anxieties. (The Adolescent knows he's overspending and worries about whether things will, indeed, "work out.") The Young Adult, while happy to be in control of current spending, wonders if there will be money enough to meet the potentially enormous cash needs of the future: college for the kids, retirement, travel, etc.

These anxieties may not be enough to keep you up at night—we are, after all, a generation of optimists—but they are likely to urge you on to the next stage.

After moving you from the Adolescent Stage to the Young Adult Stage, the Financial Sanity system poises you—in two important ways—to automatically make the transition to the Mature Adult Stage.

First, remember that, as Young Adults, part of what we're doing is paying off the extravagances of our Adolescent period; we're repaying debt. As that debt gets paid off, the monthly cash flow used to retire debt suddenly becomes available for, if you choose, longer-range funding projects, such as retirement, college and other future spending plans that characterize the Mature Adult.

Second, as you master this system, you will learn to plan virtually all of your significant spending in advance. So, over time, as additional money becomes available, regardless of source, the opportunity to fund for longer-range expenses will not be washed away in a splash of impulse spending or "emergency" expenditures. This kind of planning may not sound very enjoyable and spontaneous, but it's actually very important to keeping the magic and excitement of your dreams. The Young Adult and Mature Adult stages are where you begin to prove to yourself that you have the power to make your dreams happen.

"But my needs are far simpler than that," you may protest. "I don't want to be on the cutting edge. I just need to get my act together a little bit. Just show me the basics."

Let me give two quick answers to those of you who are protesting:

- Just because these techniques are new, sophisticated and powerful does not mean that they are difficult.
- These *are* the basics. We've been deluded for decades into thinking that personal financial management is a walk in the park. It's not. Most of us average folks have vastly more complicated financial lives than the well-to-do of a century ago. We need tools—sophisticated tools—to match the complexity of our lives.

Forgive Yourself

It's okay. Admit it. You can afford only a part of the good life. In fact, go ahead and admit that you can't even afford some of the good life that you're currently enjoying—on credit. I hope, by showing you some of the economic dynamics of the times we've lived through, that you will realize that you are not as alone as perhaps you thought you were. I hope, too, to convince you to forgive yourself for whatever mess you feel you've made of your finances—for whatever opportunities you feel you've missed.

When you do, you will be filled with a forgiving new sense of self. This cosmic understanding of the interrelatedness of humanity will create in you a sense of peace and euphoria that will last about ten minutes. After that, the pragmatic, materialistic, cynical and responsible side of you will say: "Wait a minute! I still want what I want! I still need what I need."

At that magic moment, you will be psychologically primed to master the Financial Sanity system of money management, which is about to unfold for you.

I invite you to make your hopes and dreams more important than money. I invite you to become financially responsible—on your own terms.

I invite you to Financial Sanity.

For the great enemy of the truth is very often not the lie—
deliberate, contrived and dishonest—but the myth—persistent,
persuasive and unrealistic.
  —*John F. Kennedy*

2

Money Myths

Our dreams are at risk. Among the dangers threatening the realization
of our dreams is the fact that our best efforts can be wasted by
following unproductive—or counterproductive—strategies. So, before we start down the road to Financial Sanity, we need to divest
ourselves of some treacherous yet pervasive half-truths and former
truths known as Money Myths.

Every day I talk to people who have been misled by these myths,
including a large percentage of competent and well-trained financial
professionals. More accurately, I talk to practically no one who *hasn't*
been affected by these common misunderstandings. I, too, have
suffered from each and every one of them.

You may wonder, as you read through this chapter, why I'm being so
critical of such time-honored institutions as saving and self-discipline.
But that's precisely the nature of a myth: It's got Mom and apple pie
written all over it, even though it's just an empty, treacherous promise.

Some of the myths discussed in this chapter (and these are just a sampling!) are what I call "former truths": They worked well for other generations but don't seem to fit with the psychological makeup and economic circumstances of this generation. Former truths are especially hard to shake off: We keep thinking that the rule would work if only we would do what it suggested. You may want to apply this test to any former truth you have trouble shaking:

Exercise: Shaking a Myth

Ask these questions of any former truth that still holds you in its seductive hold:
1. How long have I known this Great Truth?
2. Has it served me well so far?

The Savings Myth

The myth of savings is enshrined in statements like this: "Put 10 percent of your pretax income in savings every month" and "Pay yourself first" and in various benchmark formulas and charts indicating how much you should save at certain income levels.

I don't believe in savings. The reason I don't believe in savings is because I look around at my friends and myself and I don't see anybody saving. You remember Tom and Jennifer—my friends who were making $150,000 a year and couldn't save $50 a month. That classic, if extreme, portrait of a baby boomer saving—and stories like it—helped lead me to my disillusionment with the concept of saving.

Instead, I believe in spending. Spending is something we know how to do. We need to take our spending instincts, which are very well developed, and channel them in a healthy direction—a direction that includes good strong planning.

What is saving for, anyway? Saving is to have money set aside so that you can spend it later on. The dangerous part about traditional saving is its mindlessness. Saving for some unnamed and unquantified future need rarely succeeds in accumulating enough money for all the spending we plan to do. You might save diligently for what you think is going to be your retirement, but when it later occurs to you to start a new business you look at your savings and say, "I can start a new business—I can use the $20,000 in savings."

A committed saver will save less than a committed spender who uses a "funding system" to plan for his expenditures. Eric and Janet are a good example. When they first started using the Financial Sanity system a few years ago, their savings rate was $0 and they were overspending slightly each month. They had a credit union account with just a few hundred dollars in it.

Two years later, Eric and Janet, who had a combined annual pretax income of $60,000, were on a full-fledged Financial Sanity funding and debt reduction program. Included in their funding were the following, which might generally be considered appropriate targets for the use of savings:

- next new car—$183 per month
- new furniture—$83 per month
- retirement (IRA)—$167 per month
- child's education—$107 per month
- home improvements—$275 per month

Monthly funding for these categories totaled $815. Debt reduction (another form of saving) added another $400 (excluding interest). Eric and Janet had never been savers. Yet, as committed *spenders,* they were now putting aside an unbelievable 24 percent of their income for the kind of spending that people generally consider to be "targets" for their accumulated savings. How many committed savers do you know who are maintaining that kind of savings rate?

Compare that to Kevin and Sarah, a couple who had been saving for well over a year. They met with me to discuss how they could get their finances in order to buy a house.

"You've been saving for a year and all you've got is $850 in your checking account?" I challenged them.

"We actually had a savings account until recently," Sarah said. "It just kept getting used for everything except buying a house. Finally, last month, we had to withdraw all the money to pay a tax bill we owed from two years ago. Before that, the savings we had put away—well, once it went to pay off our credit card—and . . . " Sarah looked to Kevin for help.

"I don't know—different things," Kevin fumbled. "It's kind of embarrassing. We were setting aside $1,000 a month for this house and after a year of doing that every—well, almost every month, we have absolutely nothing to show for it."

"It's very common," I said. "I call it 'mindless saving' because we delude ourselves into thinking we are saving, when at the same time we are forgetting several major expenses which are bound to come up that we have made no provision for whatsoever."

"Yeah, well that certainly happened to us," piped up Sarah, suddenly remembering what they spent some of their savings on. "Last June we flew back East to visit Kevin's family—it was a family reunion. That ate up a couple thousand dollars."

"Yes," I said. "Exactly. And did this trip back East come up all of a sudden?"

"No," Kevin said, "we knew about it. It had been planned."

Planned, but not saved for.

To see whether you've been doing a little mindless saving of your own, try this exercise.

Exercise: The Mindless Savings Test

1. Look through the list below:

Expenditure Items:

☐ Property taxes $_____
☐ Income taxes due April 15 $_____
☐ Christmas presents $_____
☐ Vacation $_____
☐ Next new car $_____
☐ Down payment on new house $_____
☐ Insurance premiums $_____
☐ Home improvements $_____
☐ Any other upcoming major purchase $_____
☐ Car repairs $_____
☐ _____ $_____
☐ _____ $_____

2. For each item in the expenditures list, put a check mark in the box to its left if you would look to any of the sources of funds listed below to provide the funds for this particular item.

Sources of Funds:

• savings account
• going into debt (including charging on a credit card)
• selling an asset
• borrowing from family or friends
• breaking into your daughter's piggy bank
• HELP!

3. Now, estimate off the top of your head (no need to do research here) the dollar amount involved and put that on the line to the right of each item.

4. Compare what you have saved—and what you are currently saving each month—with the dollars on the right-hand side. If you're like most baby boomers, you'll discover a vast chasm between what you're saving and what you need to be saving.

The Self-Discipline Fallacy

For years I conducted my Financial Sanity Workshop in major hotels. Sometimes our seminar room would be next to a "Diets Don't

Work" seminar, and I would assure the people in my workshop that "Budgets Don't Work" either. It's not that budgets aren't useful so much as that traditional budgeting approaches depend on people applying a fair amount of self-discipline that wasn't previously in evidence.

This may sound cynical, but pinning your financial dreams on the assumption that you'll be "good" next month can lead to devastatingly disappointing results. And your personal finances are far too important to risk mishandling with optimism.

But just in case you still feel that previously absent self-discipline will save you from your financial flagrancy of past years, why not take this very brief exercise I've designed for you:

Exercise: Predicting Your Future Self-Discipline

1. See how much self-discipline you have now.
2. That's how much you'll have tomorrow.

Listen, since money is so hard to talk about, let's talk about garages. There are two types of people who have clean garages. One of them is the kind that has his garage totally organized—a place for everything and nothing out of place. You know the type. You feel uncomfortable even standing in his garage because you don't belong there. You live in fear that at any moment he may spray-paint your body outline on the pegboard wall and hang you from one of those little hooks.

Other people spend months or years saying "One of these days we've got to clean out the garage." Finally, the day dawns and everybody pitches in, getting dust in their nose and hair and having a great time cleaning out the garage, which then proceeds to look perfect for a week, darned clean for a couple of months, okay for another half a year, after which it's a mess again. Then these people start saying, "One of these days we've got to . . ."

The Financial Sanity system is made for those of us in the sporadic-garage-cleaning class, as well as for those of us who didn't do too well on the Self-Discipline Test.

Don't be misled—the Financial Sanity system isn't so much fun that it rises to the level of a recreational activity. But when getting your financial act together becomes important enough to devote some time to it, I think you'll find this system will be a worthwhile and rewarding way to spend that time.

It's been designed so that self-discipline is significantly less important in making your budget work. For instance, I discourage trying to merely spend less on everyday discretionary expenses, because that requires daily self-discipline. Instead, I advocate economizing on larger expenses (where you only have to be "good" once) and on *structural changes*—changes which result in economies without having to consciously economize over and over.

The Tax Myth

Taxation is one of the all-time favorite reasons for making completely irrational decisions.

"My CPA told me to buy a Mercedes," was the old small businessman's cliché back in the days before the Tax Reform Act of 1986. Somehow, somewhere, thousands and thousands of people seem to have developed the misunderstanding that the tax benefits of certain transactions and investments were so great that they completely paid for the cost involved—and delivered a profit to boot.

Certainly, after having spent a good part of my professional life in tax practice, I'm not going to tell you that there haven't been tax strategies that were truly advantageous; a few exist even today.

The strategies to pay attention to these days:

- Deduction for interest on personal residence. This is still the best deal around. A substantial portion of this deduction amounts to a subsidy of what is essentially the equivalent of rent on your home. Coupled with reliably rising housing values (if they exist in your area), this tax shelter for the masses can't be beat.
- Retirement plans. Whether we're talking about IRAs, SEPs, 401(k)s, Keoghs or employer-paid plans, the combination of avoiding taxes on income before it goes into the plan and not paying taxes on income while it accumulates in the plan makes a retirement plan the ideal conservative hideout from taxes and inflation. Just remember: Such a plan is good only for money you plan to actually use for retirement. If you're saving money for your kids' education or to buy a house, this is not the place to keep it. (I often counsel people who are trying to save for a down payment on a house *not* to make contributions to IRAs.)

Much of the rest of tax law consists not of finding nifty ways to avoid paying taxes you might otherwise owe, but of avoiding being taxed more than once on the same income. The completely illogical but politically expedient corporate tax is classic double taxation that affects virtually everyone. The tax on interest and dividends (a long-standing provision that one must assume reflects a carefully considered national policy discouraging saving and investing), coupled with the disallowance of interest (and, for that matter, other investment-related expenses), discourages the practice of borrowing money to invest elsewhere.

People need to remember that no one is ever in a 100 percent tax bracket when earning extra income, nor does getting a tax deduction mean the deductible expense is free. Taxes are often an important part of the equation, but they never warrant making decisions without looking at the underlying economics.

The Investment Myth

We've been conditioned to believe that becoming more responsible about finances means learning about investing. And it's easy to understand why. We equate investing with financial responsibility because it's all we ever hear.

Once we stopped listening to dear old Dad, the only real source of information we had about money was from the mass media. Frankly, a substantial portion of our investment "education" likely came from advertisements.

We learn that being a responsible adult has something mysterious to do with life insurance companies. We learn that we've "got clout," and that the amount of credit we can qualify for and use is a fundamental indicator of our worth as a human being. We learn that while we are sitting on our thumbs earning 5½ percent interest on the $1,200 in our savings account, the rest of the adult world is achieving a 17 percent risk-free yield in some mutual fund that we're too stupid and too poor to invest in.

If we get beyond the stage of flipping past ads and actually start reading the articles on financial and money matters, we get a little more balanced picture. We begin to realize that money decisions aren't quite as simple and straightforward as the ads would have us believe. But the "investment presumption" largely remains.

Yet premature attention to investment issues serves only to distract us from the real issues of spending, planning and control—the things we need to attend to in order to *have* money to invest.

The Green Eyeshade Myth

A few years ago, when I was still developing the basic Financial Sanity system's structure, some friends of mine, Fred and Marilyn, announced that they had just spent the weekend doing their budget. Eager to steal for my course any new ideas they could offer about how to wend one's way through the labyrinth of budgeting, I quizzed them about what exactly they had done.

"Oh," said Marilyn, clearly pleased with their accomplishment. "We went through all our expenses for last year and figured out how much we spent on everything."

"And . . . " I prompted, waiting to hear the good stuff.

"And you wouldn't believe how much we spent on dog food," Fred volunteered.

I was astounded. Here were two practicing attorneys spending an entire weekend collecting data barely sufficient enough to warrant putting Fido on a diet.

"That's it?" I pressed. "Did you set up any budgets for next year?"

"No," Marilyn said. "We didn't have time. But we have all the data ready to do our budget."

What were the chances, I thought, that they would spend two weekends in a row "doing their budget"? In fact, the next time they did any work on their budget was when they took my course, many months later.

Many people do start their budgeting project with a weekend-long binge of catching up on a year's worth of accounting. This makes *some* sense. You have to know, the reasoning goes, where you currently stand before you can start making any changes. But it has a fatal flaw: The weekend you spend doing accounting is very likely the *only* weekend you will have to devote to budgeting. You'll blow all of your budgeting time doing bookkeeping. Not a good idea.

There are better ways. One alternative is to do no historical accounting at all. Just forget about what has happened in the past, depend on your memory and dive right into making decisions about your future spending.

Because you're making decisions without complete and accurate information, you'll make mistakes. But what the hell—you're going to make mistakes anyway! Your budget is never going to be *right!* The best you can do with a budget is just get close—*maybe* real close. If you're fairly close in your budget planning, to the extent you make a mistake or life turns out a little differently than you thought—well, you won't be hurt that much. Bookkeeping may satisfy a compulsive need for pinpoint accuracy, but it isn't planning; it isn't forward-looking.

Doing no accounting may sound like a sloppy, almost irresponsible way to start your budgeting. But, in truth, it works rather well. It's the way my wife and I budgeted our way to financial contentment, and it's the way the people in my early workshops did their budgeting.

Anyone can tell you how to take control of your finances by slavishly spending all your weekends with a quill pen and green eyeshade. But you need a system you can live with. Decision-making—not accounting—is the primary purpose of budgeting. The goal is to achieve maximum control with a realistic amount of effort.

Because the emphasis of this system is so heavily oriented toward decision-making, I don't require you to do a lot of accounting. This doesn't mean that I'm against accounting. After all, I'm a CPA.

(There's a full, formal set of books for my family's finances, just as there is for my business.) I merely mean to say that accounting is secondary to planning and that accounting shouldn't be a distraction from your planning efforts.

The Myth of "Enough"

The notion that there is some amount of money—either a lump sum or an annual income—that will be enough to solve our financial problems is one of the most anesthetizing lies we can tell ourselves. It keeps us from dealing with the realities—and planning opportunities —at hand. Furthermore, chances are good that whatever farfetched amount of money you dream about, it probably isn't enough for what you've got in mind!

As Bill Cosby, racking up more earnings than anyone seems able to count, said when asked when enough is enough: "No one ever told J. Paul Getty to stop drilling oil wells."

Closer to the other end of the spectrum, a recent national newspaper poll suggested that 73 percent of Americans were satisfied with their income. Two thirds of those polled who had annual incomes between $15,000 and $75,000 said that they were making enough—or more than enough—to live a "comfortable" lifestyle. As individuals' incomes rose, however, so did their concepts of "enough." Only half of those making more than $75,000 said that they were not making enough to truly support a comfortable lifestyle.

My experience with clients mirrors the statistics: More money rarely seems to result in less financial uncertainty.

"When I was an $18,000-a-year secretary," a new client recently told me, "I never had any money problems. I knew exactly what I couldn't afford." But now, as a $180,000 real estate agent, she was in debt and out of control. She didn't know what she could afford and what she couldn't, so she just bought whatever appealed to her, driving herself into debt.

When I was a young auditor for an international accounting firm, we did almost all our work on the clients' premises. The client provided us with a space to work—sometimes a twenty-foot conference table, sometimes the corner of an absent employee's desk. In any case, whether we worked on a majestic expanse of mahogany or positioned ourselves between some credit manager's coffee mug and pictures of his wife and three-year-old, we always covered the work surface completely. No matter how much room we were given, it was always just a little bit less than enough.

Money is a lot like that. It seems that, as we make more money, we increase our appetite for the things that money can buy—but our appetite always increases just a bit more than our income does.

The point of this discussion is not to make you feel despondent about ever having enough. Instead, I hope to discourage the notion that "someday" your ship will come in and, until it does, you'll just have to settle with less than you really want and need. Your ship has *already* come in. It left its cargo for you on the dock and sailed away to get more. Why don't you get down to the wharf and collect what has already been delivered?

Riches do not consist in the possession of treasures, but in the use made of them.
  ·—*Napoleon I*

3

Goal Planning

A Question of Choice

Close your eyes for a moment. Pretend you're the kid in the proverbial candy store. You've just been told you can have anything in the store—*anything*. There's licorice to your left, truffles to your right. Almond bark, red vines and white chocolate. There's so many things, and you want them *all*. Suddenly, anxiety sweeps over you. You can't decide on just one. Desperate, you shove aside your doting parents clutching their pathetic little quarters. You stride up to the kindly old man behind the counter, look him squarely in the eye, whip out your credit card and say, "I'll take one of everything."

This is the classic image of the baby boomer—the spoiled yuppie who has too much spending power for his own good. As unfair and inaccurate as this image is, even we baby boomers sometimes fall prey to it. Swamped by a barrage of media and advertising, it's easy to believe that we should have it all by now and if we don't—well, we must not have our act together.

For those of you who insist on having it all—who have bumper stickers that say "He who dies with the most toys wins"—I have little to offer you. My system and my philosophy are for those who believe that some things are more important than others, that building a fortune is not a game and that money—all money—is for spending and not for keeping score.

On the other hand, minimalism—the purposeful denial of materialistic wants—is an artificial reaction to the frustration of trying to acquire what one wants. The minimalist is as enthralled and imprisoned by materialism as the guy with the bumper sticker; the minimalist is a materialist in drag.

Andrew—Art over Money

Neither the minimalist nor the materialist is paying attention to his dreams. Let me share an example with you.

A few years ago I was a guest on a money show on the largest public radio station in San Francisco. The call-in show had just moved to a new time slot, and some of the audience was apparently not used to hearing about money matters on public radio.

One of the callers was a self-described starving artist photographer from Berkeley who complained about the "incredibly materialistic" emphasis of the program.

"There are a lot of people for whom other things are more important than money," Andrew explained to me. "In other words, you do what you want to do with your life first, and then money kind of falls into place and you handle it the best you can."

I would be less than honest if I told you I hadn't spent some younger years of my life wishing it were true. Indeed, I agree with the first part of his statement: "you do what you want to do with your life first." The problem with the rest of his philosophy is that it's the rare person for whom money actually does "kind of fall into place." And my suspicion that the caller wasn't one of those people was quickly confirmed.

"I had a [photographic] project that was very, very near to coming to reality recently," the caller complained, "which was, in fact, a traveling project and the project fell apart simply because I didn't have the money for the plane fare at that point."

"Aha!" I said, almost involuntarily. "I knew that if I listened to your story long enough, I would hear about one of your projects falling victim to finances," I said. "You accused us of talking about materialism. Well, we *are* talking about materialism. Materialism is what would have bought that plane ticket. Materialism can be put to very good use. Frankly, I think that some of your art got lost for the lack of a little of our materialism."

Andrew's proud notion that he was putting his photography ahead of money looked to me like justification for his lack of financial mastery. I believed—and I told him so—that Andrew was putting his unwillingness to handle money ahead of his art. It was apparently more important to Andrew that he be protected from the pain of putting his financial life together than it was to be able to get on a plane in order to do an important shoot. You tell me—what's taking a back seat here?

Choice: The Key to Financial Sanity

Neither the materialist nor the minimalist extreme is legitimate. Both deny the fundamental human opportunity—and responsibility: choice. The world is simply full of far too many things, experiences, points of view, feelings. The candy store is infinitely stocked. Only the foolishly obsessive would attempt to corner it all. Instead, our task is to browse through this infinite collection of goods and experiences and make the *choices* that serve and please us the most.

Ortalda's First Law: *You can have just about anything you want.*
Ortalda's Second Law: *You can't have everything you see.*
Ortalda's Corollary: *You don't even want it all.*

The BMW Myth

Bear with me while I expound on one more money myth that has everything to do with choice.

I call this the "BMW Myth" because it is characterized by how we feel when someone our age shows up to the softball game in a BMW that we know we couldn't afford—so why can he?

The mind begins to juggle possibilities:

Maybe I'm in the wrong field. What does he do again? Ah, yes. He's a food broker. Sales! That's it! I knew I should have gone into sales.

Maybe he made money with his investments. Doesn't he own some apartments? Why didn't I get into real estate? I should have gotten into real estate in '75. It's too late now.

His business must be doing well. Why isn't my business doing well? I make less money than when I was working for a salary. What am I doing wrong?

Isn't he my age? How come I don't have a BMW? I'm smarter than he is. What does he know that I don't know—or is it who does he know? He joined the University Club, didn't he? Maybe I should join. How do you get invited? Why do I feel so out of it?

We all manifest envy and jealousy to some degree or another. But I see a sinister danger lurking in habitually comparing ourselves, especially negatively, to other people we view as our peers. After all, we're already comparing ourselves to our parents—often unfavorably. To tell ourselves that we are doing worse than both peers and parents will quickly convince us that we are flunking finance and may as well drop the course.

With low financial self-esteem, we may lack confidence in our ideas and lack the will to carry them through. Taken to its extreme, we risk becoming financial couch potatoes who, without a whimper of resistance, let changes in the economy roll right over us, crushing hopes, dreams and aspirations.

I don't usually advocate greater government regulation of our lives, but I could see some social benefit to requiring people to fly their Balance Sheets from the car-phone antennas of their expensive European cars. It might give the rest of us a little peace of mind to know they went $38,000 into debt to buy their $40,000 car. Or that it's leased. There could be any one of dozens of possible conditions connected with your friend's acquisition of his BMW—conditions he can, perhaps, live with but you might find unacceptable.

Maybe you live in your dream house—and he lives in a funky apartment he never lets his friends see. Maybe you've reduced your credit card debt to zero, while he juggles balances in the five figures. He might have nothing set aside for retirement, while you make maximum contributions to your IRA or Keogh account.

You don't know what choices your friend has made, so you can't judge his relative success by the car he drives. When you do, you are forgetting the rich tapestry of choice we have in this society.

What to you is an expensive luxury, far down on your list, might be a necessity in your friend's mind. He doesn't have—and doesn't need to have—the same priorities that you do.

We're all in the same boat. We all face major challenges in attaining—much less maintaining—the lifestyles we want. Thinking that you're the "only one" who has a rough time financially keeping up with his hopes and dreams only serves to keep you from realistically moving forward in your efforts to gain financial control.

The Goals Planning Timeline

The Financial Sanity system is based on the premise that the entire system must revolve around your goals—your personal set of hopes, aspirations, dreams, ambitions, promises, wishes, good ideas, "maybe somedays," commitments, intentions—anything you said you would, could or should do.

The Goals Planning Timeline is the first step in your financial-planning process, the foundation upon which the entire Financial Sanity system rests.

The timeline is a place where you can organize your thoughts about your plans for the future. You may think of it as a sort of hopes-and-dreams scratch pad.

Suzanne and Ted's Timeline

Let's go through the example in Figure 3-1 (your list will probably be longer) and see what we can learn about how to make best use of the Goals Planning Timeline.

Suzanne and Ted are expecting their second child in May. Medical insurance, gifts from the grandparents and hand-me-down furniture, clothes and equipment from their first daughter, Christine, will make the new arrival relatively cost-free. But the event is significant because of its impact on their lives, an increase in their operating expenses and a temporary decrease in Suzanne's income for a few months. Suzanne and Ted have therefore included the event on their timeline.

Notice a few negative items—the selling of their old car and getting a loan on the new one. Negative items denote income or negative expenses, since almost everything else on the schedule is an expense. (People with irregular but predictable income patterns may want to use a separate timeline form solely to track anticipated income.)

Also notice that Christine's college tuition costs (she's five years old now) are estimated at 1988 (current) cost levels. I recommend that you calculate all long-range expenditures that way. In Chapter 19 I'll show you how to avoid getting hung up in inflation predictions and worrying about what various things are going to cost twenty years from now.

Finally, Suzanne feels very strongly that she and Ted should invest locally in real estate. She's targeted 1993–95 as a time she thinks they can pull together $20,000–25,000 (again, in 1988 dollars) as a down payment on a small property or a capital contribution to a small partnership. To indicate her uncertainty about when this will happen, she has written through three blocks of years on the timeline.

Now it's your turn to create a road map of your future. Again, don't worry about making sure that everything on your list is going to happen. Just get your pencil going and start writing.

Exercise: Goals Planning Timeline

1. Make a worksheet similar to Figure 3-1. (All the blank forms mentioned in this book are available in Appendix B. You may wish to photocopy these.)

Period Covered Nov 88 through Oct 89

(Label boxes below with time periods to be covered, e.g., months, quarters, years, etc.)

(For each line item, enter the expected dollar amount, if known, or "X" if unknown)

Goal	Nov 88	Dec 88	Jan 89	Feb 89	Mar 89	Apr 89	May 89	Jun 89	Jul 89	Aug 89	Sep 89	Oct 89
(List events, income and expenditures)												
New Baby							X					
IRA		4,000										
New Car						12,000						
Sell old Car						-3,000						
New Car Loan						-6,000						
Property Taxes		750				750						
Home Improvements											2,000	
Furniture												1,000

(List events, income and expenditures)

(For each line item, enter the expected dollar amount, if known, or "X" if unknown)

Goal	1989	1990	1991	1992	1993	1994	1995	2000	2005	2010	2015	2020
Christine's College									12,000 per year (1988 cost level)			
Greek Island Vacation												
New House		15,000	X									
New Car												
Real Estate Investment					20,000 - 25,000							
IRAs		4,000	4,000	4,000	4,000	4,000	4,000	? ?	? ?		? ?	? ?

Figure 3–1

If you are married, make a second copy for your partner, and a third set to combine your individual timelines.

2. Label the first line of boxes with the time periods you're interested in planning for.

Most people feel comfortable using one timeline to cover the next twelve months and using a second form to cover the next several years. Any period of time that makes sense to you is okay. In the example in Figure 3-1, we have artificially split the form in half to demonstrate both month-by-month planning and year-by-year planning, which slips into five-year periods after 1995.

3. Down the wide left-hand column, label each line with a particular event or item of income or expense. The items don't have to be earth-shattering, but they will generally be events that will make some financial impact. Do not include items which recur every period, like your salary. You may include items that only might occur—like the bonus you might get—and mark it specially as an uncertain event.

4. Under the columns labeled with time periods, make entries related to the line items in the description column. We're after two kinds of information here: time frame and dollar amount. Sometimes you will be uncertain as to one or the other of these or both. Refer to the example in Figure 3-1. You'll see an "X" in the 1991 column, where Suzanne and Ted knew they wanted to buy a new house but didn't know the price range. You'll notice that some dollar amounts are spread over two or more time periods, indicating Suzanne and Ted's uncertainty about when some of these financial events were likely to occur.

This is not an exact process; there will be no penalty for being overly optimistic, so let your imagination fly. Don't worry now about being realistic—realism will be applied to the process in later chapters. About the only real mistake you can make here is not including an aspiration that is important to you, even if you're not sure you will be able to attain it.

5. Now that you've completed your first worksheet, this would be an excellent time to start your Financial Sanity workbook. Details about how this workbook can be organized are at the beginning of Appendix B.

Getting Your Priorities Straight

You may notice that, in talking about the Goals Planning Timeline, I don't make references to goals like "become a millionaire" or "make $150,000 next year" or even "achieve financial independence." That's because I don't consider these "real" goals. Not only that, I think that these kinds of aspirations will ruin your planning process. Here's why:

In my years of working with goals and planning, I have identified two traits of successful goal-setting that *seem* mutually exclusive. The first is that cardinal rule of goal-setting: To be a goal, an objective has to be specific as to quantity and time. "Saving money to send the kids to college" isn't specific enough. A specific goal would require something like: "We will have $10,000 on August 1, 2001 (when Christine enters college), $20,000 more in 2002 (when both Tommy and his sister will be in school), $20,000 in 2003. . . . " That's specific. It is a measurable, objective result, to be attained within a specific and knowable period of time.

It's also a trap. One way to end up in a heap of trouble is to blindly pursue a specific goal like the one cited above. We don't really care if there is $10,000 in an account and available to us on August 1, 2001. All we care about is that lack of money won't prevent Christine from getting her education.

The specifics (as to time and money) are important because they give us security to hang on to, something to work for. But the specifics are potentially false. Maybe $10,000 is not enough—or too much. Maybe 2001 won't be the right year.

What if Christine wins a scholarship? What if she undertakes a seven-year course of study? What if she graduates from high school a year early? Ten thousand dollars is *specific*—but it's potentially meaningless. A clear subjective statement about Christine's educational opportunities isn't quantifiable and measurable, but it's a *true statement* of what needs to happen for you to feel successful. As difficult as it is for these two statements to exist together, coexist they must.

F. Scott Fitzgerald said: "The test of a first-rate intelligence is the ability to hold two opposed ideas in the mind at the same time, and still retain the ability to function."

The key to holding these two ideas:

· the specific, but potentially false goal
· the true, but nonspecific objective

in balance is to remember that the specific goal—the $10,000 by 2001—is just a *representation* of the true goal. Since the true goal—"a good education"—is too unspecific to fit into any mathematical budgeting formulas, the specific goal must take its place.

The danger of having the specific "$10,000" permanently take the place of the true "college education" is prevented by periodic planning. In Financial Sanity, we ask you to sit down with long-range goals such as these at least every couple of years. This allows you to reassess whether or not your specific goal still properly represents your true objective.

For instance, you may have spent tranquil moments of youth around a North Carolina lake, fishing and helping Grandpa chop wood. Now you're a high-flying executive (literally—you spend 20 percent of your time in airplanes) and you long for the peace of those North Carolina summers. Your goals sheet has an entry for buying lakefront property in North Carolina by 1995.

It's a good goal—specific and definable—even though it isn't a *true* goal. The cabin in the pines is only a representation for you of something—something you probably can't adequately define.

Don't obsessively strive for the Carolina cabin after you've discovered that something else (who knows—maybe playing tennis with your son) satisfies the need you associated with the property at the lake. I'm not suggesting that you analyze all your wants and try to discover what you're *really* after, perhaps developing substitute goals for every aspiration on your dream list. Just don't be afraid to stop working for something after you've essentially already got it. Have the guts to admit it when you've won.

Money is good only in the spending, and only when the spending is for good things. Based on my years of experience working with people who have a lot of money and people who didn't have enough, I suggest to you that it is easier to figure out how to get more money than it is to spend it well. I also believe that merely getting more money probably won't make you any happier or more satisfied, but that learning to spend well will.

Financial Sanity is not about having money. It is about having what you want, about attaining your dreams. This system is not about amassing wealth, although you will probably build your net worth more for having applied this system. It's also not about saving, although you will probably save more as a result of your work with this system. Financial Sanity is also not necessarily about making more money, although many of you will be spurred to do so as a result of your work with this system. And, although we will spend almost all of our time talking about money, it is not about materialism.

The work you do on your Goals Planning Timeline is the first step in learning how to spend well. In the next several chapters, we'll address issues of affordability, so that you can ultimately match your financial capabilities with your goals.

Light purse, heavy heart.
—*Poor Richard's Almanack*

4

Your Financial Snapshot

The September 14, 1987, issue of *Fortune* magazine devoted its cover story to the question of whether we live as well today as our parents did in the fifties. Page 40 featured a photograph of the Stephens family of Del Rio, Texas, astride the various and sundry wheeled vehicles owned by this smiling, sunglassed clan—a car, a big rig, a boat on a trailer, a motorcycle, a lawn mower you can ride, and two small children's bicycles (with children)—spread out in front of their ranch-style brick home. No one would suggest that this picture tells a complete story of the Stephenses' financial situation, but it does paint a rudimentary, if incomplete, picture of where they stand in terms of material goods.

If you were to look in your own family album of photographs, you too would see an imperfect chronicle of the changing material fortunes of a family—*your* family. The work we'll do next to create your own balance sheet will be very much like taking a snapshot of your current financial condition—a financial snapshot, if you will.

It will be as if I asked you to haul all your worldly goods out onto your front lawn and take a picture. The picture is called a Balance Sheet and it shows what you own (*Assets*), what you owe (*Liabilities*) and how much of what you own is really yours (*Net Worth*), after paying off what you owe. Like a snapshot, it shows this information for a single point in time. Just as next month's snapshot would be slightly different, so would next month's Balance Sheet.

The Balance Sheet

Any time I talk about the Balance Sheet—whether it be to you in this book, to a client in my office or to a group of people in a workshop—I have to deal with the reality that some of you know a whole lot about Balance Sheets and some of you know practically nothing.

Anyone who takes the time to read this book from cover to cover should expect to be able to master personal financial management and control. So I'm going to lead the novice and the unsure through the basics. For those of you who are experts, you may want to skim through the definitions, then move right on to the next chapter to build your current Balance Sheet.

So, let's dive in. This chapter does two things. It tells you what a Balance Sheet does. Then it tells you about each of the different categories on the Balance Sheet and what goes in them. Then, in Chapter 5, you'll create your own Balance Sheet.

Whatcha Got There, Pal?

The Balance Sheet answers just two basic questions. The first question is "How much stuff do you have?" This question is answered on the *Assets* side of the Balance Sheet.

Look around your life and notice the stuff that you have. Those things—whether they be cars, houses, golf clubs, jewelry, stocks, IRA accounts, cash or whatever—are assets. You might be surprised at how much stuff has the same address as you do.

Once you've figured out what you've got, there's another very important question to answer: "How *much* of what you have do you really own?"

Your indebtedness—to the bank, your mother-in-law or whomever else you owe money—is basically a call on your assets. So, realistically, if you owe money you really must anticipate setting aside assets (usually money) to give to the person you owe. In effect, you don't really own that asset—they do.

The amount of your stuff that other people have a call on is called *debt* or, as used in our Balance Sheet, *Liabilities*. The remaining portion that you truly own is sometimes called *equity* or, as we call it here, *Net Worth*. Figure 4-1 shows graphically how what you have must, of course, equal the sum of the ownership of what you have. In accounting terms:

$$\text{Assets} = \text{Liability} + \text{Net Worth}$$

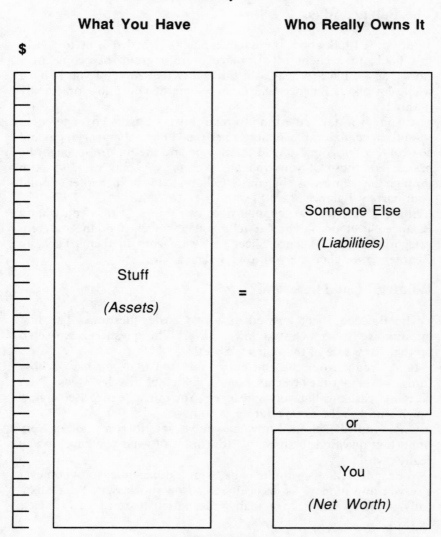

Figure 4-1

So now you have the big picture of the Balance Sheet. The left side totals up all the stuff you have (*Assets*). The right side starts off with the part of what you have that other people "own" (*Liabilities*). Whatever's left is yours (*Net Worth*). Since the right side merely explains who owns what's on the left side, *the right side must always equal the left side.* That's why it's called a *Balance* Sheet.

The Long and the Short of It

Now let's see how you will actually build your Balance Sheet. Take a look at Figure 4-2. It shows the major sections of the Balance Sheet, each with its respective categories. Notice that, on both the right and left side, Short-Term Assets or Liabilities are shown first, with Longer-Term Assets or Liabilities shown below. This reflects the fact that in the very short run—day by day—we are most aware of what might be called our Short-Term Net Worth: Short-Term Assets minus Short-Term Liabilities. The rest of Net Worth is made up of the difference between long-term assets and long-term liabilities.

The concept of classifying assets and liabilities as either long-term or short-term can be easily illustrated: Suppose Joe owes $100,000 on his home mortgage and $2,000 on his MasterCard. Joe's friend Frank, on the other hand, owes $2,000 on his home mortgage and $100,000 on various credit cards. Each has $2,000 in the bank. Even though both of these otherwise identical friends owe exactly the same amount of money, Frank's situation is much more precarious than Joe's. Frank could be insolvent in a matter of weeks, whereas Joe has essentially no debt problem at all.

The difference between these two scenarios is the difference between short- and long-term debt. The essence of short-term debt is that it is expected to be paid off soon—so soon, in fact, that you should have either short-term assets or near-term anticipated income lined up to pay it.

Now, let's take a closer look at each of the categories of the Balance Sheet in Figure 4-2.

Short-Term Assets

Cash includes checking and savings accounts, cash on hand (if there's enough of it to worry about), certificates of deposit and "near-cash" holdings, such as money market funds. Don't include any funds that are already in an IRA or other retirement fund.

Other Liquid Assets includes marketable securities, such as actively traded (exchange-listed) stocks, bonds and mutual funds. Also, include any tax refunds you have due you. Again, your IRA account

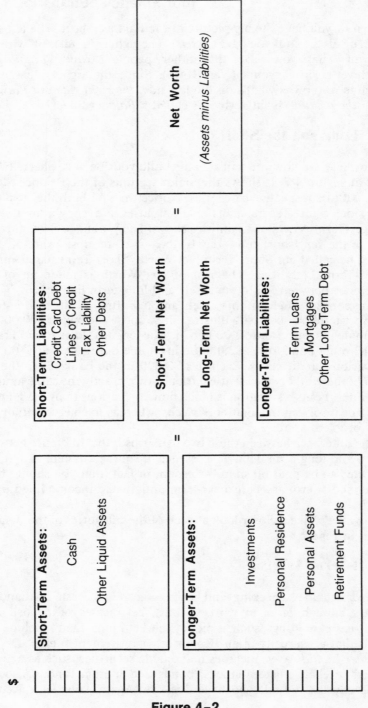

Figure 4-2

holdings don't count—they're listed in Retirement Funds, described below.

Longer-Term Assets

Investments include real estate (other than your own residence), interests in partnerships, nonliquid stock holdings (such as your 20 percent interest in the family business), money owed to you, etc.

Personal Residence is best calculated using the "net realizable value" method, which reduces the market value of your home by the costs of selling it. (See Figure 5-5 for an example of calculating net realizable value.)

Personal Assets are part of your net worth, although they are usually "nonworking" assets. They are the least likely to ever be converted into money. The value of your furniture, appliances, sporting goods and so forth is in your use of them—not in their eventual sale.

Retirement Funds include IRA, Keogh, SEP and 401(k) accounts, as well as your vested portion of your employer's pension, profit-sharing, stock and/or thrift plans. (Vesting has to do with how much of your accrued benefits you would receive if you were to leave your job today—usually based on years of service. For instance, if your employer had set aside $5,000 for you in a profit-sharing plan over two years and you were 20 percent vested, you would receive $1,000 if you left the company now. This vested amount, $1,000, is the amount you should use to value your interest in the retirement fund.)

On the Liability Side

Credit Card Debt includes the balance you owe on major credit cards and store accounts (whether a plastic card is involved or not). Do not, however, include installment agreements with stores (for example, to purchase furniture or an appliance with equal monthly payments). These belong on the Term Loans line.

Lines of Credit are open borrowing agreements with a bank that allow you to freely borrow and repay within a specified credit limit. Include only the amount you currently owe, not the entire credit limit. There are two major types of lines of credit: secured and unsecured. Secured merely means that one of your assets, usually your house, has been pledged against any outstanding balance of the loan in case you default.

Tax Liability applies if you owe money for last year (or any prior year) or if you are incurring more tax liability this year than you are paying to the government through withholding, estimated tax payments and credits. This area can be confusing, so let me show you some examples.

The easiest example is *unpaid prior-year's tax.* If you have not yet filed your return for last year but expect to owe some tax when you do, the amount you expect to pay is actually a debt you owe now—whether payment is required now or not. Include that amount on the Tax Liability line.

It's more difficult, however, to get a fix on *underpaid current-year's tax.* Let's suppose that you are in the middle of the year, paying taxes to the government through withholding—just as you have in years past. But you know that—just like in years past—you will owe about $2,000 in taxes when you file your return next April. Maybe you have a small moonlighting business or you receive significant taxable income from investments. Since you're now halfway through the year, you would estimate your tax liability at $2,000 × ½ = $1,000.

Another version of underpaid current-year's tax is *unpaid capital gains tax.** This arises when you sell—at a profit—an asset, such as stocks, a house or other property. You only pay tax on the profit (sale price less what you paid for the asset).

Other Debts should include anything that you owe (except taxes) that doesn't fit in one of the above categories, but is due soon (say, within a year). Include debts to family, friends, employers, your own corporation, your retirement plan, etc. If the debt is not to be paid for quite a while, you should include it below in the Longer-Term Liabilities section.

Longer-Term Liabilities

Term Loans are loans that have fixed payment amounts due each month. They typically include car loans, student loans and loans for furniture and other major purchases. Real estate loans are also term loans, but I'm asking you to include real estate loans in the Mortgages section.

Use the Term Loans section only for *amortized* loans: An amortized

---

*The term "capital gains tax" has recently been rendered somewhat less meaningful by the Tax Reform Act of 1986 (TRA 86). Long-term capital gains used to be taxed preferentially—at 40 percent of the normal tax on other income. TRA 86 ended that preferential treatment; now capital gains are taxed just like all other income. For the purposes of this discussion, however, it makes no difference at what rate the capital gains are taxed. The important feature of capital-gains transactions is that they rarely involve any withholding of tax, and so whatever tax is due on the transaction is usually due and payable in April of the next year.

loan is a loan whose interest payments are calculated to pay off the debt completely in a certain number of payments.

Other than amortized loans, the most common type of term loan is an interest-only loan. Most commonly associated with real estate transactions and sales of small businesses, the balance due on an interest-only loan does not decrease each month as payments are made because the payments are only large enough to pay the interest due each month. These loans, therefore, result in what can be one of the scarier of financial events: the due date of a *balloon payment.* A balloon payment is so named because, after making small interest-only payments for many months, the required payment suddenly "balloons" to include all or a significant part of the principal. "Partially amortized" loans are term loans which follow an amortization schedule—say for thirty years of payments—but become due and payable after a shorter period of time, like five years. Again, the partially amortized loan features a balloon payment.

Mortgages include first and second (and third) real estate loans on your personal residence, vacation property or rental property you own.

Other Long-Term Debt is the same kind of catch-all category that we encountered up in the short-term section, except that debts in this section are not due in the near future. An example might be a five-year, interest-only note borrowed from your pension fund.

As you get more familiar with working with Balance Sheets—or if you are a sophisticated user already—you can fine-tune your use of the categories. For instance, a line of credit is a short-term liability in Figure 5-1. But some people use lines of credit for long-term purposes, even though that may or may not be what was intended by the lending bank. For instance, you may have borrowed on your line of credit to finance your new business, or to add on to your house, or to buy a classic car. You may be retiring the line in a systematic way, much like a term loan. In cases like these, it may be more appropriate to put the amount owed on your line of credit in the long-term section—squeeze it in between two other lines—than to continue calling it short-term.

It can go the other way, too. You may find yourself reclassifying as short-term liabilities—or even assets—that normally are characterized as longer-term. Examples might include a term loan that you intend to pay off in full during the coming year, or an investment that will be sold for cash in the very near future. If *you* think of an asset or liability as short-term, then it should be reflected that way on the Balance Sheet, regardless of its usual flavor.

Similarly, you may have marketable securities (normally classified as Other Liquid Assets), such as stocks or bonds, which you have earmarked for retirement and have promised yourself you won't use for anything before that time. You might better reflect your own financial situation by including these assets in the Retirement Funds section of your Balance Sheet. (Not every retirement asset is in a tax-free retirement trust recognized by the IRS.)

Keep in mind, then, as you read the sections that follow, that your priority in classifying assets and liabilities on your Balance Sheet should be to accurately reflect your financial condition for *you*. This may not be the Balance Sheet you take to the bank to get a new line of credit. It is the Balance Sheet *you* will look at to help *you* determine your true financial condition.

Off Balance

Readers who are new to Balance Sheets might wonder what happened to some other financial tidbits that seem to have been left off Figure 4-2. These are some of the questions that have come up in the workshops I conduct.

Income, for instance. Where do I put my salary? Income is not a Balance Sheet item because it doesn't deal with a point in time—it covers a span or period of time. We cover the parts of your financial life that don't appear on a Balance Sheet in Chapter 6, where we help you analyze the *flow* of income and outgo.

How about my car lease? Where do I put that? A true lease is also not a Balance Sheet item (unless the lease is really a disguised loan). It, again, deals with a period of time—a month, for instance. Also, since you don't own the asset you're leasing—a car, apartment, rented furniture, etc.—they don't appear on your balance sheet as assets. They simply don't belong to you.

Many lease transactions, however, are really merely no-money-down loans. If, at the end of the "lease," the equipment (car, mobile phone, computer, etc.) is yours to keep, then you should treat the lease as a loan and you should show the equipment as an asset on your Balance Sheet. If, however, you have to pay a substantial amount to acquire the asset (this is typical of automobile leasing), then you are basically just renting the car. You have no asset and you have no debt.

How about credit availability? If I have $2,000 of available credit on my credit card—or a $15,000 unused line of credit with my bank— isn't that worth something? Yes, it's worth something, but it isn't an asset—or a liability, yet—until you use it. It doesn't appear on your Balance Sheet.

(Credit availability is generally a good thing. The ability to put your hands on a reasonable amount of cash in case of an emergency or opportunity can be comforting—even vital—to have. It is possible, however, to have too much credit availability. A client of mine who made $60,000 a year had two $15,000 lines of credit and seven credit cards with open lines of $3,000 to $5,000 each. In all, he had about $55,000 of credit availability, although, after working with some of the debt reduction techniques in Chapter 11, he had less than $10,000 borrowed. While applying for an auto loan, his banker told him he had "too much" credit availability. If he actually had $55,000 in debt, the banker explained to him, he wouldn't qualify for the loan. All those lines of credit made the bank nervous that he might be about to run up huge amounts of new debt.)

A Balance Sheet for Every Purpose

How important is a Balance Sheet? And what's the significance of Net Worth?

A Balance Sheet is a good, reliable and fairly standard way to measure wealth. You can't know how you're doing by looking in the driveway—that Mercedes may be leased. And even the extremely wealthy can be "cash poor" at times (meaning that they have lots of assets, but none of them have pictures of a President on the front).

Only the Balance Sheet tells the straight story (yes, you have a beautiful house, but you're mortgaged up to your eyeballs). That's why you'll rarely find yourself on the receiving end of a loan without having shown someone your Balance Sheet.

But you should understand that different Balance Sheets exist for different reasons and will have different numbers on them—and different Net Worths—depending on their purpose.

For instance, many banks, when making home equity loans, will loan up to 80 percent of the value of the home, less any existing mortgages. In our example in the next chapter, Sam and Wendy will value their residence at a net realizable value of $140,000 when they do their Financial Sanity Balance Sheet. But the number the banker expects to see on their financial statement is more like $160,000, the value placed on it by the real estate agent.

The Financial Sanity Balance Sheet is prepared for a special reader: you. Its categories are especially designed to facilitate the Financial Sanity planning process, and the way we ask you to value assets helps make sure that you don't add yourself to the long list of people willing to feed you disinformation. It's specifically designed to not fool you into thinking you're better off than you are.

The Balance Sheet is very much like a snapshot—a "financial snapshot"—of your wealth at a given point in time. It balances what you have (Assets) with two "ownership" concepts: debt (Liabilities), where someone else "owns" your assets, and Net Worth, which calculates how much of your assets you own free and clear.

Let's go to Chapter 5, where I'll guide you through the creation of your own Balance Sheet.

Wealth is well known to be a great comforter.
—*Plato*

It is preoccupation with possession, more than anything else, that prevents men from living freely and nobly.
—*Bertrand Russell*

5

Building Your Own Balance Sheet

Sam and Wendy Sheridan were one of the earliest couples to use my system. The facts I'm presenting here are largely authentic, although they have been embellished here and there in order for me to clarify as many points as possible about filling out the Balance Sheet.

Figure 5-1 reveals Sam and Wendy's Balance Sheet the first time they began using the materials of this system. In this section, I will walk you through the step-by-step creation of that Balance Sheet, pointing out finer points that you may encounter as you make your own Balance Sheet.

If you're ready to get to work on your own Balance Sheet, feel free to skip forward to the exercise at the end of this chapter and get started. If you want to feel a little more sure of your ground, however, work through the comprehensive example of Sam and Wendy Sheridan. We'll be using their case for Chapter 7, too, so the familiarity you gain here will serve you twice.

As of (Date): [ ]

	Assets			Liabilities & Net Worth			Net Worth Analysis

Assets

		Ref.	

Short-Term:

Cash	A	$	2,750

Other Liquid Assets	B		2,520

Total Short-Term Assets			5,270

Longer-Term:

Investments	C		25,000

Personal Residence	D		140,000

Personal Assets	E		25,000

Retirement Funds	F		6,375

Total All Assets		$	201,645
========

Liabilities & Net Worth

	Ref.	

Short-Term:

Credit Card Debt		$	6,450
Lines of Credit			8,000
Tax Liability			1,250
Other Debts			700

Total Short-Term Liabilities			16,400

Longer-Term:

Term Loans			10,500
Mortgage(s)			84,000
Other Debts			25,000

Total All Liabilities			135,900

Net Worth (Assets minus Total Liabilities)			65,745

Total Liabilities Plus Net Worth (Must equal Total Assets)		$	201,645
========

Net Worth Analysis

Short-Term Net Worth

-11,130

Long-Term Net Worth

76,875

= $ 65,745
========
Net Worth

Figure 5-1

Supporting Schedules

Now is an excellent time for you to learn about a little organizational trick that accountants use that will save you hours of grief. The concept is the *supporting schedule,* and it is very simple.

The first item in the Short-Term Assets is Cash. Sam and Wendy have $2,750 in cash, but it's not all in their checking account. Three months—or three years—from now, when they're looking back at the Balance Sheet, they might wonder, "Why did we think we had $2,750 back then? I can only account for about $1,800."

Now take a look at Figure 5-2. It details how Sam and Wendy added up their various cash assets to arrive at $2,750.

Figure 5-2: Supporting Schedule for Cash

A   *Cash*

Checking Account	$ 824
Credit Union	187
Money Market Fund	350
Leftover Traveler's Checks	700
Savings Account	689
	$2,750

Wendy's supporting schedule for Cash is little more than well-labeled notes on a yellow pad. Yet it provides crucial backup that is generally missing in the accounting systems of individuals and families.

Normally Sam and Wendy wouldn't bother counting up what little cash they might have on hand and adding that to their Balance Sheet. But the Sheridans had recently returned from a vacation and still had some of their uncashed traveler's checks on hand, which they were using for cash to avoid trips to the automatic teller until the traveler's checks ran out.

Leftover traveler's checks are just the kind of asset that's likely to be forgotten years later when you're trying to figure out what you were thinking when you said you had all that cash. So might one of the savings, money market or credit union accounts, if it had subsequently been closed.

The "Ref." columns on the Balance Sheet provide boxes that refer to items on the supporting schedules. In this case, Wendy used the reference "A," which appeared on the Balance Sheet, to refer to what she labeled Supporting Schedule "A," for Cash.

The supporting schedule can be used in a variety of ways. For instance, the Sheridans' Other Liquid Assets of $2,520 were supported by Schedule B (Figure 5-3), where Sam merely multiplied the number of shares of stock they had by the current market price.

Figure 5-3: Supporting Schedule for Other Liquid Assets

B   *Other Liquid Assets*

Apple Computer Stock	120 shares
	× $ 21 price
	$2,520

At this point, the Sheridans are ready to add up their two types of Short-Term Assets—Cash and Other Liquid Assets—for a total of $5,270. This means that they have $5,270 worth of funds they can get their hands on quickly.

Next, Sam and Wendy move down to attack the Longer-Term Assets portion of their Balance Sheet. The first item is Investments and, even though they only have one investment to add up—a one-sixth ownership in a small apartment building—the calculations necessary to arrive at its value are a perfect application for a supporting schedule. They label it Supporting Schedule C (Figure 5-4).

Figure 5-4: Supporting Schedule for Investments

C   *Investments*

Partnership Interest in Royal Arms Apartments:	
Estimated Market Value	$ 500,000
Less Mortgage	350,000
Net Equity	$ 150,000
Our Ownership	× ⅙
	$ 25,000

The Sheridans' investment in this small real estate partnership (put together by Sam's brother-in-law) has not done nearly as well as they had hoped. Although they enjoyed some tax deductions and they will ultimately make a small profit on the investment, they have been frustrated that the apartments could not be sold when projected.

(The value of the property in the real estate partnership has been reduced by the mortgage, and the mortgage therefore does not appear on the Mortgages line on the Liabilities side, as it would if this property were held solely by Sam and Wendy. Because Sam and Wendy do not have the same kind of control over their partnership asset—they can't, for instance, have the property refinanced without the agreement of their partners—it's more appropriate to show the "net" value of the partnership.)

Let's Not Kid Ourselves

Sam and Wendy feel much better about their other real estate "investment"—their home, purchased two years earlier. They bought the little two-bedroom, one-bath house in a San Francisco suburb for $125,000—an outrageous price, they thought at the time. In the intervening years, home prices in their area have escalated such that you can't touch a bungalow like theirs for less than $140,000.

Their friend Lillian is a real estate agent. "Oh, this is the cutest house on the block," gushed Lillian. "I'd list it for $160,000."

But Sam and Wendy would be wise to temper Lillian's enthusiasm with a little Financial Sanity. Valuing personal residences is an excellent opportunity to apply one of the basic tenets of the Financial Sanity system.

It's tempting, when assessing our net worth, to tell ourselves little white lies about the value of our assets, thereby making ourselves look better on paper. But the system I'm sharing with you in this book will become the foundation for your personal financial decision-making. You wouldn't want to foul up those important decisions with bad data.

So we have a policy in Financial Sanity called *Let's not kid ourselves.* It includes valuing assets at close to what we may actually receive for them.

Sam and Wendy, following the "Let's not kid ourselves" advice, decide that, when the deal finally closes, they're more likely to have sold the house for $150,000. So they value the house on their Balance Sheet at $150,000. Right?

Wrong! When Sam and Wendy do finally sell the house, Lillian Gush will get a commission of $9,000. Furthermore, although the house has been recently spruced up, Sam estimates that about $1,000 worth of minor repairs will have to be done to make the house salable.

By the time Sam and Wendy have subtracted the cost of repairs and both Lillian's commission and her optimism, the house is worth about $140,000. The complete analysis of this calculation is Sam and Wendy's Supporting Schedule D (Figure 5-5).

Figure 5-5: Schedule for Calculating Value of Personal Residence

D   *Personal Residence*

257 Hudson Street	
Estimated Market Value	$ 150,000
Less Commission (6%)	−9,000
Less Fixing-Up Costs	−1,000
	$ 140,000

"But It's an Investment!"

Another favorite area of confusion is the issue of personal assets that are "investments." Oriental rugs, cars, antiques and art often fall into this murky, illogical area of financial double-talk.

You've seen it. Your yuppie friend cruises art galleries on the weekend and plunks down $1,200 for a painting by a rising contemporary artist. He hangs it on the wall of his rented apartment and says, "It's really an investment."

Is it? Is your friend ever going to sell his painting? Presumably he's not an art dealer, so we can assume that, although he bought it at retail, he'll be selling it at wholesale. But that aside, will this painting ever be sold at all? Right now, it's a nice thing to have on the wall. Later, when it becomes rare and valuable, will it be merely a rare and valuable nice thing to hang on the wall? Or will it be sold to finance Megan's college education? Your friend's $1,200 painting may be worth a small fortune when he dies (thereby raising his estate taxes), but even his heirs may not turn the old heirloom into cash.

Antiques may hold their value better than new furniture, but tell me—do you own an antique shop downtown?

In keeping with our "Let's not kid ourselves" policy, unless you have clear plans to sell your collectible acquisition, I would suggest that if you walk on it, hang it over your sofa or drive it to work—it's probably not an investment. If you aren't going to sell it—and sell it like a pro—don't call it an investment. And certainly don't use the "But it's an investment!" rationale to buy something you otherwise wouldn't buy.

Valuing Personal Assets

The "investment" pitfall comes to light when you value Personal Assets. It's not that it's so all-fired important that you value Personal Assets exactly—although you should be careful not to overvalue some of the larger Personal Assets, like cars. It's just that, in valuing Personal Assets for your Balance Sheet, some of the foibles of your more optimistic days come to disenchanting light. There, for instance, is that antique oak desk you bought to fix up and resell. Judging from its position under a pile of tools in the garage, it's in danger of becoming the world's most expensive workbench. The same might go for that vintage Jaguar you were always so proud of. After seven weeks (and about $180 in advertising costs) in the classifieds, its "value" seems to have dropped about 35 percent.

Sam and Wendy had their own "it's an investment" foibles, but we won't embarrass them by dredging up the details here. Figure 5-6 shows the beginning and end of their long list of assets that they valued mostly by "armchair evaluations." Again, this list is an important one to commit to a supporting schedule. You'll find yourself constantly needing to re-create this list and its values for Balance Sheets—both for your own budgetary purposes and for applying for loans. This list can also be helpful for your insurance records.

Figure 5-6: Supporting Schedule for Personal Assets

E   Personal Assets

Stereo	$ 250
Sofa	850
TV	850
Old TV	125
Honda	2,500
VW	1,800
Armoire	700
. . .	. . .
. . .	. . .
Books	400
Jewelry	4,100
	$ 24,880
	say . . .
	$ 25,000

Retirement Funds

The amount entered for Retirement Funds for the Sheridans is, again, supported by a schedule. Even with only two components, the calculation is moderately complex.

Figure 5-7: Supporting Schedule for Retirement Funds

F   Retirement Funds

IRA		$ 2,187
Company Plan:		
Account Balance	$ 20,940	
Vesting %	20%	
		4,188
	$ 6,375	

Company-sponsored retirement funds can often be a mystery to employees. In this case, Sam had to check with the personnel department of his employer to find out what he had in his pension fund and how much vesting he had earned.

Finally, Sam and Wendy had totaled up all their assets. They found themselves in control of more than $200,000 in assets. The next question spurred them on to finish their Balance Sheet: How much of that $201,645 was really theirs—and how much was being claimed by creditors?

Liabilities

Sam and Wendy made the same use of supporting schedules for their liability items as they did for assets. But, since we're getting so familiar with supporting schedules, I won't guide you through them step-by-step. I will, however, point out a few wrinkles in the fine art of developing numbers for your Balance Sheet.

The Sheridans' credit card debt was fairly easy to calculate. It was just a matter of getting out all of their credit card statements and finding the box that says "New Balance."*

The Line of Credit was even easier: They consulted their statement from the lender. Of course, only the amounts Sam and Wendy actually borrowed on the line count as a liability. Their "line" with the bank is $15,000. This means the bank is willing to lend them $15,000 anytime the Sheridans want. The $15,000 is essentially like a credit limit on a credit card. However, Sam and Wendy have borrowed only $8,000 of the $15,000 the bank offered them. So, $8,000 is what appears on their Balance Sheet as a liability.

The Tax Liability number was a little trickier. The Sheridans had to call their tax accountant, who did a scratch pad analysis for them over

*This is the easiest and least sophisticated method for determining the balance due on a credit card. A more accurate method is to keep a balance on your credit card the same way you keep a balance on your checkbook—which, of course, requires keeping track of all your purchases, writing them down as you go. A middle road, which I recommend, is to take your latest charge card New Balance and add it to any charges you've made that don't already appear on the bill. As a practical matter, you do this by riffling through all the tissue copies (which you should *always* keep) of your recent charges and setting aside the ones that didn't appear on the last couple of statements. The set-aside tissue copies are what will probably appear on your next bill. But you are indebted for that money *now*—even though the bill hasn't come for them—because you're wearing *now* the sweater (or the Beef Wellington) that you bought with the card. If you maintain a habit of stapling the tissue copies of charges to the back of the statements they appear on, you will accomplish two worthy goals: You will have made sure that all the charges on the statements are legitimate, and you will always know that all the unstapled tissue copies you still have on hand are charges that you owe that have not yet appeared on a bill. At any time these loose tissue copies can be added to the latest available New Balance and you will quickly know your accurate liability. (In any of these calculations, be sure to subtract any payment you have made since the statement was issued.)

the phone, based on Sam's fairly clear understanding of how this particular year compared to the prior year. Had Sam had less of a grasp on their income for the year, or had there been drastic changes during the year (such as sale and purchase of a house), or had their situation been complex, the Sheridans probably would have had to spend a few hundred dollars getting an accurate tax projection from their CPA. As it was, the cost of getting a rough estimate of how much they would owe cost them only about $50.

Some readers are sophisticated enough about tax law to make their own rough projections. (A very few have sophisticated software that calculates their tax liability for them.) The majority of readers may not know enough about taxes to prepare a tax projection, but may know that their withholding is likely to be nearly correct and that they are incurring no additional unpaid tax liability. For the rest of you, however—especially those operating your own small business— unpaid tax liabilities may be a very real issue. And paying for information about your tax liability in the middle of the year may be an unfortunate product of the complexity of your life and the unnecessary and unproductive complexity of our federal and state tax systems. Sorry.

Other debts weren't difficult. Both the Short-Term and the Longer-Term Other Debts were family debts. The short-term $700 was due to Wendy's sister, who had sold the couple some antique furniture and was supposed to be paid "sometime." The Longer-Term Other Debt was the $25,000 Sam's parents had loaned the couple to help them buy their house. Its due date was informal, but the general idea was that they would not have to pay anything but interest for a very long time.

"Short-Term Net Worth"

After filling in the last of their Short-Term debts, Sam added them up: they came to $16,400.

"That must be wrong," Wendy said, so she added them up again: $16,400.

The reality that they owed, short-term, more than three times what they had in liquid (short-term) assets was sobering. It worried Wendy, who harbored hopes of taking leave from work to have a baby sometime soon.

"I would feel awfully vulnerable if we lost my income and were trying to come from so far behind," she confided to me in a session I had with the couple.

"Vulnerable is a good word," I replied. "It's not that you guys are in trouble—or even headed for trouble. Your situation is quite common, and with two incomes—at least one of them being a pretty good salary—you can work your way out from behind this short-run eight ball in just a few years," I reassured her.

"But," I continued, "you really haven't got a lot of resiliency. If you're dropped, you won't bounce, you'll crack."

Sam shifted uneasily in his seat. "What kind of bouncing are you talking about?" he asked.

Wendy interrupted, "Like if we had a baby and I stopped working for a while."

"Or," I added, "if one of you was disabled. You have no disability insurance."

Sam nodded thoughtfully, if a little glumly.

"Or, if one of you lost your job," I added. "It could be one of a hundred things—or it could be nothing."

We talked further about Sam and Wendy's somewhat precarious cash vs. debt position. Ultimately, the Sheridans didn't do anything to protect themselves from the vulnerability they felt. Nothing bad happened, either, and, a few years later, as we shall see in later chapters, Sam and Wendy had earned and restructured their way out of their precarious position.

What we are talking about here might be called "Short-Term Net Worth"—Short-Term Assets minus Short-Term Liabilities. While I think it's a good idea to consider the implications of your own Short-Term Net Worth figure, I am reluctant, as usual, to offer you any rule of thumb about what your Short-Term Net Worth should be. Keep in mind the rule "There's an exception to every rule and you're it."

Just to give you an idea of how this number can change, Figure 5-8 compares Sam and Wendy's Short-Term Net Worth for the year of this example to the year immediately prior and again to years two and three years hence.

Figure 5-8: Historical Pattern of Short-Term Net Worth

YEAR	1 YEAR PRIOR	EXAMPLE YEAR	2 YEARS HENCE	3 YEARS HENCE
Major Event	Took Cruise		Sold Investments	Bought New House
Short-Term Assets	$ 5,165	5,270	15,000	3,655
Short-Term Liabilities	5,200	16,400	0	2,000
Short-Term Net Worth	−35	−11,130	15,000	1,655

It's evident that a seriously negative Short-Term Net Worth, although perhaps alarming, is not necessarily fatal. Again, it's okay to ponder the ramifications of having an unsatisfactory Short-Term Net Worth, but don't use it to discourage yourself or make judgments about your chances of success.

Net Worth

Sam and Wendy continued their Balance Sheet. They dropped in balances due on their Term Loans (student and car), which they got from merely consulting the statements from the lenders.

Their home mortgage was a little more problematic. Their lender did not provide them with current balance information each month. Sam got the number for this analysis by calling the lender and asking for the payoff amount. Other methods of determining the balance due on mortgages include:

- getting an amortization schedule, whether by printing it on your own computer, getting one from the bank or having your tax or financial advisor produce one for you
- calculating the current balance due on a financial calculator (a regular calculator can't do the calculation)
- figuring it out by hand from the inception of the loan

Finally, Sam and Wendy had all their Liabilities totaled up. Their Short-Term Liabilities plus each of their Longer-Term Liabilities were cranked into the old pocket calculator to come up with a grand, if not glorious, total of $135,900.

With both a Total Assets number and a Total Liabilities number, Sam and Wendy could now calculate that famous measure of wealth: Net Worth.

"I can't believe we have a Net Worth of $65,000," Wendy beamed when they showed me their Balance Sheet. After her upsetting experience with the relationship of Short-Term Assets to Short-Term Liabilities, their Net Worth number was a pleasant surprise.

"Most people who've owned their own homes for a few years usually show a decent Net Worth, unless they're in a depressed housing market. In fact," I added, citing a recent statistical study, "half the people in the United States would have no Net Worth were it not for the equity they have in their home. Your Net Worth is fairly healthy because you've got more assets than just your house."

I did some quick analysis of their Balance Sheet for them:

- "The net equity in your home accounts for about $30,000 of your Net Worth." (I took the $140,000 net realizable value and subtracted the $84,000 mortgage. Then I also subtracted the $25,000 Other Debt, which had been a loan from his parents to buy the house. The net was $31,000.)
- "Your Royal Arms investment accounts for $25,000.
- "And the remaining equity (Net Worth) comes approximately from your Retirement Funds."

I assumed that all the other liabilities were generally associated with buying Personal Assets, the value of which almost offset the amounts of the loans.

The analysis helped the Sheridans to understand how they could feel poor even when they had a fairly good start at building substantial Net Worth. "When a lot of your cash is tied up—in nonliquid investments, in your house, in personal assets or in retirement plans—it's easy to feel that you have no wealth, because you can't spend any of it today."

Exercise: Creating Your Own Balance Sheet

Now it's time to create your own Balance Sheet, the same way the Sheridans did. Don't forget to use supporting schedules.

Don't be afraid to change the categories of the Balance Sheet if you need to in order to make it more meaningful to you.

In case you're not absolutely clear about how the math goes:

- *Short-Term Assets* (which is a subtotal) is the total of any and all items above it on the *Assets* side.
- *Total All Assets* is the total of all the assets listed below the *Short-Term Assets* subtotal, plus the subtotal for *Short-Term Assets*.
- *Short-Term Liabilities* is the total of any and all items above it on the *Liabilities* side.
- *Total All Liabilities* is the total of all the *Liabilities* listed below the *Short-Term Liabilities* subtotal, plus the subtotal for *Short-Term Liabilities*.
- *Net Worth* equals *Total All Assets* minus *Total All Liabilities*.
- *Total Liabilities Plus Net Worth* must be equal to *Total All Assets*. If it doesn't, you probably didn't calculate *Net Worth* correctly.

The concepts of the Balance Sheet aren't difficult for most of us, but putting one together takes a little digging around in your records. Honor the work that you do to track down accurate numbers by recording your note-taking on properly labeled supporting schedules.

In this chapter, you have defined your financial situation with respect to a single *point* in time. The next chapter will teach you to efficiently summarize your financial ebbs and flows over a *period* of time. We will return to the Balance Sheet, however, in Chapter 8, where we will use Balance Sheet information to analyze just how financially powerful you are—and find out just how much major discretionary spending you can afford.

Simplicity, simplicity, simplicity! I say, let your affairs be as two or three, and not a hundred or a thousand; instead of a million count half a dozen, and keep your accounts on your thumb-nail.
—Henry David Thoreau

6

Summarizing Your Cash Flow

When I first started teaching the Financial Sanity Workshop in San Francisco, I invited people to bring in any financial information they thought might be useful. At the very first course I conducted, one couple lugged in a big cardboard box jammed full of statements, papers and records.

"We didn't want to be missing any crucial information," they explained, "and this is what it took—this is our life."

This story points to the complexity of our financial lives. Our personal financial dealings can easily be more complex than those of a small business.

The box that the San Francisco couple dragged into the seminar room was real, but it was also a metaphor. Everyone in the room had a cardboard box full of financial confusion in their heads that evening. A cluttered mélange of numbers, balances, interest rates and terms flows around in our heads, together with subjective, nonnumerical notions of wealth, how well we're doing, affordability and deservedness. Because we generally store our financial information in our heads, it tends to be confusing and disorganized—and not subject to analysis.

This chapter will take the cardboard boxes of your life—both the real boxes and the mental filing cabinets—and reduce them to a few sheets of paper. The Inflow-Outflow Information Sheet, together with the Balance Sheet you just produced, should put an end to your need for stacks of files, statements and papers.

Sean and Maggie Bennett's Inflow-Outflow Information Sheet offers a good variety of entries, so I've reproduced theirs as an example at Figure 6-1. You may want to refer to it as you read through the explanation in this chapter.

Essentially, the Inflow-Outflow Information Sheet is nothing more than an intelligent list of information about the following kinds of financial inflows and outflows:

- Inflow
- Debt
- Funding
- Expenses

Inflow

The work we're doing throughout this section has to do with the ebb and flow of cash. (By cash we mean, typically, the balances in your checking and other cash accounts, such as credit union share accounts, savings accounts and money market accounts. We are also referring to activity involving piggy banks, wallets and mattresses, but only if that's where you keep substantial funds.)

The important thing to remember about this category is that we're talking about inflow, not income. Inflow we're defining as anything that results in cash coming into the checking account. That includes income, of course, but also includes loan proceeds, sales of assets and so forth.

One question to address is whether to include income before or after taxes. For most people whose taxes are withheld from their payroll checks and who neither owe a great deal on April 15 nor have a fortune coming back, after-tax (net) income is the best number to use. Some taxpayers can—legally—pay significantly less than they owe during the year and, of course, owe a whopping bill on April 15. If you're one of these lucky people, you should count your *gross* income as inflow and use the funding technique in Chapter 12 to accumulate funds for the tax bill you're building up. (This technique is usually most

Description	Code	Amount	Frequency	Nonmonthly When Next Payment Falls Due	Debt Repayments Debt Owed	Interest Rate	Minimum Payment
Sean's Salary	I	1,350	twice monthly				
Maggie's Salary	I	288	Weekly	Thurs.			
Haircut	E	25	once every 6 weeks	Jan. 31			
Dividends — Chevron	I	70	Quarterly	Feb			
Groceries	E	80	Weekly				
Property Tax	F	550	once every 6 months	Dec & Apr			
Clothes — Maggie	F	?					
Clothes — Sean	F	?					
Contributions	F	?					
Church	E	5	Weekly				
Phone	E	20	Monthly				
City — Garbage	E	40	every other month	Feb			
Entertainment	E	about 200	Monthly				
Auto Insurance	E	300 700 + 11	Yearly Monthly	Feb Mar			
Gasoline	E	?					
Auto Repairs	F	about 1000	Yearly				
Walking Around Money	E	100	Weekly				
Macy's	D				580	18%	25
Visa	D				1,520	21%	45
Mortgage — First	D				105,000	15%	1,365
Mortgage — Second	D				10,000	12%	100

Figure 6-1

appropriate for anyone who doesn't have withholding and, instead, pays the majority of his or her taxes primarily through quarterly estimated tax payments.)

Inflow also includes such things as:

- gifts (*to* you, of course—not *from* you)
- sale of assets
- interest earned
- borrowing

Again, we're talking about in*flow* here, not in*come.* That's why borrowing is included. Borrowing isn't income, because you have to pay it back. But it is inflow because it increases the cash in your checking account.

Just as there are *nonincome* items, like borrowing, that *do* turn out to qualify as inflow, there are also *income* items that *don't* qualify— because they don't increase the checking account balance. Examples include:

- increase in the cash surrender value of whole-life insurance
- interest earned on an IRA
- increase in the vested value of a company-sponsored pension plan
- increase in the value of marketable securities or other investments

Debt

Debt, too, is a straightforward concept. The same items of debt that appeared in your Balance Sheet should appear here, even if you aren't currently making payments.

Funding

Since we haven't talked yet about funding, for purposes of this exercise, funding includes any expenditure that isn't fairly steady, month-to-month. Such expenditures generally fall into three major categories:

- major purchases (like a new car)
- scheduled expenditures (like semiannual property taxes)
- expenses over which you want to maintain some control on a yearly basis, even though they may vary from month-to-month (like buying clothes and giving gifts)

If you do any regular saving, code that as funding also.

Expenses

In the Financial Sanity system, we do not make the usual distinction between fixed and variable expenses. There are several reasons for this.

First, those of you with financial backgrounds will remember that fixed and variable are relative concepts, depending on the scope of the decision-making cycle. Let's take an example from personal finance. Rent expense is fixed over the short term: There is virtually no effective way to economize on next month's rent. But over the course of a year or two, rent is more controllable. You could move to a less-expensive place, take in a boarder or eliminate rent altogether by buying your own home.

The second reason is related to the first: It's often hard enough to get people to reassess their ingrained patterns of spending without referring to some of them as "fixed." In Chapter 24 I'll ask you to challenge every single one of your expenses, whether fixed or variable, necessity or luxury, illegal, immoral or fattening. I'll try to convince you—for a brief, irresponsible moment, at least—that all expenses are variable.

Third, I'm encouraging you to expand your budgeting scope. I want you to look at next week and next month, but I also want you to look at next year and after.

Finally, I actually have a bias for altering fixed expenses, rather than what usually might be considered variable expenses. The term "fixed" implies that it's not to be changed—yet changing fixed expenses (what I call "restructuring") is generally significantly more effective than economizing on those variable expenses most budgets have us work on.

Exercise: Inflow-Outflow Information Sheet

1. Use a sheet of paper with headings similar to those in Figure 6-1. (Alternatively, you may photocopy this form from Appendix B.)

2. Describe the expense, debt or inflow item in the Description column. Use a new line for each item.

3. You can code each item in the Code box. Coding is actually optional, but it may help you pull together like items quickly when you're doing your Debt Reduction Planning (Chapter 11), your Funding (Chapter 17) and your Master Budget Summary (Chapter 20). Use these codes:

I = Inflow
D = Debt
E = Expenses
F = Funding

4. The next box is for the Amount of the inflow or outflow. Enter the amount exactly as you know it. If property taxes are $600 in April and December, write that. Don't artificially convert it to $100 a month or $1,200 a year.

5. Next describe the Frequency of the item. Again, be descriptive. If your auto insurance bill requires an initial payment of $300 in February and another $700 spread over eleven monthly payments, say just that. (See the example in Figure 6-1 for the treatment of precisely this set of facts.) The goal is to provide precisely the information you'll need about the timing and amount of payments. Averaging doesn't serve your purpose here; what you want is the detail.

6. As you work on the Inflow-Outflow Information Sheet, keep in mind that many of your nonmonthly items will end up on a timeline in work you'll do in later chapters. For that reason, the next box—NonMonthly: When Next Payment Falls Due—allows you to specify the starting point. This feature of the Inflow-Outflow Information Sheet is integral to putting away the cardboard box forever.

The next three columns are used only for items of debt you owe. Again, they are designed to collect enough information that you won't need to hunt up your latest Visa statement in order to plan your debt reduction program.

7. The Debt Owed column is for the principal amount of the debt—the remaining balance. The amount you customarily make in monthly payments (particularly if it is different from the Minimum Payment required) may be entered in the Amount column, or you may leave the Amount column blank for Debt items.

8. The annual interest rate is the next piece of information you'll record. If you're like some Financial Sanity participants (including me, the first time I did this), this might be the first time you paid enough attention to the interest rates on your loans to actually know which credit cards charged the highest interest rate.

9. Finally, you'll need to record the minimum payment due on this debt. This information is primarily useful for credit cards. (For some debts—such as a car loan or home loan—the minimum payment is *the* payment.) Although I generally don't advise making mere minimum payments on credit card debts, it is sometimes advantageous to make a minimum payment on one card while you aggressively work to zero out the balance on another card.

Tripping over Information Potholes

At various times throughout the Financial Sanity process, you'll stumble over "information potholes." In order to move forward with your planning, you'll need information you don't know—and can't even estimate.

Information potholes can be disastrous if you let them immobilize you. For instance, if you have no idea how much a college education costs, how can you set up a funding program for it?

Your first recourse in the absence of information is to estimate. Very often, the value of more precise information is not worth the trouble required to get it. If you don't know how much you spend on gas each month, for instance, it makes more sense to merely guess at some round number than to shut down your financial planning process to conduct a month-long test to determine the true amount. Sure—conduct the test. But use an estimate to keep you going in the meantime.

To zero in on more accurate numbers, I recommend doing a simple organizational technique utilized by many businesses and professional disciplines and known variously as "point sheet," "open items list" and scores of other names.

It is, very simply, a list of unresolved questions or items, assembled in one place rather than on scraps of paper or perched precariously in someone's memory.

Figure 6-2 is an example of an open item list for the Financial Sanity system. I call it the Information Needed List. A yellow scratch pad would do as well. The format of the list isn't nearly as important as that it exists and you keep it in an intelligent, easy-to-find place—like your Financial Sanity workbook binder.

Exercise: The Information Needed List

1. Review the exercises you've completed so far—especially the Inflow-Outflow Information Sheet and the Balance Sheet—and determine what unanswered questions you have about your personal financial life.

2. Write the question on a piece of paper with headings similar to the Information Needed List in Figure 6-2.

3. Reflect on what might be the sources for finding the answer to your question—the public library, your accountant, the personnel department of your employer, and so forth—and jot those down. Psychologically, this will help you move faster to resolve the question.

4. Place the Information Needed List in a prominent place in your Financial Sanity workbook—details about how to organize your workbook are at the beginning of Appendix B—and make plans to get started on your research.

Information Needed	Source(s)	Answer
How much will college cost for baby?	Library — Money Magazine	Newspaper says $100 per month good rule of thumb
What is tax affect when we sell duplex?	CPA	
Gas Expense	Last year's gas card records — or run 1 month test	

Figure 6-2

Moving Forward—with Less Baggage

The Inflow-Outflow Information Sheet very simply collects information efficiently and stores it in one place so that it's available for you when you do the planning and analysis of later chapters. By effectively putting your filing cabinet on a starvation diet, you have dramatically taken the initiative in clearing away the confusion around your personal financial affairs.

And by ferreting out only the essential details, you have supplied yourself with the facts pertinent to your planning efforts, and have swept away the paper fog that nonessential financial records can produce.

I'm living so far beyond my income that we may almost be said to be living apart.
— *e e cummings*

7

Your Spending Power

In this chapter, you'll find out how much financial clout you have available to make your dreams come true. I define a new term— *Spending Power.* Conceptually, it's not much different from the economist's notion of "discretionary income" or the financial planner's "investable income." But I call it by a different name because I have a very specific definition for Spending Power that I don't want confused with these other definitions of "excess" income.

In defining Spending Power, we're looking for the number, in dollars, that represents the money you have significant choice about. For example, if you made only enough money to pay your taxes and to house, feed and clothe your family, everyone would agree that you would have zero Spending Power—you have no choice about what you spend your money on. But zero Spending Power can exist at even high levels of income, if all your income is "booked up." No matter how indulgent the luxury, as long as you don't feel you can do without it, the money you spend on it is not available to you as Spending Power.

Spending Power is, simply, the excess of income over what I call your *Baseline Cost of Living.* Since it exceeds what you need to make it through the month (in the manner to which you have chosen to become accustomed), you have a significant amount of choice about where it goes.

Don't confuse your Baseline Cost of Living with merely survival costs, or true necessities. Your Baseline Cost of Living includes all the expenses that you *consider* necessities. Of course, they include food, clothing and shelter—those are Baseline Cost of Living items for everyone. But as we grow more prosperous and become entrenched in a higher standard of living, what constitutes our Baseline Cost of Living goes higher and higher. Even people who are by no means prosperous consider such things as a color television, a stereo, two cars and a few other luxuries as some of their baseline necessities. And, as you achieve greater incomes, your family's "overhead" costs can rise significantly as it maintains cleaning, gardening and pool service, semiannual trips to the cabin, ballet lessons, private schools—any of which, if lost, would be perceived as a significant blow to the family's quality of life.

(Not every habitual luxury is so important that it can't be negotiated away: A Kansas City doctor and his wife were more than willing to give up one or both of their vacation homes—they just weren't that important to them. Another family, although considerably less prosperous, viewed their vacation property as a critical link in helping the family stay together as it plays together and considered the vacation home an important part of their Baseline Cost of Living.)

If, in the normal course of your spending pattern, you go further into debt each month, then you have negative Spending Power. Most of us, however, have positive Spending Power. We have some amount of money (few of us really know how much) over which we have some choice and control. We can use it to invest in our future, maintain a better standard of living now, pay off debt, go on vacation, eat out and so forth.

When I talk about financial decision-making—budgeting, control of expenses, financial management, financial planning—I am talking about what to do and not do with your Spending Power. There's not much point in talking about managing your cost of living—that money is mostly spoken for already. The fun part of money is in the Spending Power area, so let's find out just how much Spending Power you can have fun with.

As you read this, you may be conjuring up a horrifying vision of a giant accounting project designed to carefully define your Baseline

Cost of Living. Don't despair. An entire weekend of messy old files, bank statements, ancient check registers and long laborious spreadsheets is *not* in front of you.

Instead, the techniques of this chapter let you find out what your Baseline Cost of Living really is—and very quickly. More important than saving you a weekend immersed in bookkeeping, however, the technique outlined in this chapter will allow you to plot out your financial future with a more realistic outlook than you've ever been able to have before. Here you will learn more about the dynamics of your own personal finances than you could possibly know any other way. It's the closest thing to actually living through the future and then getting to go back and plan it right.

This chapter will show you how to determine what you can afford in a "big," or macro, sense. That is, it will answer the question "What can I afford?" and be fairly accurate within about a thousand dollars or so per year. (Later, in Chapter 20, you'll answer the same question in the micro sense. You'll fine-tune your answer down to "What can I afford?" to the nearest $10–100 per month.)

Calculating Your Spending Power

Remember when we talked about your Balance Sheet? I said it was basically a "snapshot" of your current financial condition. Let me carry that financial snapshot metaphor a little further.

Let's say that your current financial snapshot is a Polaroid picture of you and your spouse and two-year-old in front of your cute three-bedroom, two-story house. In the driveway is the new car, the old car and the boat you bought last year. It's a nice picture. Everyone is smiling.

Now put this picture down in the middle of the coffee table in front of you. Next imagine a picture that represents your financial position three years ago. Let's say it shows you and your spouse—you were smiling then, too. You're standing in front of the little two-bedroom, one-bath house you used to own—your first. No baby in this picture. The old car is still in the driveway, along with the ancient VW convertible you used to love to take to the beach. (You're still sorry you sold that car.) The new car and the boat are nowhere in sight.

Put this picture on the left side of the coffee table.

Obviously, these two pictures show, in summary, what you had then and what you have now. Now let's imagine a third picture on the right-hand side of the coffee table. This picture will show just the difference between the other two pictures.

Old Picture	New Picture	Difference

```
+---------------------+
|  +----------------+ |
|  | small house    | |                              - small house
|  | VW             | |                                   -VW
|  | old car        | |          +----------------+
|  |                | |          | old car        |
|  |                | |          | baby           |    + baby
|  +----------------+ |          | boat           |    + boat
|                     |          | new car        |    + new car
|                     |          | +------------+ |
|                     |          | |large house | |    + large house
|                     |          | +------------+ |
+---------------------+          |                |
                                 |                |
                                 +----------------+
```

Figure 7–1

It will include all the things that were added: the boat, the new car and the baby. It will include the new house. It will also somehow show as negative differences the old house and the VW.

The Spending Power Analysis does in numbers what I just asked you to imagine in pictures. If we could, for example, just put a dollar value on the plus items and minus items in the Difference column in Figure 7-1—that would tell us Spending Power. That would tell us how much in big ticket items, investments and asset building this family has been able to do in the past.

It's a little more complicated than that, of course. (The example in Figure 7-1 doesn't include mortgages, for instance.) Let's look now at a realistic example. We'll look at Sam and Wendy Sheridan's situation again to see how the analysis works.

Item/Checked?/Rationale

You remember that Sam and Wendy created a Balance Sheet in Chapter 5. To help them determine their Spending Power, I had Sam and Wendy prepare another Balance Sheet—this one from about a year prior to the Balance Sheet in Figure 5-1.

You will see Sam and Wendy's prior-year Balance Sheet as the left-hand part of Figure 7-2, Spending Power Analysis. It was prepared using exactly the same rules and techniques as the current Balance

Major Events During Period **Cruise**

	Balance Sheet			Difference
	Earlier Date	Later Date	√	Period Covered
	Year Ago	*Now*		*12 mos.*

ASSETS
Short-Term
Cash	845	2,750	√	+	1,905
Other Liquid Assets	4,320	2,520		+	

Longer-Term
Investments	25,000	25,000		+	
Personal Residence	130,000	140,000		+	
Personal Assets	22,000	25,000	√	+	3,000
Retirement Funds	2,000	6,375		+	

Total Assets	184,165	201,645	

LIABILITIES
Short-Term
Credit Card Debt	5,200	6,450	√	–	1,250
Lines of Credit		8,000	√	–	8,000
Tax Liabilities		1,250	√	–	1,250
Other Debts		700	√	–	700

Longer-Term
Term Loans	7,500	10,500	√	–	3,000
Mortgage(s)	84,700	84,000	√	–	- 700
Other Debts	25,000	25,000	√	–	0

Total Liabilities	122,400	135,900	

NET WORTH	61,765	65,745	

Extraordinary Expenditures/Adjustments
Normal New Personal Assets	+	- 2,500
	+	
Vacation	+	8,750
	+	

Spending Power for This Period — - 2,345

Adjustments to Calculate Spending Power for Next Period
	+	
	+	
Estimated Income Increase Next Y	+	3,000
	+	

Projected Spending Power for Next Period — 655

Monthly* Spending Power for Next Period — 55
(* Divide Spending Power by number of months in period covered.)

Figure 7–2

Sheet. Sam prepared the same carefully labeled Supporting Schedules for the old Balance Sheets as he had for the current one. The Sheridans did find it a little more difficult preparing the year-old Balance Sheet, just because the information was not quite so readily available. It took Wendy "forever" to find their old check register, and one of their credit card statements could not be found at all—they had to estimate the balance on it.

(Many less-organized readers of this book may, in fact, find the notion of reconstructing years-old records laughable. They will have to stick to more recent prior-period Balance Sheets—perhaps just a few months. Other readers will have old Balance Sheets already prepared —in the form of loan applications made months or years before. With a few adjustments to bring the treatment of assets into line with our rules, these people will have "instant" prior-period Balance Sheets to feed into the Spending Power Analysis.)

In the middle column (labeled "Now") the Sheridans entered their current-year Balance Sheet information in each of the appropriate spaces.

Armed with their two side-by-side Balance Sheets, Sam and Wendy were eager to sink their budgeting teeth into the Spending Power Analysis.

"We just subtract the differences between the two Balance Sheets, right?" Sam asked.

"That's true," I said, "but we're only interested in some of the differences." That's what the check boxes are for, I explained. You simply check the box if you are going to use the difference number in your calculation of Spending Power. Then calculate the difference between the old and new Balance Sheets only on those lines where the box is checked.

"How do you tell which items should be checked?" Wendy asked.

The key, I explained, was to ask, "Could I have used this money to buy Spending Power (discretionary) items?" If the answer is yes, the difference for that line item probably represents Spending Power.

Let's run through the items on Sam and Wendy's Spending Power Analysis and briefly review the rationale for checking or not checking each item:

Cash	Yes	The cash could have been spent on discretionary items.
Other Liquid Assets	No	The decrease in asset value was due to market-value loss and so had no cash effect. Also, paper losses in volatile markets have little, if any, value in predicting Spending Pow-

er for the future, which is what the Spending Power Analysis is designed to accomplish. If the change in value had been due to a partial sale of the assets, then the line item would have been included.

Investments	No	Aside from the fact that no change in value makes the point moot, changes in the value of this real estate partnership investment have no affect on spendable dollars unless the investment is sold.
Personal Residence	No	No effect on spendable dollars unless the residence is sold. The values of replacement residences are presumably rising just as fast. However, the portion of the increased value attributable to improvements paid for in cash may be included in Spending Power.
Personal Assets	Yes	Money spent here could have been spent elsewhere.
Retirement Funds	No	These increases represented employer-paid contributions and changes in the vested value of prior-year contributions. Had Sam and Wendy made cash contributions to an IRA, that may have been includable in Spending Power. Also, if Sam and Wendy's spending plans included providing for their retirement, then the buildup of retirement assets *would* be included in the computation of their Spending Power.
All Debt	Yes	Increasing debt provides funds for discretionary spending and decreasing it requires application of discretionary spending dollars.
Net Worth	Never	Since the changes in Net Worth are already mirrored in the changes in the Assets and Liabilities category balances, there is no need to duplicate those changes by using Net Worth in the Spending Power calculation.

Different Spending Powers for Different Purposes

When determining your Spending Power, you must always define what kind of spending you're talking about.

Most of the time, people are talking about devoting money to major purchases (house, car, vacation, furniture, investment, debt repayment and the like) in the coming year. I say "devoting money" and not "spending" because I am including people's ability to save up for a down payment on a new car, a house, and so forth. Spending Power, then, is the yearly or monthly amount of money that is available—or can be made available—to devote to these major expenditures or discretionary expenses.

Sam felt that it was wrong to exclude the increased value of their residence from the Spending Power formula. "One of the things we're planning to buy is a new house," he argued, "and the equity in our old house is *very* important to our efforts to buy a new one."

"True," I admitted. "But to the extent that the market value of your old house goes higher, so will the cost of the new house you want to buy."

(Even if you've found your dream home and plan to live there forever, the increase in its value, again, is superfluous to your Spending Power—simply because you won't be selling the house. The increase in value of any asset is merely *interesting;* it becomes *important* if you sell it.)

Adjustments to Spending Power

Balance Sheet changes were not the only source of information relating to the Sheridans' Spending Power. The remaining changes were recorded in the Extraordinary Expenditures/Adjustments section at the bottom of the analysis.

I had asked the Sheridans if there were any extraordinary expenses they had incurred during the year between the two Balance Sheets we were analyzing. I was looking for expenses that were nonrecurring and which didn't result in an increase in assets that would therefore already be reflected in the Spending Power formula. They mentioned a few minor items too small to worry about, then suddenly remembered their biggest single expense in years—a Mediterranean cruise, made all the more memorable by the fact that they were still in debt for it. I penciled the $8,750, the cruise cost, onto the analysis.

"Isn't that supposed to be a minus number?" Sam asked, looking over my shoulder.

"No," I said, "it adds to your Spending Power."

"It does?" Wendy challenged me. "Seems to me we haven't had a bit of Spending Power ever since we took that cruise."

"Remember," I said, "what we're trying to do here."

I waved the Spending Power Analysis as I talked. "This analysis is designed to give you some guidance about how much you can spend on major purchases in the future. All other things being equal—like cash and credit card balances—any money you spent last year on a major discretionary purchase—well, a similar amount should be available *this* year for some *other* major discretionary purchase."

"I don't know," said Wendy, squinting at the analysis. "Are you saying that *because* we spent so much money last year on this cruise, we will have more money this year to spend on luxuries?"

"No. It's not *because* you spent the money last year. The fact that you spent the money last year is only an *indicator* of the fact that you have Spending Power. For instance, you mentioned that this cruise really drove up your credit card balances. Well, up here in the Liabilities section"—I waved my pencil over the $1,250 increase in credit card debt and the $8,000 increase in Lines of Credit balances—"the increases in these liabilities served to *lower* your calculated Spending Power."

Sam and Wendy nodded their heads up and down in a way that convinced me that they didn't have the faintest idea of what I was talking about.

"Let's put it this way," I said. "The Spending Power Analysis already knows you spent this money."

"How does it know that?" asked Wendy, suspicious.

"It sees that debt has gone up, and it also 'knows' that your assets have not gone up accordingly. The analysis assumes that any money spent is spent on annual, habitual living expenses—your Baseline Cost of Living. What we're trying to do here in the Extraordinary Expenditures/Adjustments section is to isolate the nonrepeating reasons for spending money.

"For instance," I continued, "if you went on an expensive vacation *every* year, I wouldn't be adding the cost of your cruise back here."

"Yeah," said Wendy, "this year we may not go on a vacation at all."

"Exactly," I said. "You might spend that money instead on buying your next house, or a new car, or starting an education fund. All those things are the kinds of things we all devote our Spending Power to."

"And if we were able to spend $8,750 on a cruise last year, we would presumably be able to spend $8,750 on something else this year," Wendy said. "I think I understand. The hardest part to understand is realizing that this analysis already assumes that we spent the money on our regular cost of living—unless we tell it differently."

"Exactly," I agreed. "We have to 'tell' the analysis that some of the money was spent on an extraordinary item and will be available this year for something else."

Up in the assets section of the Spending Power Analysis, we had added $3,000 into our computation of Spending Power because that's how much the Sheridans' Personal Assets had increased in that year.

But when I asked them, Sam and Wendy admitted that they would do a certain amount of new Personal Asset purchases every year, no matter what.

"I think that's true for most of us," I said, "and that's why it's appropriate to subtract out some of the Spending Power that is represented by these purchases."

"I get it," Sam interjected. "You're saying that since we buy this much in Personal Assets every year anyway, it's not really quite like discretionary money."

"Right," I said. "You wouldn't really be able to choose not to spend the money on these items, just like you wouldn't really be able to cut out, say, your entire entertainment budget for the year."

We subtracted the $2,500—which might be called "baseline" purchases of Personal Assets—from the calculation of Spending Power.

Negative Spending Power

After selecting the line items Sam and Wendy would include (check) in their calculation of Spending Power, they next simply needed to calculate the difference between the current Balance Sheet (middle column) and the prior-year Balance Sheet (left column). When calculating the differences between the old and the new, always take the newer and subtract the old from it, and don't make any calculation at all on those lines where the box hasn't been checked.

Sam and Wendy had, as it turns out, negative Spending Power for the year we were analyzing. When they added up all the pluses and minuses in the Difference column, the net result was negative Spending Power of $2,345. Sam and Wendy's Baseline Cost of Living was $2,345 more than their income. Nothing was left for discretionary expenditures like vacations, cars and other personal assets (except for the "normal" $2,500 in personal assets). When they did spend money on these things (like the $8,750 Mediterranean vacation), they went into debt. If you've ever wondered why things just don't seem to add up in your personal budget, do this analysis for yourself.

Negative Spending Power is not uncommon. In my experience, it is more common among young, high-income, two-earning couples than it is among couples with more modest incomes, who somehow manage to maintain a clearer picture of their financial limits.

As higher-income college-educated people start to make decent money for the first time, they want to begin buying the things they've done without for so long, perhaps through years of Spartan lifestyles as they pursued their medical, law and other graduate degrees. They don't feel that their habitual level of purchases is extravagant, but, if it results in negative Spending Power, it is extravagant. In fact, purchasing in excess of available Spending Power could easily be a *definition* of extravagance.

For most people, the slack is taken up by assuming more debt. We've all done that before, and that's why we so often end up habitually overspending and not really understanding why. Debt is a buffer. We don't really experience disappointment or loss when we add a little to our credit card balance.

Calculating Next Year's Spending Power

Although Sam and Wendy had just suffered through a year in which they experienced negative Spending Power, they could fortunately look forward to the following year, in which they had positive Spending Power.

The calculation of next year's Spending Power is made at the bottom of the current year's calculation in Figure 7-2. The last few lines of each year's Spending Power Analysis describe how next year will differ from the current year, due to projected increases in income, increases or decreases in expenses and so on.

Sam and Wendy told me what increases they were expecting in their incomes for the coming year. After deducting an estimated amount for taxes, we calculated that $3,000 would be available. We added that to the calculation for Spending Power.

After adjusting for the $3,000 net (after taxes) anticipated increase in earnings this coming year, Sam and Wendy are looking forward to a very meager $655 of Spending Power for the year. That works out to about $55 a month.

"Boy," said Wendy, shaking her head in disbelief, "if I hadn't seen these numbers . . ." She interrupted herself: "I was all ready to start loosening up the old purse strings when Sam and I got our raises," she said. "You know, an extra night out each month, maybe more expensive clothes. I had no idea we were spending so much more than we were making."

"Or," said Sam, "that after our raises we won't be making enough to cover anything we were planning to do this coming year."

As grim as Sam and Wendy's situation looked, they actually had two viable options in front of them in their quest to upgrade their personal residence. One was to make a significant restructuring in their financial lives to cause a radical shift in their Spending Power. This strategy, which I call Creative Alternatives, is discussed in Chapter 24.

Their other alternative was to work their way into the financial position sufficient to buy the house they wanted. But how long would that take? Would their salary increases keep pace with the rising cost of the home they wanted to buy? Would they ever get there, or would they be like greyhounds, constantly chasing a mechanical rabbit that was always two lengths ahead? Find out how they did in the next chapter, where we follow the Sheridans as they plan their financial future.

The techniques for determining your Spending Power are perhaps your first opportunity to truly grasp how much you can afford in the macro, or large, sense. And for those of you who want to improve what you see, the work you do in the next chapter will allow you to determine just what kind of improvement is required for you to attain what you really want. It's a vision of the future that few people have. And it's a grasp of reality that can make you extraordinarily effective in making decisions about income, levels of monthly expenses and affordability of major purchases.

The only way to predict the future is to have power to shape the future.
—*Eric Hoffer*

8

Creating Your Future —on Paper

Before we return to Sam and Wendy's story, let's get you started by having you calculate your own Spending Power. The first exercise in this chapter will have you calculating your current Spending Power, just as the Sheridans did in the last chapter. Then, after checking in with Sam and Wendy to see how their house plans are progressing, we'll lead you through a second exercise that will tell you more about your own future than you thought possible.

The Spending Power Analysis will tell you what you can afford and what you can't. You can use it to find out how fast you'll reach your goals and what it will take for you to make sure you are successful.

Exercise: Analyzing Your Spending Power

1. Make a worksheet with the same headings as the Spending Power Analysis worksheet in the last chapter (Figure 7-2) or use a copy of the worksheet in Appendix B.

2. Find the Later Date box and label the box with the current date, or with the date from the most recent Balance Sheet you have produced.

3. Below that date, fill in all the amounts from that Balance Sheet. The descriptions on the left-hand side of the Spending Power Analysis are the same as those on the Balance Sheet form. At this point, you now have the "anchor" of your Spending Analysis—your financial position as of right now. To the left of this anchor you will be putting information about the past.

4. You may also want to make a notation in the Major Events During Period box at the top of the form. This notation will help remind you of significant spending events in the time frame the analysis applies to, which will be especially useful as you start working with several analyses, each representing different periods of time.

5. Pick a date in the past for which you have or could produce a Balance Sheet. If you're producing a fresh Balance Sheet, use the Balance Sheet form and make full use of Supporting Schedules. If you're using a Balance Sheet that you already had on hand (say, from a loan application), be sure to adjust the amounts of some assets to correspond to the way you filled out your current Balance Sheet. For instance, if you valued your Personal Residence at net realizable value, as I have urged you to, but you valued it at full current market value on your loan application from the past, you should revalue the old Balance Sheet to correspond with the method you used for the current one.

6. In the box under the Earlier Date, enter the date of the prior-period Balance Sheet. Then figure out how much time elapsed between the old and the current Balance Sheet and put that number of months in the box under Period Covered.

7. Just as you did for the current Balance Sheet, enter in numbers from your old Balance Sheet in the column under its date.

8. Use the check boxes to the left of the Difference column to indicate whether you will include the particular item in the calculation of Spending Power. Typically, you would want to exclude (by *not* checking the box) any items that aren't generally available for spending in the categories you are doing your spending planning for. As we discussed in the example, common candidates for noninclusion in the calculation include Other Liquid Assets (if earmarked or self-restricted), Investments (if self-restricted or illiquid or if valuations are of spurious merit), Personal Residence (unless it's being bought or sold in the period being analyzed) and Retirement Funds (unless retirement funding is included in your plans for your Spending Power).

9. Subtract the Earlier Date Cash amount from the Later Date amount and enter the result in the Difference column for Cash. If Cash has gone down, the number you entered would be negative, of course. Then perform the same subtraction for each line that has a check mark in the box to the left of the Difference column. Remember always to subtract the old from the new: Later minus Earlier. If the number you obtain is negative, be sure to put a minus sign in front of it in the Difference column.

10. In the boxes set aside for Extraordinary Expenditures/ Adjustments, enter the descriptions and amounts of any extravagant purchases or onetime expenses that occurred during this period. These add to your Spending Power, because they represent income that was available for discretionary expenditure in the last period, so therefore would likely be available for some other use in the upcoming period. (However, be sure not to include extraordinary expenditures that are already represented by changes in the Balance Sheet accounts, such as an extraordinary Personal Assets purchase.)

11. Total the Difference column, including amounts in the Extraordinary Expenditures/Adjustments section. When adding up the column, pay attention to both sets of signs: the pluses and minuses provided on the form and any minus signs you put in the Difference column when your subtraction yielded a negative number. Following is a key for translating multiple signs:

$$+ \; + \text{ is the same as } +$$
$$- \; + \text{ is the same as } -$$
$$+ \; - \text{ is the same as } -$$
$$- \; - \text{ is the same as } +$$

The total of all the pluses and minuses should be entered in the Spending Power for This Period box.

12. Next, write down in the Adjustments to Calculate Spending Power for Next Period section the descriptions and amounts of any factors that would alter your Spending Power from the period you just analyzed. Include increases in income over that period. Also include any expenses that were regular expenses during the period between Balance Sheets but have now disappeared. (For instance, if you have dropped your health club membership since your old Balance Sheet, and therefore no longer pay dues of $100 a month, you would include the total of all the health club dues you did pay during the period.) You might even have negative numbers here, for income that occurred during the period that no longer exists, or if you expect your Baseline Cost of Living expenses to rise.

13. Using the same sign rules as discussed above, add the Spending Power for This Period to the items in the Adjustments to

Calculate Spending Power for Next Period and put the answer in the Projected Spending Power for Next Period box.

14. Divide the Projected Spending Power amount by the number of months in the Period Covered to obtain Monthly Spending Power for Next Period. Spending Power can be either positive or negative.

The number that results for the Spending Power Analysis may be a revelation—or it may mean nothing to you, standing on its own.

Certainly, if your projected Spending Power is negative, you know you're in some kind of trouble. Unless you change your earning and spending pattern, you will go further into debt next year, or you will eat away at your savings—or both.

You may have positive projected Spending Power, but be shocked at how low it is.

But if your Spending Power is not exceptionally low and is not negative, you may find the predicted number totally mystifying. "A thousand dollars a month," you may say. "What does that *mean?*"

Later in this chapter, as you work with planning your future using the Spending Power Analysis, you'll see how this number becomes all-important.

Sam and Wendy—Brush Clearing

Sam and Wendy's Goals Planning Timeline was dominated by one large and overriding ambition: to buy a larger, nicer house. Almost all of their other goals were subordinate to this objective.

It was pretty clear to Sam and Wendy that they weren't going to be able to buy the house they wanted in the coming year. Their projected Spending Power for the coming year was only $55 a month—hardly sufficient to support a larger mortgage payment. They had no excess cash, and they were saddled with five-figure consumer debt.

They faced a year of what Sam called "brush clearing"—paying off debt and getting rid of some investments they really wished they had never made. The Spending Power Analysis could help them predict what kind of shape they'd be in at the end of the year.

I first had the Sheridans start a fresh Spending Power Analysis worksheet (see Figure 8-1). Instead of calculating Spending Power for a prior year, however, this Spending Power Analysis would take Sam and Wendy into the future. They wrote "Sell Investments" and "Repay Debt" in the Major Events box at the top of the column.

I asked the Sheridans the same question for each of the categories on the Spending Power Analysis: "How much do you expect (or need, or want) to be in this category at the end of the upcoming year?"

"How much do you want to see in your checking account at the end

	Major Events During Period	Sell Investments and Repay Debt		
	Balance Sheet			**Difference**
	Earlier Date	Later Date		Period Covered
	Now	*Year 1*	√	*12 mos.*

ASSETS

Short-Term

	Earlier Date	Later Date	√	Difference
Cash	*2,750*	*12,725*	√ +	*9,975*
Other Liquid Assets	*2,520*	*0*	√ +	*- 2,520*

Longer-Term

Investments	*25,000*	*0*	√ +	*- 25,000*
Personal Residence	*140,000*	*155,000*	+	
Personal Assets	*25,000*	*27,500*	√ +	*2,500*
Retirement Funds	*6,375*	*10,500*	+	

Total Assets	*201,645*	*205,725*		

LIABILITIES

Short-Term

Credit Card Debt	*6,450*	*0*	√ −	*- 6,450*
Lines of Credit	*8,000*	*0*	√ −	*- 8,000*
Tax Liabilities	*1,250*	*0*	√ −	*- 1,250*
Other Debts	*700*	*0*	√ −	*- 700*

Longer-Term

Term Loans	*10,500*	*9,500*	√ −	*- 1,000*
Mortgage(s)	*84,000*	*83,200*	√ −	*- 800*
Other Debts	*25,000*	*25,000*	√ −	*0*

Total Liabilities	*135,900*	*117,700*		

NET WORTH	*65,745*	*88,025*		

Extraordinary Expenditures/Adjustments

Normal New Personal Assets	+	*- 2,500*
	+	
	+	
	+	

Spending Power for This Period	*655*

Adjustments to Calculate Spending Power for Next Period

Estimated Income Increase for Yr 2	+	*4,500*
	+	
	+	
	+	

Projected Spending Power for Next Period	*5,155*

Monthly* Spending Power for Next Period	*430*

(* Divide Spending Power by number of months in period covered.)

Figure 8-1

of the year?" I started. Sam and Wendy wanted to build up their cash reserves, they said, but didn't know how much they'd be able to accomplish, so we left Cash blank for the time being and moved on to Other Liquid Assets.

"How about your stocks?" I asked.

Sam and Wendy wrinkled their noses at each other and laughed. "That investment was a turkey. Let's get rid of it."

Zero went onto the Other Liquid Assets line.

"How about your Investments—that would be the real estate thing."

"We hope to sell out this coming year," offered Wendy.

Zero.

"Okay. Personal Residence?"

Home prices in their neighborhood have been rising about 10 percent each year lately, and the Sheridans assumed that trend would hold. I rounded up the calculation to $155,000, from the current net realizable value of $140,000.

We had earlier decided that the Sheridans tended to spend a minimum of $2,500 each year on personal assets. Since they were intent on gearing up to buy a new house, I suggested they try to limit themselves to $2,500 of new asset purchases this year. That made Personal Assets $27,500 at the end of the year, up from $25,000 now.

Based on the earnings of their retirement funds and employer-paid contributions, Sam and Wendy calculated their Retirement Funds to have a value of $10,500 at the end of the upcoming year.

When we got to Short-Term debt, Sam and Wendy were adamant about paying it all off with the proceeds from the sale of their $25,000 real estate investment. I put a zero in each slot.

The longer-term investments (home mortgage and term loans) would be paid down making the regular monthly payments. We consulted amortization schedules to see what their balances would be at the end of the upcoming year. The $25,000 Other Debt—an interest-free family loan—required no payments, and its balance would therefore remain unchanged.

At this point, we had predicted balances for every item on the balance sheet except for Cash—and we could calculate the cash buildup based on predicted Spending Power.

First, we needed to calculate, line by line, the Differences between the Now Balance Sheet and the one for a year from now. As we did before, if the balance for the upcoming year was larger than this year, we entered the difference as a positive number; if smaller, as a negative.

I also wrote in one of the adjustments we made to the prior year's Spending Power calculation—the Normal New Personal Assets base of (minus) $2,500. Again, what we're saying by subtracting this figure from the calculation of Spending Power is that the first $2,500 of new personal assets purchased is not really part of Spending Power because Sam and Wendy don't really have much choice about spending it.

Next, I checked off the check boxes to the left of the Difference column. I made a check mark whenever the change in the asset or liability represented something that added to or subtracted from Spending Power.

Notice that the Spending Power for This Period near the bottom of Figure 8-1 is $655. It's no coincidence that this number is identical to the $655 Projected Spending Power for Next Period that Sam and Wendy had predicted on their first Spending Power Analysis, Figure 7-2.

In fact, the Sheridans forced their Spending Power to come out to the predicted $655 by adjusting their predicted Cash balance to the $12,725 you see in Figure 8-1. Accountants call this "plugging," while you may remember it being called "solving for the unknown variable" in high-school algebra.

For those of you who aren't used to doing this kind of "backward math," here is a short worksheet that will allow you to calculate this for Sam and Wendy's Cash as well as for your own unknown variables when you're working on your own Spending Power Analysis.

Exercise: "Plugging" Your Spending Power Analysis

1. Combine all the pluses and minuses in the Difference column, ignoring the line for the category that you're trying to plug. Include any numbers in the Extraordinary Expenditures/Adjustments section. In the Sheridans' case, these numbers totaled a negative $9,320.

2. Take the Monthly Spending Power for Next Period that you calculated in the Spending Power Analysis for the period immediately preceding this one. Multiply the monthly amount by the number of months covered in the current Spending Power Analysis. The Sheridans' prior Spending Power Analysis (Figure 7-2) showed a monthly Spending Power of $55. Since this Spending Power Analysis is for twelve months, 12 times $55 is $655. This number is entered on the Spending Power Analysis on the Spending Power for This Period line.

3. Subtract the number derived in the previous step from the number derived in Step 1. For Sam and Wendy, it looked like this:

$$655 - -9,320 = 9,975$$

4. Enter the number obtained in the Difference column on the line for the category you're trying to plug. If the Difference column for that line is in the Liability section, change the sign (from positive to negative, or from negative to positive) of the number obtained in the step above.

5. Add the number (subtract it if its sign is a minus) to the amount in the Earlier Date column and enter that result in the Later Date column. Sam and Wendy added $9,975 to $2,750 to equal $12,725, which became their prediction of the Cash balance they would have a year from now.

6. That completes your plugging operation. If you check the math on your Spending Power Analysis, you'll find that it all adds up to the Spending Power for This Period figure you've already entered.

For Sam and Wendy, all that was left to do was account for anything about the following year (which we're calling Year 2) that would be different from Year 1. Sam and Wendy estimated their increases in incomes to total $4,500 after taxes, so we entered that amount, yielding a Projected Spending Power for Next Period of $5,155 for the year, or $430 per month. This is the Spending Power (for Year 2) that the Sheridans would carry into their next Spending Power Analysis.

We'll follow the Sheridans through their quest for a new home in the next chapter. For now, however, it's time for you to predict your own financial future, using the Spending Power Analysis. This exercise is incredibly powerful. It will give you an understanding of the dynamics of your personal finance that nothing else can match, except living through the future and getting to come back and fix it up.

Exercise: Predicting Next Year's Spending Power

1. Make another worksheet with the headings for a Spending Power Analysis, or use a copy of the worksheet from Appendix B.

2. Label the Earlier Date box with the date corresponding to your most current Balance Sheet, the same Balance Sheet that was used for the Later Date column in the last Spending Power Analysis you did.

3. Below that date, fill in all the amounts from that Balance Sheet.

4. Select a point in the future and write the date in the Later Date box. The Later Date should not be too far out: It should cover a period of time that is somewhat comparable to your current situation. Depending on the stability of your income and expense pattern, six months to a few years is probably a reasonably appropriate range.

5. In the Major Events During Period box, write in a milestone or two that you expect to characterize this period—whether it be making a major purchase, consolidating and reducing debt, selling an asset, taking an expensive trip or reducing your living expenses dramatically.

6. Calculate the number of months between the future point you selected and the current Balance Sheet and enter that in the Period Covered box.

7. Now comes the fun part: Begin fantasizing about what you'd like to see happen to each of your asset and liability balances. Perhaps you'd like to see a healthier cash account, a new retirement account, a bigger investment portfolio, lower debt. Select numbers you think you'd like to shoot for and put them in the column under the future date. You are, essentially, creating a Balance Sheet you hope will exist in the future.

It's difficult to envision your entire future Balance Sheet all at once. So take the most important change you want or expect to see in your Balance Sheet and record that change first. For instance, you might start with the changes in your Balance Sheet that you would anticipate in connection with the events in the Major Events box.

8. As you go, decide which items are to be included in your Spending Power calculation and check the box for each of them. For items you are including in Spending Power, subtract the left-most column from the right (the Earlier Date from the Later).

9. Periodically, as you decide what Balance Sheet balances you're hoping for in each category, you'll want to add the differences to come up with hoped-for Spending Power. The Spending Power amount you come up with should be compared with the Spending Power you predicted in your last Spending Power Analysis. If your financial aspirations for the coming period are too ambitious (that is, if your calculated Spending Power on this analysis is greater than the Spending Power predicted in the last analysis), you'll need to do some paring back of your plans—or figure out a way to increase your Spending Power by making more income or reducing your Baseline Cost of Living.

Adjust the amounts in your Balance Sheet of the future until the resulting Spending Power for This Period matches the Spending Power you predicted, perhaps using the plugging technique we discussed earlier.

Planning Power at Your Fingertips

At this point, you have done some excellent work that will allow you to do extremely powerful financial planning. The readers of this book are likely to be busy people. Knowing that, I have sometimes encouraged you to work swiftly, or to skip steps.

This is not one of those times. This is a time to savor some of the best financial information you may ever see about your future all on one piece of paper. This is a time to experiment, to "what-if," to try out different scenarios.

What would happen, for example, if you moonlighted to make some extra money? Presumably it would help you do more of what you wanted to do—but how much would it help? Would it, for instance, allow you to add on the new breakfast nook one year earlier than you currently have planned?

Or, if you or your spouse quit full-time work in order to raise kids or write the Great American Novel—what would happen? Would you be sinking or swimming?

Later in this book, as you learn more about the ways you can make more financial flexibility for yourself (especially in Chapter 24), you may want to return to this Spending Power Analysis and what-if your future a little more.

It takes a heap o' livin' in a house t' make it home.
—Edgar A. Guest

9

Buying a New House

A Case Study in the American Dream

For many people, financial success or failure is measured in their ability—or inability—to buy their own home. And, once the first tiny bungalow or fixer-upper has been successfully purchased, attention is often turned toward the purchase of the home they *really* wanted to buy.

Because buying and upgrading our personal residences is so important to so many of us, I felt it particularly important to make sure the subject was amply covered in this book. But rather than merely pass out tips and strategies that are so commonly available in newspaper and magazine articles, I want to lead you to some information that few people are going to show you. Specifically, I want to show you how *you're* going to buy that house, with precisely *your* financial circumstances.

The foundation of your analysis will be the Spending Power Analysis. With it and a few other analytical tools, you will be able to predict *when* and *how* you will make your purchase.

There are few real estate markets in the country that are as exciting, fast-moving and expensive as the San Francisco Bay Area, where it has been my privilege to practice and my pleasure to live. My perspective on real estate is colored by my experience and the experiences of my clients in this geographic area. Other areas of the country experience strikingly different dynamics in their real estate markets, so if Sam and Wendy's situation seems unrealistic to you, please pardon—and make adjustments for—the regional differences they bring to this case study.

Sam and Wendy, as you will recall, had high hopes for buying a new home soon. They felt good, however, about their year of financial brush-clearing. They felt, after ridding themselves of both their nonproductive investments and their consumer debt in Year 1, that they would be ready to buy sometime in Year 2.

The house they wanted would cost them now about $230,000, but, because homes in their area were appreciating at the rate of 10 percent per year, the $230,000 house they wanted would be priced at about $280,000 by the end of Year 2.

Let's follow carefully the Sheridans' attempt to plan for the purchase of their $280,000 house in Figure 9-1.

Of course, we start with a beginning-of-the-period Balance Sheet in the left-hand column. Here the Sheridans merely copied the Year 1 projected Balance Sheet from Figure 8-1 into the Earlier Date column of Figure 9-1.

Next we attack the step-by step process of predicting various balances in the Later Date (Year 2) Balance Sheet. We start with what's most important—the house, at $280,000.

With every new house comes a new mortgage, which Sam and Wendy calculated to be $150,000. Why $150,000, you might ask, especially since you know that mortgage lenders are typically willing to lend at least 75–80 percent of the value of the house?

The answer lies in Spending Power. Sam and Wendy knew they had only $430 per month of additional Spending Power (based on their calculations in Figure 8-1) to apply to their new mortgage payment. Together with their current mortgage payment of $875, adding, say, an additional $400 a month provides for up to $1,275 in mortgage payments. At the prevailing interest rate of 9½ percent, $1,275 would support only a $150,000 mortgage.

Major Events During Period	Try to Buy $280,000 House			

	Balance Sheet			**Difference**
	Earlier Date	Later Date		Period Covered
	Year 1	Year 2	√	12 mos.

ASSETS

Short-Term

	Earlier	Later		Difference
Cash	12,725	2,000	√ +	- 10,725
Other Liquid Assets			√ +	

Longer-Term

Investments			√ +	
Personal Residence	155,000	280,000	√ +	125,000
Personal Assets	27,500	32,500	√ +	5,000
Retirement Funds	10,500	15,500	+	

Total Assets	205,725	330,000		

LIABILITIES

Short-Term

Credit Card Debt	0	0	√ −	0
Lines of Credit	0	0	√ −	0
Tax Liabilities	0	0	√ −	0
Other Debts	0	0	√ −	0

Longer-Term

Term Loans	9,500	8,300	√ −	- 1,200
Mortgage(s)	83,200	150,000	√ −	66,800
Other Debts	25,000	25,000	√ −	0

Total Liabilities	117,700	183,300		

NET WORTH	88,025	146,700		

Extraordinary Expenditures/Adjustments

Normal New Personal Assets	+
	+
	+
	+

Spending Power for This Period	53,675

Adjustments to Calculate Spending Power for Next Period

	+
	+
	+
	+

Projected Spending Power for Next Period	53,675

Monthly* Spending Power for Next Period	4,473

(* Divide Spending Power by number of months in period covered.)

Figure 9-1

The Mortgage Calculation Table

The size of the mortgage that the Sheridans' $1,275 would support could be discovered by either using a calculator programmed with financial functions or consulting a realty blue book, a fat little handbook full of loan tables. Instead, Sam used the chart reproduced in Figure 9-2, which allowed him to calculate the mortgage using, at most, a simple four-function calculator.

The Mortgage Calculation Table tells you the monthly payment required to retire a $100,000 mortgage of a given interest rate and term. To calculate the payment for a loan of a different face amount, merely apply the same percentage to the payment as the desired loan is to $100,000.

For instance, a 12 percent 15-year $100,000 loan requires monthly payments of $1,200.17. This is determined by reading down the interest rate column until you reach 12.00%, then reading across until you get to the 15 years column, where the amount shown is $1,200.17. If you wanted to calculate the monthly payment for an $80,000 loan, merely take the ratio of $80,000 to $100,000 (which is .8) and multiply it by the mortgage payment from the table:

$$
\begin{array}{r}
\$1{,}200.17 \\
\times\ .8 \\
\hline
\$\ \ 960.14
\end{array}
$$

which yields $960.14, precisely the mortgage payment required to retire a fifteen-year $80,000 mortgage at 12 percent.

Sam used a similar technique to work back the other way on the chart—*from* the mortgage payment *to* the principal. He found from the Mortgage Calculation Table that a 30-year $100,000 mortgage at 9½ percent interest would require a $840.85 monthly payment. Since Sam and Wendy felt they had about $1,275 available for mortgage payments, Sam took the ratio of $1,275 over $840.85—about 1.5—and multiplied that by $100,000 to derive a principal of $150,000.

Throughout my years of buying real estate personally and advising clients in their efforts to purchase real estate, I don't know how I would have survived without a calculator programmed with financial functions. These kinds of calculations are so important to budget planning as well, that I seriously considered providing financial calculators to every one of my Financial Sanity Workshop participants.

Fortunately, however, you will not have to master a new machine in order to pursue your own Financial Sanity program. In this and two

Monthly Payment Required to Retire a Loan of $100,000 Over Life of Loan

Interest Rate	Life of Loan (in Years)						
	10	12	15	20	25	30	40
6.00%	1,110.21	975.85	843.86	716.43	644.30	599.55	550.21
6.25%	1,122.80	988.84	857.42	730.93	659.67	615.72	567.74
6.50%	1,135.48	1,001.92	871.11	745.57	675.21	632.07	585.46
6.75%	1,148.24	1,015.10	884.91	760.36	690.91	648.60	603.36
7.00%	1,161.08	1,028.38	898.83	775.30	706.78	665.30	621.43
7.25%	1,174.01	1,041.76	912.86	790.38	722.81	682.18	639.67
7.50%	1,187.02	1,055.23	927.01	805.59	738.99	699.21	658.07
7.75%	1,200.11	1,068.79	941.28	820.95	755.33	716.41	676.62
8.00%	1,213.28	1,082.45	955.65	836.44	771.82	733.76	695.31
8.25%	1,226.53	1,096.21	970.14	852.07	788.45	751.27	714.14
8.50%	1,239.86	1,110.06	984.74	867.82	805.23	768.91	733.09
8.75%	1,253.27	1,124.00	999.45	883.71	822.14	786.70	752.17
9.00%	1,266.76	1,138.03	1,014.27	899.73	839.20	804.62	771.36
9.25%	1,280.33	1,152.16	1,029.19	915.87	856.38	822.68	790.66
9.50%	1,293.98	1,166.37	1,044.22	932.13	873.70	840.85	810.06
9.75%	1,307.70	1,180.68	1,059.36	948.52	891.14	859.15	829.56
10.00%	1,321.51	1,195.08	1,074.61	965.02	908.70	877.57	849.15
10.25%	1,335.39	1,209.57	1,089.95	981.64	926.38	896.10	868.82
10.50%	1,349.35	1,224.14	1,105.40	998.38	944.18	914.74	888.57
10.75%	1,363.39	1,238.80	1,120.95	1,015.23	962.09	933.48	908.40
11.00%	1,377.50	1,253.56	1,136.60	1,032.19	980.11	952.32	928.29
11.25%	1,391.69	1,268.39	1,152.34	1,049.26	998.24	971.26	948.26
11.50%	1,405.95	1,283.32	1,168.19	1,066.43	1,016.47	990.29	968.28
11.75%	1,420.29	1,298.33	1,184.13	1,083.71	1,034.80	1,009.41	988.36
12.00%	1,434.71	1,313.42	1,200.17	1,101.09	1,053.22	1,028.61	1,008.50
12.25%	1,449.20	1,328.60	1,216.30	1,118.56	1,071.74	1,047.90	1,028.69
12.50%	1,463.76	1,343.86	1,232.52	1,136.14	1,090.35	1,067.26	1,048.92
12.75%	1,478.40	1,359.20	1,248.84	1,153.81	1,109.05	1,086.69	1,069.20
13.00%	1,493.11	1,374.63	1,265.24	1,171.58	1,127.84	1,106.20	1,089.51
13.25%	1,507.89	1,390.13	1,281.74	1,189.43	1,146.70	1,125.77	1,109.87
13.50%	1,522.74	1,405.72	1,298.32	1,207.37	1,165.64	1,145.41	1,130.26
13.75%	1,537.67	1,421.38	1,314.99	1,225.41	1,184.67	1,165.11	1,150.69
14.00%	1,552.66	1,437.13	1,331.74	1,243.52	1,203.76	1,184.87	1,171.14
14.25%	1,567.73	1,452.95	1,348.58	1,261.72	1,222.93	1,204.69	1,191.62
14.50%	1,582.87	1,468.85	1,365.50	1,280.00	1,242.16	1,224.56	1,212.13
14.75%	1,598.07	1,484.83	1,382.50	1,298.36	1,261.46	1,244.48	1,232.67
15.00%	1,613.35	1,500.88	1,399.59	1,316.79	1,280.83	1,264.44	1,253.22
15.25%	1,628.69	1,517.00	1,416.75	1,335.30	1,300.26	1,284.46	1,273.80
15.50%	1,644.11	1,533.20	1,433.99	1,353.88	1,319.75	1,304.52	1,294.40
15.75%	1,659.58	1,549.48	1,451.31	1,372.53	1,339.29	1,324.62	1,315.02
16.00%	1,675.13	1,565.83	1,468.70	1,391.26	1,358.89	1,344.76	1,335.65
16.25%	1,690.74	1,582.24	1,486.17	1,410.05	1,378.54	1,364.93	1,356.30
16.50%	1,706.42	1,598.73	1,503.71	1,428.90	1,398.24	1,385.15	1,376.96
16.75%	1,722.17	1,615.29	1,521.32	1,447.82	1,418.00	1,405.40	1,397.64

Figure 9–2

later chapters, you will find a chart that looks something like Figure 9-2. Each chart meets a specific need and allows you to derive an accurate answer with, at most, a four-function calculator to perform simple multiplication.

Sam and Wendy Onward

After determining the new Mortgage and Personal Residence amounts, most of the other predictions about Year 2 are easy. As you can follow on Figure 9-1, Sam and Wendy want a minimum of $2,000in cash reserves, so $2,000 goes onto the Cash line. Although they normally buy only $2,500 in Personal Assets, they expect that, with the purchase of a new house, they'll need to buy more personal assets this year. They add $5,000 to the earlier year's bal- a ance of $27,500, for total of $32,500. Retirement Funds are again adjusted based on information Sam and Wendy got from their employers.

On the Liabilities side, the Sheridans do not aspire to going back into consumer debt—although they might be slightly tolerant of a little debt if it meant the difference in buying this house. They'll go through the analysis and, if they find themselves a few thousand dollars short, they can make up the difference by accessing their Line of Credit. As we shall soon see, "a few thousand dollars" doesn't begin to describe how short the Sheridans came up.

Having determined the amount of their new mortgage, Sam and Wendy treated the other debts in the Longer-Term Liabilities section as they had in their last Spending Power Analysis: Term (student) Loans were reduced as anticipated by the amortization schedule and Other Debts (parent loan) were left alone.

With their side-by-side Balance Sheets for Years 1 and 2 completed, Sam and Wendy next needed to determine which categories of Assets and Liabilities should be included in the Spending Power formula. This time, all categories except Retirement Funds were included in the formula. This represents a change from how we handled Figure 8-1, where the change in the market value of the Personal Residence was not included in the calculation. Any time there is a sale or purchase, however, the change must be reflected, since it generally requires or generates cash.

Now the Sheridans were ready to compute their Spending Power for This Period, to see if it matched the Projected Spending Power from their analysis last chapter. As you have probably already figured out, they weren't even close. Figure 8-1 said the Sheridans *had* a projected

$5,155 of Spending Power going into Year 2; Figure 9-1 said that they *needed* about ten times that Spending Power to pull off the house purchase.

Certainly the Sheridans were frustrated by this answer. What they had thought was near their grasp now seemed totally out of reach, and they were tending toward despair. They complained about the "insanity" of the local housing market and were frustrated that—even with two incomes—they couldn't afford a home like the house they grew up in.

It was not as if they didn't understand the economics of their situation. A $195,000 mortgage loan would solve their problem, but they wouldn't have the cash flow to support the payments. Or, they could stick with the affordable $150,000 loan if they had an extra $45,000 in cash reserves—which they didn't.

"I suppose," remarked Sam, "that you can be short on cash flow or you can be short on accumulated reserves, but you can't be short on both."

You, too, may become discouraged in the course of your calculations. I urge you, however—just as I urged Sam and Wendy—to stick with the analysis. Let's see what happened to the Sheridans when they did.

Sam and Wendy Face Reality

Since Sam and Wendy clearly could not swing a house purchase in Year 2, they redid their Spending Power Analysis for that year. The new Spending Power Analysis in Figure 9-3 conforms with the $5,155 Spending Power predicted in Figure 8-1. The Sheridans also predicted their Spending Power for Year 3 at $10,155, based on anticipated increases in their incomes. Figure 9-3 was calculated much as Figure 8-1 was, so if you have questions about how it was derived, you may want to review the explanation of the earlier analysis.

Moving into Year 3, the Sheridans were determined to keep their Spending Power in line as well as provide for only as much mortgage as they could afford to service.

Their first move was to do a proposed Spending Power Analysis for Year 3 (Figure 9-4), making sure that they stayed within the $10,155 Spending Power constraint predicted by Figure 9-3. At this point, the estimated cost of their new residence had risen another 10 percent to $308,000, but their ability to service a loan had risen even more dramatically: They could now handle a $200,000 mortgage.

	Major Events During Period	Sit Tight and Save		

	Balance Sheet			**Difference**
	Earlier Date	Later Date	√	Period Covered
	Year 1	Year 2		12 mos.

ASSETS

	Earlier	Later	√		Difference
Short-Term					
Cash	12,725	15,680	√	+	2,955
Other Liquid Assets			√	+	
Longer-Term					
Investments				+	
Personal Residence	155,000	170,500		+	
Personal Assets	27,500	30,000	√	+	2,500
Retirement Funds	10,500	15,500		+	
Total Assets	205,725	231,680			

LIABILITIES

	Earlier	Later	√		Difference
Short-Term					
Credit Card Debt		0	√	–	
Lines of Credit		0	√	–	
Tax Liabilities		0	√	–	
Other Debts		0	√	–	
Longer-Term					
Term Loans	9,500	8,300	√	–	- 1,200
Mortgage(s)	83,200	82,200	√	–	- 1,000
Other Debts	25,000	25,000	√	–	
Total Liabilities	117,700	115,500			
NET WORTH	88,025	116,180			

Extraordinary Expenditures/Adjustments

Normal New Personal Assets	+	- 2,500
	+	
	+	
	+	

Spending Power for This Period	5,155

Adjustments to Calculate Spending Power for Next Period

Estimated Income Increase for Yr 3	+	5,000
	+	
	+	
	+	

Projected Spending Power for Next Period	10,155

Monthly* Spending Power for Next Period	846

(* Divide Spending Power by number of months in period covered.)

Figure 9–3

	Major Events During Period	Attempt to Purchase House, Now $308,000		

	Balance Sheet			**Difference**
	Earlier Date	Later Date	√	Period Covered
	Year 2	Year 3		12 mos.

ASSETS

Short-Term

Cash	15,680	2,335	√	+	- 13,345
Other Liquid Assets			√	+	

Longer-Term

Investments			√	+	
Personal Residence	170,500	308,000	√	+	137,500
Personal Assets	30,000	35,000	√	+	5,000
Retirement Funds	15,500	21,000		+	

Total Assets	231,680	366,335	

LIABILITIES

Short-Term

Credit Card Debt			√	–
Lines of Credit			√	–
Tax Liabilities			√	–
Other Debts			√	–

Longer-Term

Term Loans	8,300	7,000	√	–	- 1,300
Mortgage(s)	82,200	200,000	√	–	117,800
Other Debts	25,000	25,000	√	–	

Total Liabilities	115,500	232,000	

NET WORTH	116,180	134,335	

Extraordinary Expenditures/Adjustments

Normal New Personal Assets	+	- 2,500
	+	
	+	
	+	

Spending Power for This Period	10,155

Adjustments to Calculate Spending Power for Next Period

	+	
	+	
	+	
	+	

Projected Spending Power for Next Period	10,155

Monthly* Spending Power for Next Period	846

(* Divide Spending Power by number of months in period covered.)

Figure 9–4

But the gap between the purchase price of their new home and the mortgage left a very wide gap. Would the ever-rising equity in their existing house, together with their cash savings, close that $108,000 gap?

To find out, I led Sam and Wendy through a short calculation that specifically addressed the financing requirements of buying the new house. It appears in Figure 9-5.

Figure 9-5: Cash Requirements for $308,000 House in Year 3

Cash Requirements

Cost of New House		$ 308,000
LESS		
Net Proceeds from Old House	$ 170,500	
Less: Selling Costs	−1,000	
	169,500	
Less: Old Mortgage	−82,200	
	87,300	
New Mortgage	200,000	
Noncash Funds Available		287,300
Cash Required		20,700
Sources of Cash		
Changes in Cash Balance		13,345
Shortfall		$ 7,355

Sam and Wendy felt that they were close enough in Year 3 to buying their new house that they could almost reach out and grab it. But the analysis showed that they would be short more than $7,000 in cash when it came time to make the down payment.

In my experience watching California residential real estate, people in the Sheridans' situation often "go for it"—borrowing the extra $7,000 (either on the mortgage or through short-term debt) in the hope that future increases in Spending Power can bail them out in a year or so.

Wendy expressed similar tendencies when she saw this analysis.

"What would happen if we just borrowed that $7,000 from the Line of Credit and bought the house right here in Year 3?" she asked.

"Well," I said, "I wouldn't recommend the line of credit because you'll want to be paying that back over a couple of years. There's no chance you'll have any Spending Power to make any true reduction in the first year (Year 3); we already know you'll be using all your

Spending Power to make mortgage payments. That means you'll be wanting to retire a debt which would by then have grown to over $8,000 in one year. But you aren't expecting anywhere near $8,000 of additional Spending Power (due to income increases) in Year 4, so it would probably take you all of Year 4 and Year 5 to clear that Line of Credit balance."

Sam indicated that he was not too thrilled about having all the increases in Spending Power "booked up" through Year 5. "That means," he correctly pointed out, "that we could spend no money raising our standard of living, and it means we couldn't set aside funds for any new major purchases, like a new car."

"There must be another way," Wendy pressed.

"There is," I answered. "You could increase the mortgage by, say, $7,500—and still be well within the lending limits the bank would like to see." I referred to the table in Figure 9-2. "Another $7,500 would require an additional monthly payment of about $63.

"Now you don't have $63 a month of available Spending Power, so you'd end up borrowing the $63 every month from your Line of Credit. At the end of the year, you'd have a balance of approximately $800. Assuming you'd want to pay that off in about a year— we're into Year 4 now—you'd need $70 per month for that, in addition to the $63 per month for the mortgage. In all, you'd require $143 a month, which probably represents only a fraction of the additional Spending Power you'll experience in Year 4, leaving some money to start applying elsewhere in your budget."

Waiting Until It's *Really* Affordable

The aggressive plan I outlined above seemed attractive to the Sheridans but, at my urging, they went ahead and analyzed the situation assuming they waited until Year 4 to buy the house.

Their first step was to redo their Year 3 Spending Power Analysis. Their work is reproduced in Figure 9-6.

Next, they moved to Year 4, where they began by planning for their new house, its cost again inflated by 10 percent. They soon discovered, however, that purchasing a $340,000 house would not use up all their Spending Power for Year 4. Their Spending Power would support a $250,000 mortgage which, together with the equity in their existing home, would allow them to "cash out" of the deal—put no cash into the purchase and still receive about $15,000 cash out of the sale of their existing home:

Major Events During Period | Sit tight for yet another year

	Balance Sheet			Difference
	Earlier Date	Later Date	√	Period Covered
	Year 2	Year 3		12 mos.

ASSETS

Short-Term

Cash	15,680	23,335	√	+	7,655
Other Liquid Assets			√	+	

Longer-Term

Investments			√	+	
Personal Residence	170,500	187,550		+	
Personal Assets	30,000	32,500	√	+	2,500
Retirement Funds	15,500	21,000		+	

Total Assets	231,680	264,385

LIABILITIES

Short-Term

Credit Card Debt			√	−
Lines of Credit			√	−
Tax Liabilities			√	−
Other Debts			√	−

Longer-Term

Term Loans	8,300	7,000	√	−	- 1,300
Mortgage(s)	82,200	81,000	√	−	- 1,200
Other Debts	25,000	25,000	√	−	

Total Liabilities	115,500	113,000

NET WORTH	116,180	151,385

Extraordinary Expenditures/Adjustments

Normal New Personal Assets	+	- 2,500
	+	
	+	
	+	

Spending Power for This Period	10,155

Adjustments to Calculate Spending Power for Next Period

Estimated Income Increase for Yr 4	+	5,500
	+	
	+	
	+	

Projected Spending Power for Next Period	15,655

Monthly* Spending Power for Next Period	1,305

(* Divide Spending Power by number of months in period covered.)

Figure 9–6

Figure 9-7: Cash Requirements for $340,000 House in Year 4

Cash Requirements

Cost of New House		$ 340,000
LESS		
Net Proceeds from Old House	$ 187,550	
Less: Selling Costs	−1,000	
	186,550	
Less: Old Mortgage	−81,000	
	105,550	
New Mortgage	250,000	
Noncash Funds Available		355,550
Cash Available from Transactions		$ 15,550

Conventional real estate wisdom in California being what it is ("Always try to buy as much real estate as you can when you buy"), Sam and Wendy were finally seduced, in their planning, by yet another option: buying a $375,000 house—the maximum they could afford in Year 4.

Their purchase funding requirements analysis follows in Figure 9-8 and their Spending Power Analysis is in Figure 9-9.

Figure 9-8: Cash Requirements for $375,000 House in Year 4

Cash Requirements

Cost of New House		$ 375,000
LESS		
Net Proceeds from Old House	$ 187,550	
Less: Selling Costs	−1,000	
	186,550	
Less: Old Mortgage	−81,000	
	105,550	
New Mortgage	250,000	
Noncash Funds Available		355,550
Cash Required		19,450
Sources of Cash		
Changes in Cash Balance		−$ 20,000
Shortfall		None

Sam and Wendy have—at least on paper—reached their goal. They can look forward to the next few years with confidence, knowing that their plan to buy a new house will work, even if they aren't in that new

Major Events During Period:	Buy $375,000 House			

	Balance Sheet			**Difference**
	Earlier Date:	Later Date:		Period Covered:
	Year 3	Year 4	√	12 mos.

ASSETS

Short-Term

Cash	23,335	3,335	√	+	- 20,000
Other Liquid Assets			√	+	

Longer-Term

Investments			√	+	
Personal Residence	187,550	375,000	√	+	187,450
Personal Assets	32,500	47,500	√	+	15,000
Retirement Funds	21,000	26,000		+	

Total Assets	264,385	451,835

LIABILITIES

Short-Term

Credit Card Debt		695	√	–	695
Lines of Credit		1,000	√	–	1,000
Tax Liabilities			√	–	
Other Debts			√	–	

Longer-Term

Term Loans	7,000	5,600	√	–	- 1,400
Mortgage(s)	81,000	250,000	√	–	169,000
Other Debts	25,000	25,000	√	–	

Total Liabilities	113,000	282,295

NET WORTH	151,385	169,540

Extraordinary Expenditures/Adjustments:

Normal New Personal Assets	+	- 2,500
	+	
	+	
	+	

Spending Power For This Period | 10,655

Adjustments to Calculate Spending Power For Next Period

+	
+	
+	
+	

Projected Spending Power For Next Period | 10,655

Monthly* Spending Power For Next Period | 888

(* Divide Spending Power by number of months in period covered.)

Figure 9–9

house right away. They have faced the specter of despair—the hopelessness of the Great American Down Payment Race—and beaten it. And, just as effectively, they have licked uncertainty. They can say to themselves—to anyone—with confidence: "We know when we're buying our new house, we know about what kind of house we'll be able to buy, and we know we'll be able to afford it. We have a plan."

Armed and No Longer Dangerous

No one would suggest that carrying out this long plan will be an easy process for the Sheridans. They came in, after all, "ready" to buy their new house *now*. Their planning, however, shows that they will have to wait not merely the one year they were expecting, but four years: one year of liquidating their debts and living—perhaps for the first time—within their means; two more years of *not expanding their cost of living,* even though their income is rising; and a final year in which they reach their dream and are able to purchase the house they've been wanting—and then some.

The Sheridans are now armed with what might be the most valuable single piece of financial information they could possibly have. They know *what* they can afford, *when* they can afford it and *how* to prepare for it. This information will help them avoid making the following mistakes:

· spending expected increases in income on lifestyle and other expenses between now and the time they purchase their new home
· taking action and making decisions based on the flawed assumption that they would be moving in a year or so
· spending countless hours looking seriously for real estate that they, as it turned out, would not be able to afford for another few years
· getting their hopes up unrealistically

The Sheridans' story is a classic picture of a couple building their financial strength in order to buy a nicer or larger home. What they can't afford now they can afford later, the product of a combination of the following:

· wages rising faster than the rate of inflation, such that there are real, after-tax increases in spending power
· no or minimal increases in the cost of living, so that the increases in wages are available for higher housing costs and so that the extra Spending Power is accumulated as cash available for investing in the new home.

These forces must counteract the upward trend in the cost of the new home, which—even if both homes are appreciating at the same rate—is rising faster (in dollars) than the value of the existing home.*

If you are facing a situation like the Sheridans' (and it's a very common scenario), you may find yourself impatient with the "answer" your Spending Power Analysis offers you. You may be unwilling to wait four years for a house you want right now; you may be unwilling to maintain your current cost (and standard) of living throughout the four-year wait.

Faster results can be obtained, but it takes some creative juggling of alternatives—assuming you have viable alternatives—by increasing income or making permanent changes in the level of expenses. Creative alternatives are explored in Chapter 24.

Using the techniques in this chapter, you can now predict when and how you will be able to make such major financial acquisitions as your first or your next house. Although we've focused here on buying residential real estate, the Spending Power Analysis can obviously be used to plan any major purchase.

Exercise: Projecting Your Financial Activity into the Future

1. Make a few worksheets with the same headings as the Spending Power Analysis, or use a copy of the worksheet in Appendix B.

2. Working forward from your latest Spending Power Analysis, create your financial future on paper for the next few years, using the Spending Power Analysis and any supporting analyses you need.

Experiment a bit. Play with different possibilities. Have fun. You're writing your own future.

---

*The analysis we followed for Sam and Wendy's home purchase was simplified somewhat, in that it did not take into account some factors that can further complicate the analysis. These can include the effect of inflation on baseline living costs, the tax effect of increasing mortgage interest payments, points and other closing costs and their tax deductibility, increases in property taxes, increases in homeowner's insurance and so forth. Readers should take into account, however, how important each of these factors is before working them into their computations. It makes no sense, for instance, to analyze in great detail the tax effect of increased mortgage payments if the resulting information will affect the size of the payments by just a few dollars. Keep in mind that the entire process is an estimate and is therefore subject to some error. Further techniques for analyzing the economics of a planned home purchase can be found in Chapter 19.

'Tis against some Men's Principle to pay Interest, and seems against others' Interest to pay the Principal.
—*Poor Richard's Almanack*

10

Your Best Investment

Debt is like a dangerous and destructive romantic relationship that's both passionate and painful. When you know credit is available to you, it's exciting to think about the possibilities it offers. And actually incurring debt is almost intoxicatingly easy. But paying it back can be painful, and the pain sometimes goes on for a period of time all out of proportion to the value of what you bought with the money you borrowed.

Debt is the financial version of a regrettable fling: While many of us love *running up* debt, no one really enjoys *owing* the debt the morning after.

Your initial reaction to debt was very possibly irrational—"Live for now, the future be damned," or some variation on that theme. Just because you now are committed to leaving your bad habits behind doesn't mean you're required to adopt an equally irrational attitude of fear and loathing of debt. You will, I predict, still make good use of debt as a financial convenience. But, if you adopt the philosophy and system of this book, you'll master debt. Tamed and controlled, debt will become your servant. And because you will be in control of your debt, you won't be afraid of it and you won't have to hate it.

Debt Theory

Debt isn't bad—it's just dangerous when it's misunderstood. And we misunderstand it a lot.

Most debt is predicated on the notion of *converting income into assets*—specifically, converting *future* income into *current* assets. This notion is both logical and risky. It's logical because a person's need for acquiring assets occurs relatively early in his adult life, while his ability to pay for it occurs later—when his spending needs are considerably smaller. It's risky because no one actually knows how much "excess income" there will be in the future and, therefore, how much debt one can safely incur now.

In the early years of financial self-reliance, we tend to have a greater need for assets than ability to pay for them. Ability to pay is equal to the excess of income over periodic expenses.

Our early years of economic independence are characterized by asset purchases, chief among them, perhaps, the purchases and upgrading of our personal residences. These purchases inevitably outstrip our ability to pay in cash accumulated from income in excess of normal living expenses. We borrow—we must borrow. If the only debt we have is the mortgage on our home, we're nonetheless in debt to finance asset purchases.

Ideally, however—ten or twenty years after we start out in the real world—we enter a period of time when our "excess" income significantly outstrips our ability to spend money on asset acquisitions. During this period, we expect to reverse the trend of buying more than we can afford and start paying off debt we accumulated in the earlier years. At the same time, we begin to build our financial assets for retirement.

Retirement represents a return to a time when our income is less than our periodic monthly expenses—a situation that has to be covered by the excess funds accumulated in our high-earning years.

Based on this three-stage cycle, it seems rational to take on a reasonable amount of debt in our early adult years, with the anticipation of bolstering our financial position in our high-income years. And, looking ahead, it also seems logical to depend on the high-income years to prepare for the deficit-spending retirement years.

If you've ever said "I want to enjoy my life now—not when I'm too old to appreciate it," you had this cycle in mind. You were making a deal: "Let me have my fun now, and I promise I'll pay it back ten or fifteen years from now."

There is one little issue baby boomers must face, however. Careful recollection will reveal the awful truth: For some of us, it *is* ten or fifteen years from the time we made that deal.

If you've recently felt the sudden urge to become more responsible for your personal finances, it may have something to do with where you are in the three-stage earnings cycle. If you are just entering your most financially productive years, you may instinctively understand that it's time to adjust your thinking—away from borrowing against the future and toward getting your financial house in order, paying off the debt of your asset-acquisition years and maybe even preparing for retirement (although that still seems far away for many of us).

A Model for a Healthy Relationship with Debt

Not fully understanding the dynamics represented by the three-stage earnings cycle, many people of our generation are reacting to their "portfolios" of debt with unwarranted panic and guilt. Building up debt is what you're *supposed* to have been doing up until now. You don't have to feel guilty. And, even if you ran up too much debt during your "borrowing years," you need not panic. You may be surprised at how powerful a set of financial options you have available to you to fix whatever is wrong with your current financial position in surprisingly few years.

In place of panic and guilt, this chapter hopes to instill in you a new, healthy outlook on debt, one that allows you to do two key things:

· work your way out of excessive debt
· establish a set of financial habits—a "system"—for staying in control on how much new debt you incur

I will try to lead you to a critical milestone in creating your new relationship with debt. You will develop sufficient control over your own debt management that you will be able to say something like:

· "Except for my mortgage, I will be completely out of debt by February of next year."
· "I will have all my credit cards paid off in seven months, my student loan paid off in twenty-eight months, and my line of credit down to zero by June of next year."

The person who can set a date for the payment of his debts—without new borrowing—has taken the first step toward complete control of his debt management. It is the aim of the Debt Reduction

Planner, to which I will introduce you shortly, that you become able to make such statements—with confidence.

We've talked so far in this chapter about debt in a very theoretical, cosmic sort of way. Now it's time to touch down on earth and get very familiar with debt in the real world—specifically, your debt. The first time I sat down to chart out my own debt reduction planning, I was amazed that I didn't even know how much I owed or what the interest rates were on the various credit cards and lines of credit I had.

John and Kathy—Coming to Grips

John and Kathy Fitzpatrick were both in their late twenties when they came to see me. Kathy, a recent law-school graduate, had worked in a large law firm for just over a year. John was an analyst for a real estate development company.

The Fitzpatricks told me they had never felt in control of their finances from the time they were married four years earlier. In the year since Kathy had passed the bar and started work, their income had shifted dramatically upward, but their debt level, too, went up instead of down.

"We sort of figured that our troubles would be over when Kathy started bringing in income," John had confided in me at our first private consultation.

"But it didn't," Kathy continued. "We're worried that if we blow it now with all this income, we'll never be able to get out of debt."

"We have some friends who did exactly that," John agreed.

"And," added Kathy, "we want to be able to have kids. I don't want to be under terrible pressure to work full time, just to make ends meet."

Their timing was perfect, I thought as I listened to the Fitzpatricks. I, too, had seen two-income couples peg their standard of living too high and "max out" their borrowing potential. The result was a complete loss of flexibility. They became slaves to their dual incomes.

First, of course, I had John and Kathy gather all the facts on each of their debts on the Inflow-Outflow Information Sheet discussed in Chapter 6. For each debt I asked them for the:

· name of the debt
· principal amount owing right now
· interest rate
· minimum payment required

I also asked them to provide:

Description	Code	Amount	Frequency	Non-Monthly Next Payment Falls Due:	Debt Repayments		
					Debt Owed	Interest Rate	Minimum Payment
First Mortgage	D	1,261	monthly		124,169	11.75%	1,262
Second Mortgage	D	250	monthly - int only balloon 10/1/92		25,000	12%	250
Visa	D		monthly		2,588	21%	116
Loan from Parents	D	1,000	yearly int only - forever?	Dec.	10,000	10%	1,000
Car Loan	D	455	monthly		10,478	4%	455
Student Loan	D	155	monthly		1,358	6%	155
Furniture Financing	D	163	monthly		3,259	18%	163
MasterCard	D		monthly		4,511	19%	203

Figure 10-1

· any special circumstances about the debt, such as variable interest rate or balloon payment due.

The debt portion of their Inflow-Outflow Information Sheet is in Figure 10-1.

Kathy eyed me as I looked over their list of debts. "We have too much debt, don't we?" she asked.

I didn't answer her right away. I don't believe in benchmark levels of debt or hard-and-fast percentages of cash flow going to debt service.

"The existence of debt, in and of itself, doesn't mean so much. The key is whether you have the income to support your debt load, and whether the two other elements of your budget can stand all this money going out in debt service."

"Two other elements?" John asked. "What are the two other elements?"

"In the Financial Sanity system, there are basically three broad categories of outflow, which of course, have to be balanced with income."

Figure 10-2: The Three Ways to Spend Money

$$\text{Income} \;\Diamond\; \begin{array}{l} \cdot \text{Expenses} \\ \cdot \text{Funding} \\ \cdot \text{Debt Service} \end{array}$$

"All income goes into one of these places or another. And when one area takes more money, the funds going to another area are decreased."

"Unless you borrow," John pointed out.

"Unless you borrow," I agreed. "And that's largely what you've been doing up until now."

John looked a little annoyed at my comment, but I knew he knew what I meant. We had both, after all, seen his Inflow-Outflow Information Sheet.

"Don't worry," I reassured them both. "This will be easier than it looks."

First, I had John and Kathy transfer their debt information onto the Debt Reduction Planner. They filled out the first month (which was June), and I asked them to fill it out in pencil. It looked essentially like Figure 10-3. It made use of minimum payments on all debts and reflected pretty much what they were currently paying to support debt. The schedule showed that the total of all monthly payments to service debts was $2,604. Not included in that total was $1,000 due to Kathy's parents each year.

Before working with the Fitzpatricks' "regular" debt, I helped John and Kathy make decisions about how to handle their annual payment to Kathy's parents and the looming balloon payment on their second mortgage. We used funding techniques to handle these two debts. Funding is discussed in Chapters 12 through 19, and a detailed description of how to handle this kind of debt through funding is treated in Chapter 19.

Of Priests and the Holy Books:
How We Keep Our Partners in the Dark

"Next," I said, waving my pencil at the remaining debts, "we need to balance two things:

· your goals for paying off each of your debts; and
· the amount of money you can make available for debt retirement."

John, I could tell, had been somewhat taken aback by the amount of monthly income he had to allocate to Funding to handle the second mortgage. "I think we could spend about $250 more each month paying off debt," he offered. "That's about as much as we can spring free for this."

"I'd really like to see all of our credit card debt paid off within two years—a year and a half would be even better," Kathy said.

John's embarrassment at how little they could apply to debt reduction was turning into thinly veiled hostility.

He scowled at Kathy. "That's ridiculous," he almost yelled. "You don't know what you're talking about! We have $10,000 on our credit cards and it took us four years to build them up. What makes you think we can just pay them off in a couple of years?"

So much for veiled hostility. John folded his arms on his chest and looked at me across my desk. I looked at Kathy. She looked straight ahead, her mouth a straight line across her face, silent.

Something important—and very damaging—was happening here. I wasn't about to become their marriage counselor, but if this event was allowed to pass unchallenged, I thought that John and Kathy's ability to plan together would be seriously impaired. Fortunately, I felt sure that both John and Kathy also sensed this, and were ready to cooperate in undoing the damage.

"Don't let him talk to you that way," I said quietly.

I didn't look at John. Kathy's eyes got watery and she blinked several times.

"Even if he's right," I said, "and he may not be, you can't afford to get kicked out of the discussion because you got intimidated. John's trying to be the priest here." I glanced over at John. He wasn't mad; he was just listening. "A priest is someone who has all the answers, so no

Month	June		
	Planned	Actual	Difference

Debt: Visa
Interest Rate: Annual: 21 % | Monthly: 1.75 % | Min.Pmt.: $ 116

	Planned	Actual	Difference
Balance Forward	2,588		
Interest	45		
Payment	116		
New Charges			
New Balance	2,517		
Principal Reduction	71		

Debt: MasterCard
Interest Rate: Annual: 19 % | Monthly: 1.583 % | Min.Pmt.: $ 203

	Planned	Actual	Difference
Balance Forward	4,511		
Interest	71		
Payment	203		
New Charges			
New Balance	4,379		
Principal Reduction	132		

Debt: Furniture Financing
Interest Rate: Annual: 18 % | Monthly: 1.5 % | Min.Pmt.: $ 163

	Planned	Actual	Difference
Balance Forward	3,259		
Interest	49		
Payment	163		
New Charges			
New Balance	3,145		
Principal Reduction	114		

Debt: Car Loan
Interest Rate: Annual: 4 % | Monthly: 0.333 % | Min.Pmt.: $ 455

	Planned	Actual	Difference
Balance Forward	10,478		
Interest	35		
Payment	455		
New Charges			
New Balance	10,058		
Principal Reduction	420		

Debt: Student Loan
Interest Rate: Annual: 6 % | Monthly: 0.5 % | Min.Pmt.: $ 155

	Planned	Actual	Difference
Balance Forward	1,358		
Interest	7		
Payment	155		
New Charges			
New Balance	1,210		
Principal Reduction	148		

Debt: First Mortgage
Interest Rate: Annual: 11.75 % | Monthly: 0.979 % | Min.Pmt.: $ 1262

	Planned	Actual	Difference
Balance Forward	124,169		
Interest	1,216		
Payment	1,262		
New Charges			
New Balance	124,123		
Principal Reduction	46		

Debt: Second Mortgage
Interest Rate: Annual: 12 % | Monthly: 1. % | Min.Pmt.: $ 250

	Planned	Actual	Difference
Balance Forward	25,000		
Interest	250		
Payment	250		
New Charges			
New Balance	25,000		
Principal Reduction	0		

Debt: Loan from Parents
Interest Rate: Annual: 10 % | Monthly: 0.833 % | Min.Pmt.: $

	Planned	Actual	Difference
Balance Forward	10,000		
Interest	83		
Payment			
New Charges			
New Balance	10,083		
Principal Reduction	-83		

Total — All Debts

	Planned	Actual	Difference
Balance Forward	181,363		
Interest	1,756		
Payment	2,604		
New Charges	0		
New Balance	180,515		
Principal Reduction	848		

Figure 10-3

one else can argue with him and no one else can get into the holy books to find out the answers for themselves."

Kathy nodded and managed a smile. She knew exactly what I was talking about. "John has an MBA."

I smiled at John and he chuckled back: "—which means I can foul up our financial planning in half the time it takes Kathy to foul it up," he admitted.

"Very efficient," I observed. "Listen, this priest thing is very important. You can't afford to have either one of you be the only one who knows about any part of the financial planning process. If you keep the checkbook, for instance, Kathy, and John wants to make such-and-such a purchase, you don't have to even listen to his argument. You're the priest—or priestess—of the checkbook. All you have to say is 'We can't—there isn't enough money' and he won't have a thing to say about it. It would take him a week to study the checkbook long enough to refute your argument."

Kathy nodded in familiar agreement. I could tell she had used that trick before.

"That's why I insist that both partners in a couple learn the entire Financial Sanity system," I continued. "Then, since all planning is done with the system, it won't matter that one person knows all about the checkbook and another doesn't—because the checkbook is not where financial decisions are made anymore.

"So," I said cheerily. "Let's really see how fast we can pay off those credit cards."

Pay what you owe, and you'll know what is your own.
 —*Poor Richard's Almanack*

11

Your Debt Reduction Plan

This chapter provides you with some analytical shortcuts to help you decide how fast to pay off your debts to achieve the results you want. It will help you target the debts you want to pay off first, and will tell you precisely when you can expect to achieve the results you have planned for.

Most important, this chapter will help put you in the driver's seat with regard to your debt.

Picking Your Shots: Targeting Debts for Payoff

In the very early days of the Financial Sanity Workshop, people had to do their debt planning by trial and error. Using only the Debt Reduction Planner, they had to calculate by hand their interest and principal reduction on each of several debts for twenty or thirty months. And if they didn't like how fast their debt was going down, they had to do the whole analysis over, with a new monthly payment amount.

People needed to be able to calculate the amount of monthly payment necessary to completely pay off a debt in a specific targeted period of time. For that reason, I devised the Payoff Planning and Prediction Tables in Figures 11-1 and 11-2. They essentially do the job that a pocket calculator with financial functions would perform— except the most sophisticated calculator you'll need to use these charts is a simple, four-function calculator.

I showed John and Kathy the chart in Figure 11-1, which is a payoff table for short-term debt. (Figure 11-2 provides a similar tool for long-term debt.)

"Let me show you how the tables work," I said. "First, why don't we figure out how long it will take to pay off each debt, given the minimum payments you've put on your Debt Reduction Planner?" (Figure 10-3). "The Visa account has a balance of $2,588 and a minimum payment of $116. What's 116 divided by 2,588?"

We tapped out our answer on our pocket calculators: .0448, or 4.5 percent.

"And the interest rate is 21 percent, so let's look on the chart. Read across the chart until you get to the interest rate of 21%, then read down until you match up with the line that's labeled 4.5 percent in the Payment as % of Debt column."

"It says 28.4," noted Kathy. "Twenty-eight-point-four what?"

"That means 28.4 months to pay off the loan, if you keep up payments of $116 per month," I said.

"Oh," said Kathy, intrigued. "Now what if I wanted to pay it off in eighteen months?"

"Okay," I said. "Read down the page in the 21% column until you get to something close to 18."

"Oh, look," she said. "Here's 18.1."

"Good," I said. "Now follow that line all the way to the left-hand column and read the percentage that's there."

"Six-point-five?" she asked.

"Exactly," I said. "That means if you pay 6.5 percent of the $2,588 each month—instead of the 4.5 percent you have planned now— you'll have that debt completely paid off in 18.1 months instead of 28.4."

John was tapping at his calculator, multiplying $2,588 times 6.5 percent. "That's $168," he announced. "So, you're saying that monthly payments of $168 will get this $2,588 paid off in 18.1 months."

"Right."

John had a calculator with financial functions. He was busy tapping

NUMBER of MONTHLY PAYMENTS REQUIRED to RETIRE DEBT

Payment as % of Debt	5%	6%	7%	8%	9%	10%	11%	12%	13%	14%	15%	16%	17%	18%	19%	20%	21%	22%
								Stated Annual Interest Rate of Debt										
1.0%	129.6	139.0	150.5	165.3	185.5	215.9	272.3	*	*	*	*	*	*	*	*	*	*	*
1.5%	78.3	81.3	84.7	88.5	92.8	97.7	103.5	110.4	118.9	129.7	144.2	165.9	205.5	*	*	*	*	*
2.0%	56.2	57.7	59.3	61.0	62.9	64.9	67.2	69.7	72.4	75.5	79.0	82.9	87.6	93.1	99.9	108.4	119.9	136.8
2.5%	43.8	44.7	45.7	46.7	47.7	48.9	50.1	51.3	52.7	54.2	55.8	57.5	59.4	61.5	63.9	66.5	69.4	72.8
3.0%	36.0	36.6	37.2	37.8	38.5	39.2	40.0	40.7	41.6	42.5	43.4	44.4	45.4	46.6	47.8	49.1	50.5	52.0
3.5%	30.5	30.9	31.3	31.8	32.3	32.8	33.3	33.8	34.4	35.0	35.6	36.2	36.9	37.6	38.3	39.1	40.0	40.8
4.0%	26.5	26.8	27.1	27.4	27.8	28.2	28.5	28.9	29.3	29.7	30.2	30.6	31.1	31.6	32.1	32.6	33.2	33.7
4.5%	23.4	23.6	23.9	24.1	24.4	24.7	25.0	25.3	25.6	25.9	26.2	26.5	26.9	27.2	27.6	28.0	28.4	28.8
5.0%	20.9	21.1	21.3	21.5	21.8	22.0	22.2	22.4	22.7	22.9	23.2	23.4	23.7	24.0	24.2	24.5	24.8	25.1
5.5%	18.9	19.1	19.3	19.4	19.6	19.8	20.0	20.2	20.4	20.6	20.8	21.0	21.2	21.4	21.6	21.8	22.1	22.3
6.0%	17.3	17.4	17.6	17.7	17.9	18.0	18.2	18.3	18.5	18.6	18.8	19.0	19.1	19.3	19.5	19.7	19.9	20.1
6.5%	15.9	16.0	16.2	16.3	16.4	16.5	16.7	16.8	16.9	17.1	17.2	17.3	17.5	17.6	17.8	17.9	18.1	18.2
7.0%	14.8	14.9	15.0	15.1	15.2	15.3	15.4	15.5	15.6	15.7	15.8	16.0	16.1	16.2	16.3	16.5	16.6	16.7
7.5%	13.7	13.8	13.9	14.0	14.1	14.2	14.3	14.4	14.5	14.6	14.7	14.8	14.9	15.0	15.1	15.2	15.3	15.4
8.0%	12.9	12.9	13.0	13.1	13.2	13.3	13.3	13.4	13.5	13.6	13.7	13.8	13.9	13.9	14.0	14.1	14.2	14.3
8.5%	12.1	12.2	12.2	12.3	12.4	12.4	12.5	12.6	12.7	12.7	12.8	12.9	13.0	13.0	13.1	13.2	13.3	13.4
9.0%	11.4	11.5	11.5	11.6	11.6	11.7	11.8	11.8	11.9	12.0	12.0	12.1	12.2	12.2	12.3	12.4	12.5	12.5
9.5%	10.8	10.8	10.9	11.0	11.0	11.1	11.1	11.2	11.2	11.3	11.4	11.4	11.5	11.5	11.6	11.7	11.7	11.8
10.0%	10.2	10.3	10.3	10.4	10.4	10.5	10.5	10.6	10.6	10.7	10.7	10.8	10.9	10.9	11.0	11.1	11.1	11.1
11.0%	9.3	9.3	9.4	9.4	9.5	9.5	9.5	9.6	9.6	9.7	9.7	9.8	9.8	9.8	9.9	9.9	10.0	10.0
12.0%	8.5	8.5	8.6	8.6	8.6	8.7	8.7	8.7	8.8	8.8	8.9	8.9	8.9	9.0	9.0	9.0	9.1	9.1
13.0%	7.8	7.9	7.9	7.9	8.0	8.0	8.0	8.0	8.1	8.1	8.1	8.2	8.2	8.2	8.3	8.3	8.3	8.4
14.0%	7.3	7.3	7.3	7.3	7.4	7.4	7.4	7.4	7.5	7.5	7.5	7.6	7.6	7.6	7.6	7.7	7.7	7.7
15.0%	6.8	6.8	6.8	6.8	6.9	6.9	6.9	6.9	7.0	7.0	7.0	7.0	7.1	7.1	7.1	7.1	7.2	7.2
20.0%	5.1	5.1	5.1	5.1	5.1	5.1	5.1	5.2	5.2	5.2	5.2	5.2	5.2	5.2	5.3	5.3	5.3	5.3
25.0%	4.0	4.1	4.1	4.1	4.1	4.1	4.1	4.1	4.1	4.1	4.1	4.1	4.1	4.2	4.2	4.2	4.2	4.2
30.0%	3.4	3.4	3.4	3.4	3.4	3.4	3.4	3.4	3.4	3.4	3.4	3.4	3.4	3.4	3.5	3.5	3.5	3.5
35.0%	2.9	2.9	2.9	2.9	2.9	2.9	2.9	2.9	2.9	2.9	2.9	2.9	2.9	2.9	2.9	3.0	3.0	3.0
40.0%	2.5	2.5	2.5	2.5	2.5	2.5	2.5	2.5	2.5	2.6	2.6	2.6	2.6	2.6	2.6	2.6	2.6	2.6
45.0%	2.2	2.2	2.2	2.2	2.2	2.3	2.3	2.3	2.3	2.3	2.3	2.3	2.3	2.3	2.3	2.3	2.3	2.3

NUMBER of PAYMENTS

* Payment results in negative amortization: Loan never gets repaid because principal balance rises each month, instead of falling.

Figure 11-1

NUMBER of MONTHLY PAYMENTS REQUIRED to RETIRE DEBT

When payment is this small and interest rate this high, the loan never gets repaid.

The payments don't cover the monthly interest charge, so the principal balance rises each month, instead of falling.

This is known as negative amortization.

NUMBER of PAYMENTS

Payment as % of Debt	Stated Annual Interest Rate of Debt																	
	6.0%	6.5%	7.0%	7.5%	8.0%	8.5%	9.0%	9.5%	10.0%	10.5%	11.0%	11.5%	12.0%	12.5%	13.0%	13.5%	14.0%	14.5%
0.60%	359	431	616															
0.65%	294	332	392	523														
0.70%	251	275	308	358	458													
0.75%	220	237	259	288	331	409												
0.80%	197	209	225	244	270	307	371	579										
0.85%	178	188	199	213	231	254	286	340	474									
0.90%	163	170	180	190	203	219	240	268	314	411								
0.95%	150	156	164	172	182	194	209	227	253	291	367							
1.00%	139	144	151	157	165	175	186	199	216	239	272	333						
1.05%	130	134	139	145	152	159	168	178	190	206	226	256	306	467				
1.10%	122	126	130	135	140	146	153	161	171	182	196	215	241	283	389			
1.15%	114	118	122	126	130	136	141	148	155	164	175	188	205	228	264	342		
1.20%	108	111	114	118	122	126	131	137	143	150	158	168	180	195	216	248	309	
1.25%	102	105	108	111	115	118	123	127	132	138	145	153	162	173	187	206	233	283
1.30%	97	100	102	105	108	112	115	119	123	128	134	140	147	156	166	179	196	221
1.35%	93	95	97	100	102	105	109	112	116	120	125	130	136	142	151	160	172	188
1.40%	89	91	93	95	97	100	103	106	109	113	117	121	126	132	138	145	154	166
1.45%	85	87	88	91	93	95	97	100	103	106	110	113	118	122	128	134	141	149
1.50%	81	83	85	87	88	91	93	95	98	100	104	107	110	114	119	124	130	136
1.55%	78	80	81	83	85	87	89	91	93	95	98	101	104	108	111	116	120	126
1.60%	75	77	78	79	81	83	85	87	89	91	93	96	99	102	105	109	113	117
1.65%	72	74	75	76	78	79	81	83	85	87	89	91	94	96	99	102	106	110
1.70%	70	71	72	74	75	76	78	79	81	83	85	87	89	92	94	97	100	103
1.75%	67	69	70	71	72	74	75	76	78	80	81	83	85	87	90	92	95	98
1.80%	65	66	67	68	70	71	72	73	76	77	78	80	81	83	85	88	90	93
1.85%	63	64	65	66	67	69	70	71	73	74	76	77	78	81	82	84	86	88
1.90%	61	62	63	64	65	66	68	69	70	72	73	74	75	78	78	80	82	84
1.95%	59	60	61	62	63	64	66	66	68	70	71	71	72	75	75	77	79	80
2.00%	58	58	59	60	61	62	64	64	66	67	68	68	70	72	72	74	75	77
2.05%	56	57	58	59	59	60	62	62	64	65	66	66	67	70	70	71	73	74
2.10%	55	55	56	57	58	59	60	60	62	63	64	64	65	67	67	69	70	71
2.15%	53	54	55	56	56	57	58	59	60	61	62	63	63	64	65	66	67	69

Figure 11-2

away at it to check the accuracy of my table. "It works out to 18.1075 payments. That's dead on."

"It won't always be quite that accurate," I warned. "Anytime you use a table you're likely to end up between columns and rows and making estimates. But this table is precise enough for planning purposes, definitely to the nearest month."

"Now let me get clear on this one thing," Kathy interjected. "When you say to make a payment of $168 each month, you assume we're not charging on the card, right?"

"That's right," I said. "And if you do make charges on the card, I expect that you will pay them off the same month they appear on your bill."

"—in addition to the $168," added John.

"Exactly. You don't have to stop using your cards, even if you are on a rapid-payoff program."

"So," Kathy asked, "you don't go around telling people to cut up their credit cards?"

"Not usually," I replied. "Credit cards can be very convenient."

"But you pay them off in full every month," John confirmed.

"Yes. All of my credit cards have zero balances. I just use them for convenience, so I don't have to waste time pawing through my wallet for several pieces of identification in order to entice some salesclerk to accept my check."

John and Kathy looked at each other, seemingly making a silent pact to follow this new system.

Since these two clients liked playing with the payoff table so much, I left them for a few minutes to analyze the rest of their short-term loans. By the time I walked back into my office, they had just finished up a chart that summarized when each of their short-term debts would be paid off, according to the table. I have reproduced their analysis in Figure 11-3.

Figure 11-3: Payoff Periods for Debts

	Visa	Master-Card	Furniture	Car Loan	Student Loan	Total
Interest Rate	21%	19%	18%	4%	6%	
Payment	$116	$203	$163	$455	$155	$1,092
Debt	$2,588	$4,511	$3,259	$10,478	$1,358	$22,194
Payment Percent	4.5%	4.5%	5.0%	4.3%	11.4%	
Months to Pay	28.4	27.6	24	24	9.3	28.4

"It really makes a difference, just knowing these numbers!" Kathy gushed. "I feel like we're actually in some kind of control. If we just make these payments every month, all these debts will be gone in less than two and a half years. If that's the best we could do, that would be okay. I'm just happy to know what's going on."

But that wasn't the best John and Kathy could do.

John had said he thought that he and Kathy could come up with still another $250 monthly, which would make approximately $1,342 available for short-term debt ($250 plus the $1,092 of monthly payments from Figure 11-3).

With this extra monthly money, I cheered them on: "Let's see about meeting your eighteen-month goal."

I left John and Kathy alone again to come up with a new chart—one that took advantage of the extra money they had available for monthly debt service and that tried to get the credit cards paid off in eighteen months. They came up with this revised plan:

Figure 11-4: Targeted Periods for Payoff of Debts

	Visa	Master-Card	Furniture	Car Loan	Student Loan	Total
Interest Rate	21%	19%	18%	4%	6%	
Payment	$168	$293	$204	$455	$155	$1,275
Debt	$2,588	$4,511	$3,259	$10,478	$1,358	$22,194
Percentage	6.5%	6.5%	6.3%	4.3%	11.4%	
Months to Pay	18	18	18	24	9.3	18

Not only were they able to pay off their Visa and MasterCard, but they also decided to reduce the time on their furniture loan from two years to eighteen months. And they still had an additional $67 a month in available funds left to reduce other debt: $1,342 was available, and the payments in the plan in Figure 11-4 total only $1,275.

Choosing the Debts to Pay Off First

"Where should we put the extra money?" Kathy asked, feeling giddy. "We were thinking about reducing the car loan, but John says we shouldn't because it has such a low interest rate."

"I'd agree with John," I said. "Let me tell you my biases for prioritizing the retirement of debt."

I briefly outlined for them my opinions about which debt should get paid off first. Following is the order I recommend (review Chapter 4 for definitions of any terms you find unfamiliar):

- Credit Card Debt—usually as fast as possible. Credit cards have a bad habit of being grossly overpriced in terms of interest rates. Furthermore, credit card debt is the kind that drives people nuts. It's too easy to let new charges slip onto the card and not pay them off immediately. This makes credit card balances seem to go on forever. Credit cards should ideally be used only for their convenience and, second, for short-term, emergency credit. But if there's a balance on the card, there's likely to be little credit availability.
- Line of Credit Debt. A line of credit is supposed to be used to smooth out short-term cash flow shortages. If you need to leave the bulk of the balance on, year after year, you probably needed a term loan. Also, there is no risk, in terms of liquidity, to paying down a line of credit balance: You can always change your mind and re-borrow the money at any time. This is not true for most other loans.
- Any high-interest loans.
- Any loans that are not fully amortized term loans.
- Fully amortized loans with moderate interest.

I would never accelerate the payment of a loan with a sub-market (below what you can get when you invest) interest rate.

"So, you're saying that you would never try to speed up the payoff of the car loan?" John asked.

"And you wouldn't try to pay this furniture loan off so fast?" asked Kathy.

"Right," I said. "I'd start attacking that furniture loan right after I had paid off the cards completely."

John and Kathy accepted this idea and calculated, using the Payoff Table, that they could pay off both of their credit cards in about fourteen months if they concentrated their extra monthly payments on the cards.

"Now I have an even better idea," I said. "Concentrate all your extra money on the card with the lowest balance—the Visa card—making only minimum payments on the MasterCard and every other debt."

"What will that accomplish?" Kathy asked, looking dubious.

"Try it," I said, directing them to the Payoff Table again.

They added together the minimum payments of all their short-term debts from Figure 10-3 *except* the Visa payment. This amount totaled $976. They subtracted $976 from the $1,342 total available funds for short-term debt payments. That left them with $366 they could devote toward paying off their Visa card. Using the table, they estimated a complete payoff of their card in 7.7 months:

Figure 11-5: Using the Payoff Table to Calculate Months of Payments

	Visa
Interest Rate	21.0%
Payment	$362
Debt	$2,588
Payment Percentage	14.0%
Months to Pay	7.7

"This leaves you with a credit card with no balance on it," I pointed out. "You can then use the Visa for all your charges and, since you'll pay them off every month as they appear on your bill, you won't be charged any finance charges." (Most credit cards charge interest on your purchases if you are carrying a previous balance on the card. This means that the card is providing you with no "float"—interest-free use of money between the time you purchase and the time you pay the credit card bill.)

"But won't it now take forever to pay off the MasterCard?" Kathy looked worried.

"Nope," I reassured her. "As soon as you pay off the Visa, you can take what was going to Visa and add it to what you're already sending to MasterCard."

John calculated that number to be $565 (the $362 former Visa payment plus the $203 minimum MasterCard payment).

After plotting out the payments of both credit cards on the Debt Reduction Planner, we determined that—after eight months of giving priority to the Visa—it would take only six more months (remember that we were making minimum payments on the MasterCard, so the balance did go down in eight months) to pay off the MasterCard. In the end, the MasterCard would be paid off in fourteen months.

The rule is: *If the interest rates are approximately the same, it will take approximately the same amount of time to retire multiple debts one by one as it will to retire them all at the same rate.*

Taking an Interest in Interest

"You know," said Kathy, examining the short-term payoff chart, "I would have thought that interest rates would have had a bigger effect on how long it takes to pay off a debt."

"What do you mean?" John asked, looking over her shoulder at the chart.

"Well, look at this 15.0 percent payment line on the chart," she said, referring to Figure 11-1. "At 5 percent interest it takes 6.8 months to pay off a loan, and at 22 percent interest it takes just 7.2 months. To my way of thinking, both those time periods are 'about 7 months.'"

"She's got a point," I agreed. "During shorter payback periods—with a high percentage of the principal being paid each month—high interest rates have so little time to do their dirty work that the time difference seems inconsequential." I was riffling through my files as I talked. "I ran a graph of that once—let me try to find it."

The graph I showed them is at Figure 11-6. It plots payback periods for monthly payments ranging from 5 percent ($50 on the graph) to 25 percent ($250).

"Interesting," John mused. "By the time you get to a 10 percent monthly payment [$100 on the graph], the lines representing different interest rates are running so close together that you can't tell them apart."

"Now," I said, putting another graph in front of them, "it's a different story for longer-term debt." A similar chart, showing payments ranging from 1.2 percent ($1,200 on the graph) to 2 percent ($2,000), is reproduced in Figure 11-7. "There's clearly a big difference in payout times for each of these lines, representing different interest rates. The difference in interest rates is getting a chance to make a difference over these longer terms."

The Debt Reduction Planner in Action

Having made their decisions about which debt to retire with what level of payments, John and Kathy made changes to their Debt Reduction Planner. The first five months of their revised version, showing total payments of $2,850 that include both long-term and short-term debt payments, is reproduced in Figure 11-8.

The Actual and Difference columns, I explained to them, were rather self-explanatory. For each month they would be entering what actually happened in the Actual column and draw off the difference in the Difference column.

The main things that will turn up different between the Actual and Planned will be New Charges. And the New Charges may make your Interest a little higher than you had calculated. As you plot these differences, be on the lookout for getting behind. If the Actual New Balance is significantly higher than the Planned New Balance, you may want to find some extra money in your budget to make a one-time extra payment.

The Fitzpatricks were immensely pleased with their payoff plan. They hadn't realized they were going to be able to accomplish so much over so few months and feel so confident about the implementation of their plan.

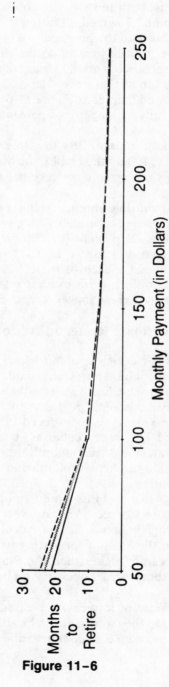

**Months to Pay Off $1,000 Debt
by Payment Amount
at Various Interest Rates**

6%

15%

21%

Months
to
Retire

Monthly Payment (in Dollars)

Each line represents a different interest rate. Interest rates are a tiny factor in determining the length of time it takes to retire short-term debt, while the size of the monthly payment has a dramatic effect.

Figure 11-6

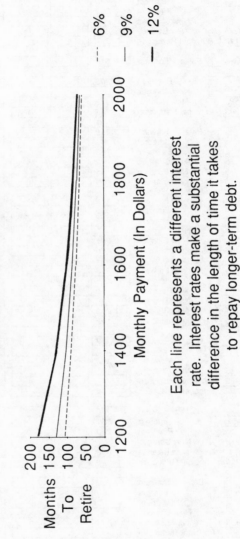

Figure 11-7

Month	June			July		
	Planned	Actual	Difference	Planned	Actual	Difference

Debt: Visa
Interest Rate: Annual: 21 % — Monthly: 1.75 % — Min.Pmt.: $ 116

	Planned	Actual	Difference	Planned	Actual	Difference
Balance Forward	2,588			2,271		
Interest	45			40		
Payment	362			362		
New Charges						
New Balance	2,271			1,949		
Principal Reduction	317			322		

Debt: MasterCard
Interest Rate: Annual: 19 % — Monthly: 1.583 % — Min.Pmt.: $ 203

	Planned	Actual	Difference	Planned	Actual	Difference
Balance Forward	4,511			4,379		
Interest	71			69		
Payment	203			203		
New Charges						
New Balance	4,379			4,245		
Principal Reduction	132			134		

Debt: Furniture Financing
Interest Rate: Annual: 18 % — Monthly: 1.5 % — Min.Pmt.: $ 163

	Planned	Actual	Difference	Planned	Actual	Difference
Balance Forward	3,259			3,145		
Interest	49			47		
Payment	163			163		
New Charges						
New Balance	3,145			3,029		
Principal Reduction	114			116		

Debt: Car Loan
Interest Rate: Annual: 4 % — Monthly: 0.333 % — Min.Pmt.: $ 455

	Planned	Actual	Difference	Planned	Actual	Difference
Balance Forward	10,478			10,058		
Interest	35			33		
Payment	455			455		
New Charges						
New Balance	10,058			9,636		
Principal Reduction	420			422		

Debt: Student Loan
Interest Rate: Annual: 6 % — Monthly: 0.5 % — Min.Pmt.: $ 155

	Planned	Actual	Difference	Planned	Actual	Difference
Balance Forward	1,358			1,210		
Interest	7			6		
Payment	155			155		
New Charges						
New Balance	1,210			1,061		
Principal Reduction	148			149		

Debt: First Mortgage
Interest Rate: Annual: 11.75 % — Monthly: 0.979 % — Min.Pmt.: $ 1262

	Planned	Actual	Difference	Planned	Actual	Difference
Balance Forward	124,169			124,123		
Interest	1,216			1,215		
Payment	1,262			1,262		
New Charges						
New Balance	124,123			124,076		
Principal Reduction	46			47		

Debt: Second Mortgage
Interest Rate: Annual: 12 % — Monthly: 1. % — Min.Pmt.: $ 250

	Planned	Actual	Difference	Planned	Actual	Difference
Balance Forward	25,000			25,000		
Interest	250			250		
Payment	250			250		
New Charges						
New Balance	25,000			25,000		
Principal Reduction	0			0		

Debt: Loan from Parents
Interest Rate: Annual: 10 % — Monthly: 0.833 % — Min.Pmt.: $

	Planned	Actual	Difference	Planned	Actual	Difference
Balance Forward	10,000			10,083		
Interest	83			84		
Payment						
New Charges						
New Balance	10,083			10,167		
Principal Reduction	-83			-84		

Total — All Debts

	Planned	Actual	Difference	Planned	Actual	Difference
Balance Forward	181,363			180,269		
Interest	1,756			1,744		
Payment	2,850			2,850		
New Charges	0			0		
New Balance	180,269			179,163		
Principal Reduction	1,094			1,106		

Figure 11–8

August			September			October		
Planned	Actual	Difference	Planned	Actual	Difference	Planned	Actual	Difference
1,949			1,621			1,287		
34			28			23		
362			362			362		
1,621			1,287			948		
328			334			339		
4,245			4,109			3,971		
67			65			63		
203			203			203		
4,109			3,971			3,831		
136			138			140		
3,029			2,911			2,792		
45			44			42		
163			163			163		
2,911			2,792			2,671		
118			119			121		
9,636			9,213			8,789		
32			31			29		
455			455			455		
9,213			8,789			8,363		
423			424			426		
1,061			911			761		
5			5			4		
155			155			155		
911			761			610		
150			150			151		
124,076			124,029			123,981		
1,215			1,214			1,214		
1,262			1,262			1,262		
124,029			123,981			123,933		
47			48			48		
25,000			25,000			25,000		
250			250			250		
250			250			250		
25,000			25,000			25,000		
0			0			0		
10,167			10,252			10,337		
85			85			86		
10,252			10,337			10,423		
-85			-85			-86		
179,163			178,046			176,918		
1,733			1,722			1,711		
2,850			2,850			2,850		
0			0			0		
178,046			176,918			175,779		
1,117			1,128			1,139		

John and Kathy left my office smiling—tough to do when you've spent the afternoon talking about debt. They took their Debt Reduction Planner home and followed it.

When I called them several months later they had wiped out all their credit card debt, well ahead of schedule. (They used some of the restructuring techniques I talk about later in Chapter 24.) This is not at all unusual among good debt planners using the Financial Sanity system. Because they know so much about the dynamics of their debt situation, it's easy for them to jump at any opportunity to pay off debt in a hurry. And they do so knowing that there isn't some important cash need coming up that they're forgetting to consider.

Once you've settled on a debt reduction plan, you are playing from a position of strength. You've already got debt licked—any new solutions (such as refinancing, selling assets or rearranging your budget) can be evaluated against the solution you already have in place.

Making Your Own Debt Reduction Plan

Now I'd like to get you started on your own debt reduction program, just as John and Kathy did. The purpose of the Debt Reduction Planner—used together with the two charts given earlier in this chapter:

- Figure 11-1, which provides the number of monthly payments required to retire short-term debt
- Figure 11-2, which provides the number of monthly payments required to retire long-term debt

—is to allow you to map out fairly precisely when and how you are going to pay off the debt you now have. The schedule allows you to take into account interest charges precisely so that you will know exactly how much cash flow your debt reduction plan will require. As a final result of your debt reduction planning, you should be able to pinpoint precisely when each of your debts will be paid off.

Exercise: Debt Reduction Planner

1. Get the Inflow-Outflow Information Sheet you prepared in Chapter 10. Update it for any changes that may have occurred in debt balances since you prepared it.

2. Format a worksheet with column headings and captions like Figure 11-8, or copy the form in Appendix B. You may find that you have more debts than your worksheet can accommodate. Don't feel bad—most of us do. If that's so, make several copies. You'll also want to make copies to accommodate more months.

3. On your Debt Reduction Planner, fill in the names of your various debts and the annual interest rate. Also, on the Balance Forward line in the first Planned column, fill in the amount owing for each debt. Put the minimum payment required each month in the Minimum Payment (Min. Pmt.) box.

4. After you've filled in all your debts, the annual rates, the beginning balance and the minimum payment, divide the annual rates by 12 and put those figures in the appropriate Monthly boxes.

Now you're ready to start reducing debt—on paper, anyway. You've set up the framework for mapping out the details of your debt repayment schedule. Next we'll have you use the payoff prediction tables to plan your overall debt payoff strategy, after which you will return to and complete this Debt Reduction Planner.

Using the Debt Payoff Prediction Tables

Every month you get charged interest on each of your debts. It's important to include these interest charges in your planning, because they often eat up a very large portion of your payments.

For instance, assume you have a $3,000 MasterCard debt which you are paying off at $100 a month. Simple arithmetic would suggest that 30 payments of $100 each would pay off the principal. But you know that interest will eat up a portion of those payments. How many additional payments must you make to cover both interest and the principal?

Those of us with financial calculators can quickly figure out that 40 payments will just about do it. But since we don't all have financial calculators (and those who do don't always know how to work them), the debt payoff prediction tables in Figures 11-1 and 11-2 are provided to accomplish the same task. Here's how to use them:

Exercise: Payoff Planning and Prediction

To determine how large your monthly payments should be:
1. Read horizontally across the top to find the vertical column that most closely corresponds to the interest rate of your debt.
2. Scan down the column until you reach the number that most closely corresponds to the number of months over which you would like to retire this debt.
3. Look to the far left-hand column to see what percentage of the amount owing you need to pay against this debt each month.
4. Multiply this percentage by the total amount of debt currently due.
5. The number obtained is the approximate amount of your

monthly payment. Pay this amount each month and the debt will be retired completely in approximately the time you desired.

Example:
   You have a credit card with a $4,000 balance due. The interest rate is 19.5 percent. You want to pay off the debt in about two years. How much do you need to pay each month to get the job done?
   First, you'll read across the top of the chart at Figure 11-1 until you find the 19% and 20% columns. Since 19.5 percent is halfway between both interest rates, read down both columns until you find a number that's close to 24 (24 months being the length of time you want to make payments). In this case, you'll find 24.2 and 24.5 on the ninth line down.
   You'll look to the left to see what payment percentage is called for. In this case it's 5%. Now take 5% and multiply it by the principal balance of $4,000.

Principal Balance	$ 4,000
Percentage from Payoff Chart	
(Payment as % of Debt Column)	× 5%
Monthly Payment Indicated	$ 200

You should pay $200 a month for about two years and your debt will be wiped out.
   (This chart gives you an approximate answer. Let's see what we could have done with a financial calculator: The dead-accurate answer is that payments of $202.61 will retire the debt in exactly 24 months. Don't take the $2.61 difference too lightly—after two years of $200 monthly payments, you'll owe $75.80 on this debt due to that $2.61 monthly shortage. Nonetheless, this chart should allow you to get very close in your planning—and save you the cost of a $45 financial calculator and an hour of learning how to use it.)
   In the example and directions above, we assumed that you had decided how fast you wanted to pay off the debt, and were interested in knowing how much you had to pay each month to accomplish that goal. But often you'll know how much you can afford to pay toward the debt each month—and want to know how long it will take.

To determine how many months it will take you to pay off the debt:

   1. Divide the monthly payment you are making by the total amount of the debt.

2. Take the derived percentage and match it as closely as possible to one of the numbers in the left-most column.

3. Find the vertical column for the interest rate of your debt.

4. The number at the intersection of your vertical column and horizontal row represents the months needed to retire the debt.

Example:

You just bought a house and have a $100,000, 30-year mortgage loan at 10 percent. You checked with your lender and found out that you could make extra payments toward principal each month, thus reducing the total number of payments you'll have to make.

Your regular mortgage payment is $877.57 per month. After doing your budget planning, you determine that you could free up an extra $150 each month for an additional principal payment. You want to know how much faster you'll pay off your loan this way.

First, you need to determine what percentage your extra-large mortgage payment will be of your loan:

Regular Mortgage Payment	$ 877.57
Additional Money Available	150.00
New Monthly Payment	$ 1,027.57

Your new loan payment will be $1,027.57. Divide the $1,027.57 new monthly payment by the $100,000 total loan:

Regular Mortgage Payment	$ 1,027.57
Loan Balance	÷100,000.00
New Monthly Payment (as %)	1.02757%

The payment is 1.02757 percent of $100,000.

Since this is a long-term loan, use the Long-Term version of the Debt Retirement Prediction Schedule in Figure 11-2. Read down the left-hand column of the chart until you get to 1.00% and 1.05%, which are the closest to your percentage. Then read across until you get to the column headed 10.0%, which is the interest rate of the loan.

The chart's answers are 216 and 190 for 1.00% and 1.05%, respectively. Your percentage is almost 1.03%, which is closer to 1.05% than to 1.00%. You estimate that had there been a 1.03% on the chart it would have read about 200 months, meaning that the loan would be paid off in about 16½ years, instead of the original 30 years. (A financial calculator would have yielded 200.7 months.)

You get so excited about the prospects of an early payoff of your loan that you want to test out what an extra $225 can do, instead of $150:

Original Payment	$ 877.57
Extra Payment	+ 225.00
Total Payment	1,102.57
Loan Balance	÷100,000.00
Percent of Debt	1.103%

This time, your derived percentage of 1.103% comes very close to a percentage on the left side of the chart, specifically, 1.10%. Reading across to the 10.0% interest rate column, you derive 171 months (14¼ years) to pay off the debt. (Your financial calculator would have yielded 169.9 months.)

The example we just went through covers a new $100,000 loan. What if you have a loan that you've been making payments on for five or so years and is partially paid down?

The technique is just the same as for a new loan. All you need to know is the remaining balance on the loan at the time you do your planning. For instance, if the $100,000 loan in our example was four years old, the remaining balance due on the loan would now be about $97,400. Of course, since four years of the 30-year mortgage have passed, you have 26 years of $877.57 payments left. This is exactly the same as having a brand-new mortgage loan of $97,400 and a term of 26 years. The payments for such a loan would be $877.57. Using this set of facts, you can use the loan payoff tables to experiment with different monthly payments exactly as we did in the example above.

With the Payoff Planning and Prediction Tables in Figures 11-1 and 11-2, you can quickly estimate one or the other of the following:

- how long it will take to retire a debt, given a specific monthly payment; or
- what sort of payment will be required to retire a debt in a specific period of time.

The ability to answer these questions will be invaluable as you complete your Debt Reduction Planner.

Completing Your Debt Reduction Planner

Now that you've decided how fast to pay off each debt, you're ready to fill out the rest of your Debt Reduction Planner. (We'll pick up numbering the steps where we left off on page 123.)

5. Enter the anticipated payment amount for each debt on the Payment line in the Planned column.

6. Calculate the Interest line by multiplying the Balance Forward by the Monthly interest rate for each debt.

7. In the Planned column, I generally recommend leaving the New Charges line blank.

8. Calculate the New Balance by adding the Balance Forward and Interest lines together (and the New Charges line, if not zero) and subtracting the Payment line.

The calculator key guide for the calculation is as follows:

+ Balance Forward
+ Interest
− Payment
+ New Charges
= New Balance

9. Calculate the Principal Reduction line by subtracting the Interest line (and the New Charges line, if any) from the Payment line.

The calculator key guide for the calculation is as follows:

+ Payment
− Interest
− New Charges
= Principal Reduction

10. Add each line for each debt together and put the sum in the appropriate line of the Total lines at the bottom of the Planner. As a check of your math, the two formulas in steps 8 and 9 should also work with the figures entered in the Totals section.

11. Copy the New Balance at the end of each debt's Planned column to the Balance Forward Line of the Planned column for the next month.

12. Repeat steps 5 through 11 for each new month on your Planner.

Exercise: Monitoring Your Debt-Reduction Planner

1. Each month, separately total up the charges made to each credit card on your debt schedule (and any borrowings from your line of credit). Enter these amounts on the appropriate New Charges line for each debt in the Actual column.

2. If this is the first month of your Debt Reduction Planner, take the beginning balance from your charge card statement or other statement from your creditors (or from an amortization schedule) and enter that number in the Balance Forward column. (If you reconcile, or balance, your charge accounts the same way people reconcile their checking accounts, use the actual calculated balance from that reconciliation.)

If this is not the first month, merely take the Balance Forward from last month's Actual New Balance.

3. Take the interest charge shown on your statement and enter it in the Actual Interest block for each debt.

4. Take the amount you actually paid to the creditor that month and enter it on the Payment line.

5. You are now ready to do the math involved in calculating the New Balance and Principal Reduction lines, which are calculated the same way as they were for the Planned column. Be sure that your New Balance calculation agrees with the New Balance on your statement, amortization or reconciliation.

6. Next, subtract the Actual amount from the Planned amount and enter the difference in the Difference column. While minor differences can be safely ignored, large differences and trends should be investigated and analyzed for their ultimate affect on your debt retirement plans.

7. The totals of all the above lines should be entered in the Total section at the bottom of your Planner. They will eventually be transferred to the Master Budget, discussed in Chapter 20.

Stop Using Your Credit Card to Borrow Money!

In all of our discussions about debt reduction, there is one prevailing assumption: that your days of borrowing any additional money on credit cards are over for good. This doesn't mean you can't use your credit cards—it simply means that you will be paying off all the new charges every month.

It also doesn't mean that you will never borrow money again, but there are a number of borrowing options that are far better than credit cards. These include

- home loans
- second mortgages (home equity loans)
- home equity lines of credit
- unsecured lines of credit
- car loans
- credit union loans

and others.

Credit card borrowing is sometimes appropriate for very short-term needs. As we work through chapters on funding, we will discuss the possibility of funding shortfalls, which might appropriately be "covered" for a month or two by credit card borrowing (although an unsecured line of credit would be better). And relatively small short-term timing differentials (expense arrives two months before the income that's supposed to go with it, for example) would be another appropriate use. (Again, a line of credit would be better, but it may not be worth your while to shop and apply for a line of credit for a two-month borrowing need.)

Those of you who have been led down the garden path by credit card borrowing before may be hard-pressed to see how the borrowing I'm advocating is any different from the "temporary" borrowing that got you into trouble in the past.

The difference is that, when you're working with the Financial Sanity system, any short-term borrowing you do (and most of you will do none at all) will be pitted against specific funds that you *know* you will have in the future.

As "safe" as short-term borrowing is under the Financial Sanity system, it is still rare. The important thing to keep in mind as you do your debt planning—and your bill paying—is this simple rule: *All new charges get paid off every month.*

Debt reduction likely looms large on your current list of priorities. For that reason, I am very happy to be able to share the techniques of this chapter with you—techniques that can earn you your independence from undesirable debt in a matter of months.

Debt will still be with you, of course, perhaps for the rest of your life. There is nothing sinister about the presence of well-managed debt, and there is nothing healthy about a single-minded drive to rid oneself of all debt.

I predict, however, that, as important as debt seems now to you, two years from now it will be an almost-dead issue. It certainly has become so for me. It's not that I no longer have anything to do with debt; in the weeks that I wrote this particular chapter, my wife and I were applying for a loan to refinance our house at a lower interest rate. It's merely this: The nice thing about getting rid of undesirable debt is that once it's done—it's done! And as long as you use enough of the Financial Sanity system to stay out of trouble, you are unlikely to work your way back into a pile of debt.

While concerns about debt disappear from the scene over time, other more enjoyable concerns take precedence. One segment of my system that I hope will be your financial companion for life is funding. I introduce you to funding in the next chapter. Don't put off reading about it—it's a whole lot more fun than debt!

A man who has a million dollars is as well off as if he were rich.
  —*John Jacob Astor*

12

Funding: Spending Like a Millionaire

My grandmother came to California from northern Italy and lived on a ranch in Silicon Valley. Back then it was only known as the Santa Clara Valley, and more acreage was devoted to orchards than to asphalt and cement.

My grandmother—everyone called her "Nonnie"—wanted to manage the family's finances in a way that ensured that the most important expenses were taken care of. She didn't live in a world where, if she came up a little short one month, she could run down to the automated teller and get a cash advance on her credit card.

Nonnie took the family's income each month and divided it into several envelopes. One was for the milk-and-egg man, another for the butcher, others for the mortgage and the power company and so forth. That money was never found rattling around in Pop's pocket. As soon as it came in the door, it went into the envelopes.

Then, when the milk-and-egg man made his delivery or when

Nonnie went into town to shop for food, she always had her money ready, in its own little envelope. She was not likely to be caught short, and the important family expenses were always taken care of. There were envelopes, too, that didn't get spent each month—envelopes for a new car or tractor, and an envelope for emergencies that everyone hoped wouldn't happen.

Many of us in the booming boomer generation might covet the simplicity and organization of Nonnie's envelope system. Instead, we find ourselves scrambling each month to get one expense or another paid. We live in fear of what might show up in the mailbox. And when even a small emergency arises, we find ourselves strapped.

Many years ago, I decided that I would employ a variation of Nonnie's envelope system myself. I trotted down to the neighborhood savings and loan and opened up seven savings accounts. I had one for auto repairs and one for buying clothes. There was one for charitable contributions and another for getting out of debt. I allocated one for "major purchases" and had two investment accounts—one designed to help make me financially independent. The New Accounts Manager thought I was crazy and, as it turned out, she wasn't far off the mark.

My plan was to put aside a certain amount of money each month, so that it would be there when that kind of purchase arose. The problem was, I couldn't get money *into* the accounts as fast as I wanted to take it *out*.

In the very first month, for instance, I needed minor repairs on my little BMW—about $60. Well, I had only the $15 I had opened the account with! The repairs couldn't wait, of course, so I took the money that I otherwise would have put in various savings accounts and used that to pay Helmut. Here I was, in the first month of my modern envelope system, and already the whole plan was falling apart. It never did work, but I have those seven little savings passbooks as souvenirs of my early attempt at financial management.

I often ask people who take my workshops about the envelope system. Most have grandparents or parents who have used it, and some workshop participants have even tried it themselves. They all ran across the same problem I encountered—trying to take too much out of the envelope too soon. It seems as if the system would work if you could just make it past the first few months and give the envelopes a chance to build up.

Well, it's been ten years since I embarrassed myself down at the savings and loan. And over that ten years, I've had a chance to do a little thinking about the problem—and I've come up with something a little more workable.

I won't ask you to hide little envelopes full of cash all over the house, and I won't suggest that you go down to the bank asking to open ten or twelve savings accounts. The funding program I'm about to show you is a sophisticated and flexible system, designed to work for a sophisticated and fast-moving generation. But I think Nonnie would approve.

Funding is designed to accommodate four special—but very common—types of expenses:

- Major Purchases
- Scheduled Expenditures
- Annual Control Expenditures (expenditures which don't necessarily occur every month, but which you still need to control)
- Unscheduled Contingencies

What Funding Is

Funding, as defined in this book, is a system of setting aside *specified* amounts of money each month for *specified* expenditures. All the money set aside for all the funded expenditures are collected into one account. Funding allows for the *organized* borrowing of money between funds, while avoiding spending more than is in the entire funding bank account.

Let's take apart that definition line by line.

We're talking about *specified* expenditures here. Gone is the concept of merely "saving." (See my criticism of saving in Chapter 2.) Every dollar saved is destined for a particular expenditure. And every expenditure you can think of is accounted for.

The money we set aside each month is a specified amount. The "bill" your funding account "sends" you each month is a bill that has to be paid. No more paying all your other bills first and then seeing how much is left over for you. The overly simplistic concept of "pay yourself first" is at work here. But, we're not merely committed to paying ourselves *first*. Funding gives us confidence that we are paying ourselves *enough*.

When we talk about setting aside money, we mean in a separate savings, checking or money market account. I generally prefer an account that bears some interest, but it also needs to have liquidity— you need to be able to access your cash quickly. Commingling your funding money with your regular checking account is a prescription for disaster. Don't do it.

On the other hand, you need only one account for all your individual funds. You don't have to worry about one fund stealing from another because you will be controlling the funds with a special Funding Tracking Ledger that I will tell you about in the next chapter.

Just because my funding system allows you to temporarily borrow money from your daughter's College Education Fund to get your Alfa

Romeo fixed does not mean that you are out of control. The Funding Tracking Ledger keeps you honest about "paying back" the money, and a special Crash Analysis makes sure that you don't try to take money out of your funding account faster than you put it in.

How Funding Works

Let's construct a very simple example to show you how funding works.

Let's say that all you're worried about are

- property taxes ($600 twice a year)
- clothes ($2,400 a year)
- Christmas presents ($900)

You've just been through a horrendous Christmas crunch for the third straight year in a row, and your New Year's resolution is that you are going to get control of these three expenditures once and for all.

First you add up the above annual costs. They total $4,500 altogether. (Remember that the property taxes are $600 *twice* a year.)

Then you divide the $4,500 by 12 months in the year. The result is $375. At its simplest level, funding suggests that, by putting $375 in the bank each month, you'll always have enough money to pay for these three items.

Let's see how that actually works out:

Figure 12-1: A Simple Funding Example

Month	Monthly Allocation	Expenditures for Taxes	Clothes	Christmas	Ending Balance
January	$ 375		$ 200		$ 175
February	375				550
March	375		450		475
April	375	$600			250
May	375		75		550
June	375				925
July	375				1,300
August	375		1,200		475
September	375				850
October	375		175		1,050
November	375			$900	525
December	375	600	300		0

Isn't this a pretty little picture! Money is always there for every little need and always a little to spare in the funding account, until the very last month, when you go out and blow all the money you have left in the account on clothes.

Well, it *is* a pretty little picture. And, although our example is simplistic, this is precisely how funding works. The feeling of organization and control you get by reviewing the above example is the same feeling of organization and control you will personally experience when you put in your own funding program.

Let's go through the same chronology of funding activity. But this time, let's review some of the typical psychology of the first-time funder. (The comments interspersed among the months in the chronology below are taken from comments I have heard from participants in my workshops as they discover the wonderful world of funding.)

Month	Monthly Allocation	Taxes	Clothes	Christmas	Ending Balance
January	$ 375		$ 200		$ 175

"It felt good to spend just what I was supposed to for clothes this month ($2400 ÷ 12 months = $200). Before, it didn't matter how much or how little I spent. I always felt guilty."

Month	Monthly Allocation	Taxes	Clothes	Christmas	Ending Balance
February	$ 375				$ 550

"It was fun not to spend any funding money at all and watch the account grow. I can't remember the last time I had $550 lying around that didn't have a bill all ready to gobble it up."

Month	Monthly Allocation	Taxes	Clothes	Christmas	Ending Balance
March	$ 375		$ 450		$ 475

"I thought I'd feel sinful spending $50 more on clothes than I should have by now. But I know that I'll make it up next month, and the money was there (borrowed from the Christmas account)."

Month	Monthly Allocation	Taxes	Clothes	Christmas	Ending Balance
April	$ 375	$ 600			$ 250

"This is great! Property taxes came and went and all I had to do was write a check. No scrambling around for the money. No cash advances on credit cards. No wondering if I would make the deadline. Just write a check and there's still money left in the account!"

Month	Monthly Allocation	Taxes	Expenditures for Clothes	Christmas	Ending Balance
May	$ 375		$ 75		$ 550
June	375				925
July	375				1,300

"You know, this funding system is fun! It's fun when I'm *not* spending money, because it's fun to watch the account grow. And it's fun when I *am* spending money because I'm only spending what I'm supposed to spend."

Month	Monthly Allocation	Taxes	Expenditures for Clothes	Christmas	Ending Balance
August	$ 375		$ 1,200		$ 475

"I thought I would have to be rich and famous before I could go out and buy over a thousand dollars of clothes in one shopping trip."

Month	Monthly Allocation	Taxes	Expenditures for Clothes	Christmas	Ending Balance
September	$ 375				$ 850
October	375		$ 175		1,050
November	375			$ 900	525
December	375	$ 600	300		0

"I can't believe I got through the whole year with enough money to hit the after-Christmas sales. This system really works. I'm going to do it again next year, only this time I'm going to add more items to my funding program."

Spending Like a Millionaire

When I contemplate what it would be like to be a millionaire—or otherwise wealthy beyond my needs—I imagine being able to spend money for things I wanted and, as I did, *know that I could afford what I was buying.* I would *always know that I had the money* when I went to buy something.

I don't imagine being able to spend money on every little whim—a million dollars is a long, long way from being an unlimited amount of money. (Most of the readers of this book will have had a million dollars pass through their hands before they're through; some have already.) But I do think a millionaire could *spend money comfortably* —without fear or anxiety.

The title of this section is Spending Like a Millionaire because it's about funding, and funding is going to allow you to *spend money comfortably.* Funding will allow you to know that *you can afford what you're buying.* Furthermore, funding will allow you to know that *you can spend money on almost anything you want*—it's just a question of priorities.

Funding also gives you some advantages the millionaire doesn't have—knowing that, with your limited resources (remember that our millionaire's resources are limited, too), you can know that *you are spending money on the right things.*

So, I hope you're ready to change the way you spend money. I hope you're ready to change your life permanently such that you

- will always know that you can afford to be spending what you're spending
- will always know that you have the money to make the purchases you are making
- will know that you can afford just about anything you truly want
- can spend money comfortably
- will know that you're spending it on the right things

When we've completed our work—and you can confidently sally forth, spending money with a clear eye and a clear conscience—you'll be spending like a millionaire!

Almost any man knows how to earn money, but not one in a million knows how to spend it.
—*Henry David Thoreau*

13

How to Spend Money

A few months ago I was visited by Denise, a friend and client.

"I've heard about this funding system," she said, "and that it's supposed to be magical and will solve all my spending problems. So tell me about it in *great* detail, because I'm totally committed to using this system. I'm going to get my finances together once and for all!"

Apathy was never Denise's problem.

"But remember," Denise warned me. "I know *nothing*. Pretend I'm stupid, because I really want to learn this."

Well, Denise wasn't stupid, but I'm glad she asked for a detailed explanation of funding. Because the explanation of the system I gave Denise was so detailed, and because she asked such good questions, I am repeating it for you here.

As you'll recall from Chapter 12, in my early attempts at what I now call funding, I tried to establish a separate savings account for each item I was funding for. I showed my old passbook collection to Denise, and we chuckled about how quickly that system had failed.

"Imagine, though," I told Denise, "what those passbooks would have looked like if it had worked.

"Each month," I said, "there would have been a contribution floating into the account." I began sketching out a facsimile passbook. "Some months there would also be money moving out, indicating an expenditure was being made. And in any month, we could see the balance in the account."

"Oh, and that would tell us how much we could spend on that category?" Denise asked.

"Exactly!" I was cutting up three months' worth of "play" passbook pages and laying them on my desk. They looked something like Figure 13-1.

"Well," said Denise, "this is really clear. I think I could stay in control if I had something like this. With this I could see how much I had to spend in each area."

"Yep," I said. "That's what it's designed to do."

"You say it didn't work? What's wrong with it?"

"Well," I said, "it has a couple of problems. It's kind of cumbersome having seven to twenty-seven different savings accounts, for one thing. And it doesn't allow for borrowing between the funds. . . ."

"You don't allow that, do you?" Denise looked horrified. She was counting on me to be fiscally conservative, and here I was telling her to rob her retirement account to buy her new car.

"Sure," I said cheerily. "It's allowed."

Denise looked at me suspiciously.

"Don't worry," I reassured her. "We have a special analysis that makes sure you won't get into any trouble when you borrow from Peter to pay Paul. I'll explain how that analysis works—after I show you how the Funding Tracking Ledger works."

Denise still looked suspicious and petulantly unconvinced. But she let me go on with the explanation.

The Funding Tracking Ledger

"Basically," I went on, "the Funding Tracking Ledger I'm going to set you up with is going to look just like those passbook pages, laid side by side."

"Let's use an easy example," I suggested. "Let's say that we want to fund for the following items:

· Property Taxes, due twice a year—$600 each installment; and
· Clothes, which we are trying to limit to $1,800 per year . . ."

Auto Repairs

First Funding Bank

SAVINGS PASSBOOK

Date	Transaction	Amount	Balance
1-7-87	Allocation	$75.00	$75.00
1-28-87	Expenditure	12.50	62.50

Auto Repairs

First Funding Bank

SAVINGS PASSBOOK

Date	Transaction	Amount	Balance
2-1-87	Bal. Fwd.		62.50
2-4-87	Allocation	75.00	137.50
2-12-87	Expenditure	125.66	11.84

Auto Repairs

First Funding Bank

SAVINGS PASSBOOK

Date	Transaction	Amount	Balance
3-1-87	Bal. Fwd.		11.84
3-3-87	Allocation	75.00	86.84

Figure 13-1

Denise rolled her eyes.

". . . and

· the down payment on a New Car, to be made fourteen months from now, for $4,200."

First, Denise and I had to calculate how much money we needed to set aside each month for each of these categories. This was fairly simple:

Property Taxes

$ 600

  ÷6 months between payments

$ 100 per month

Clothes

$ 1,800 per year

  ÷12 months per year

$ 150 per month

New Car

$ 4,200

  ÷14 months before purchase

$ 300 per month

Next Denise and I filled in our simplified Funding Tracking Ledger for the month of July.

"Let's assume that there were no Clothes expenditures that month—"

"No Clothes expenditures?" asked Denise, incredulously.

"No Clothes expenditures," I continued, "and Property Taxes are due in December and April, so no funding expenditures were made in July in any category—only contributions, which we call Allocations on the Tracking Ledger."

Figure 13-2 shows what the first month's activity looked like: Balance Forward in each fund of $0; full contributions (Allocations) for each fund at the amount calculated above; and a New Balance in each fund equal to the month's Allocation.

"The person in this example is obviously a man," noted Denise, still contemplating the notion of spending no money on clothes for a whole month.

"Now let's see what happens in August. First, see how we bring forward the ending balances from July as the beginning balances for August?

Month	July	
Fund		

Property Taxes		
Balance Forward	0	
Allocation	100	
Expenditure	0	
Adjustments +/-		
New Balance	100	

Clothes		
Balance Forward	0	
Allocation	150	
Expenditure	0	
Adjustments +/-		
New Balance	150	

New Car - Down Payment		
Balance Forward	0	
Allocation	300	
Expenditure	0	
Adjustments +/-		
New Balance	300	

Figure 13-2

"Again," I said, pointing to the August column in Figure 13-3, "notice that the Allocation is added to the fund, exactly as it was in July."

"Now what's happening here?" Denise interrupted. "Are these Allocations real money? Are you actually taking real money and setting it aside?"

"Yes," I explained. "In this example we'd actually be taking $550 each month ($100 for Property Taxes, $150 for Clothes and $300 for the New Car) and putting it in a savings account or a money market fund."

"What happens when you want to spend the money? Do you have to go down to the bank and make a withdrawal?" Denise looked a little dubious about the mechanics of accessing her funding money.

"You might," I said, "but I don't. I just spend money on funding items out of my regular checkbook. Then, at the end of the month, when it's time for me to send some money to my funding account, I just deduct whatever I spent that month on funding items."

"Oh," said Denise. "So, in August here, when you spent $205 on Clothes, you would have written a check for that?"

"Yes. Or charged it," I said. "Then, at the end of the month, how much would I have sent to my savings account?"

"Oh boy, a word problem," joked Denise. "Let's see, you normally send $550 to the bank account, but you already spent $205 on Clothes—that leaves $345 that you need to send to the savings account."

"Exactly."

Denise examined the calculation of the Clothes Fund for August: starting out at $150, adding another $150 for August's Allocation; subtracting the $205 spent on Clothes that month; to end up with $95 to carry over to next month. (In the Funding Tracking Ledger, I recommend that you round everything to the nearest whole dollar, and leave off the pennies.)

"Well," sighed Denise, "that's pretty easy. I think I can handle that every month. How do you keep track of how much of your savings account is supposed to be for what, though?"

I pointed back to the Funding Tracking Ledger. "With just this. Here. Let me show you how the Total section works at the bottom. It sort of ties everything together."

In Figure 13-4, we see the Funding Tracking Ledger as I had filled it out for the whole six months. I also added the section for Total—All Funds.

"In the month of July," I explained, "all that happened was that we made our allocations to the three different funds and sent all the money to the savings account. As we calculated earlier, that's $550.

Month	July	August
Fund		
Property Taxes		
Balance Forward	0	100
Allocation	100	100
Expenditure	0	0
Adjustments +/-		
New Balance	100	200
Clothes		
Balance Forward	0	150
Allocation	150	150
Expenditure	0	205
Adjustments +/-		
New Balance	150	95
New Car - Down Payment		
Balance Forward	0	300
Allocation	300	300
Expenditure	0	0
Adjustments +/-		
New Balance	300	600

Figure 13–3

Fund

	July	August	September	October	November	December
Property Taxes						
Balance Forward	0	100	200	300	400	500
Allocation	100	100	100	100	100	100
Expenditure	0	0				600
Adjustments +/-						
New Balance	100	200	300	400	500	0
Clothes						
Balance Forward	0	150	95	160	310	385
Allocation	150	150	150	150	150	150
Expenditure	0	205	85	0	75	955
Adjustments +/-						
New Balance	150	95	160	310	385	-420
New Car - Down Payment						
Balance Forward	0	300	600	900	1,200	1,500
Allocation	300	300	300	300	300	300
Expenditure	0	0	0	0	0	0
Adjustments +/-						
New Balance	300	600	900	1,200	1,500	1,800
Total - All Funds						
Balance Forward	0	550	895	1,360	1,910	2,385
Allocation	550	550	550	550	550	550
Expenditure	0	205	85	0	75	1,555
Adjustments +/-						
New Balance	550	895	1,360	1,910	2,385	1,380

Figure 13–4

That total shows down here." I pointed to the New Balance line of the section I had labeled Total—All Funds.

"See the Allocation of $550?" I asked. "And the total of $550? This simply means that there should be $550 floating around in that account at the end of July."

"Okay," said Denise. "Let me try August. Balance Forward is $550, because that's what last month's New Balance showed."

"Yes," I agreed. "And it's also the total of all the Balance Forward lines for the three funds in August."

"Okay," said Denise carefully. "Then the Allocation is $550, the same way it was last time."

"Yes."

"And the Expenditure is $205 because that's the total of all the expenditures in the three funds, which means just the expenditures for Clothes, since there were no expenditures in the other funds."

"That's right," I said.

"And then," she went on cautiously, "the total for New Balance is $895 because that's the total of the New Balances in the three funds."

Property Taxes	$ 200
Clothes	95
New Car—Down Payment	600
	$ 895

"And," I pointed out, "the math also works within the Total section."

Balance Forward	+ 550
Allocation	+ 550
Expenditure	− 205
Balance	$ 895

We then reviewed the six-month Funding Tracking Ledger in its entirety.

Property Taxes progressed in an extremely neat and orderly manner. Every month we put aside $100, so that in the sixth month there was $600 available to be sent to the tax collector. At the end of the six-month period, the fund is empty, ready to start all over again.

"Simple," I said.

"Yet elegant," quipped Denise.

We skipped Clothes for a moment and looked at New Car—Down Payment. This was also simple. At the end of six months, we'd saved $1,800 toward our goal. By the time we've done this for fourteen months, we'll have the $4,200 we need.

Borrowing Between Funds

"Now let's look at Clothes," I said. I showed Denise the erratic, low-level spending pattern for the months of September through November, which left a November New Balance of $385. "That's about two and a half months' worth of Allocations," I pointed out. "Then a December shopping spree rang up $955 worth of spending. This leaves a negative New Balance of $420 at the end of the month."

Denise looked perplexed. "How can there be a negative balance in a savings account?"

"Well, of course," I pointed out, "if we had the old system of a separate savings account for every fund"—I waved the seven experimental passbooks at her—"then we *couldn't* have a negative balance in any of them at any time. But in the Financial Sanity system, the positive balance in the Car Fund is cushioning the $420 negative balance in the Clothes Fund," I explained. "Essentially, we're borrowing money from the Car Fund to 'cover' the Clothes Fund."

This concept still offended Denise's sensibilities. "I don't see what good it does to have a budget if you can spend over your budget any time you want to and just take the money from someplace else and never pay it back and—"

"Wait," I said. "That's the key. We *do* pay it back. Automatically."

"We do?"

"Yes," I insisted. "The automatic action of the funding system restores negative balances and makes money available for unspent allocations—without any attention on your part."

Denise still looked uncomfortable about borrowing between funds.

"Listen," I said. "You and I are from a generation that knows how to borrow better than just about anything else we do. If I tell you to stop borrowing money, you won't stop."

Denise shook her head earnestly and started to protest, but I interrupted her.

"You may agree that borrowing is bad. You may want to stop. You may promise me you'll stop. But you won't stop borrowing money. You already heard 'Neither a borrower nor a lender be.' Your dad has told you a million times not to get into debt. If you were going to take advice like that, you would have taken it years ago."

Denise nodded her head silently.

"The truth is," I pontificated, "that's what you're good at—borrowing and spending."

Denise looked depressed.

"So," I said cheerily. "Let's *play to your strengths!*"

"What?"

"Listen," I said. "Since you're so good at borrowing and spending, let's design your financial control system around your talents. Let's make a system in which all you have to do is borrow and spend!"

"I don't get it."

"Okay," I said. "How are you at saving money?"

"Terrible," she admitted.

"But you know that saving money is a good thing to do."

"Sure," she said. "I just never seemed to be able to do it."

"Well, what's more fun—saving money or spending it?"

Denise smiled, embarrassed. "Well, of course I like spending it. . . ."

"Right," I said. "Now you aren't going to be able to believe me until you've tried it, but sending money off to your funding account for all these fun things like Clothes and a New Car . . ."

Denise laughed. "And Property Taxes. Fun!"

She had a point, but I was a determined cheerleader on this point. "Trust me," I continued earnestly. "Sending money off to your funding account *feels* like spending."

Denise pondered that for a moment. "Sort of like layaway?"

"Sort of," I said, never having bought anything on layaway.

"Okay," said Denise. "You tell me that sending money to my savings . . ."

"Funding," I corrected her.

". . . to my *funding* account will feel just like spending. And I see how I can borrow money to my heart's content from— Hey! I'm really borrowing money from myself!"

"Exactly." I smiled. "I don't mind you being a borrower—as long as you're the lender, too."

"So it's not 'Neither a borrower nor a lender be,'" quoted Denise, "but *'Both* a borrower *and* a lender be!'"

"You could say that," I agreed.

"But, still," said Denise, "what's to keep me from overspending on clothes?"

"You've got a good point. If your monthly funding for Clothes is $150, you obviously can't spend $150 most months and then spend $900 every so often—you'll never catch up," I said.

"So at this point in our example," I continued, "you would have to look long and hard at whether and how you'll be able to hold off buying clothes until the $420 negative balance disappears. It would take about three months."

"What if I didn't think I could do it?" she asked me.

"You'd either need to make a conscious decision to change your monthly funding allocation—divert $50 or $100 per month from some other expense—or learn to live with the reality of your Clothes budget as you have defined it."

I looked at Denise. "The bottom line still must be: *On the average,* you have to stay within the monthly Allocation amount. There may be high months and low months, but *on the average,* it must settle down to—in this case—$150 per month."

"How is this different from just regular old budgeting?"

"Well," I said, "in regular budgeting, when you go over your budget one month you don't have to 'pay it back' in later months. Also, you can't 'save up' spending like you can in these funding accounts."

"That's true," agreed Denise. "Whenever I tried to control this kind of spending before, I would go on binges every once in a while, then I'd be 'real good' for a while and then, since I'd been 'real good,' I would deserve to splurge a little—by the end of the year I had spent far more, on the average, than I had said I wanted to."

She looked at the example I had sketched out. "At least with this system, I can keep track of how up or down I am. I can know whether I have to go easy, or can go all out, or whether I have to abstain altogether—and for how long."

"Right," I said. "And that's very valuable information to have."

"Okay," Denise said. "There's one thing that still bothers me. What would have happened if I wasn't saving for a car? Or what if I was saving slower—say, I didn't have $1,800 in the Car Account, but only $300? There wouldn't be $420 worth of cushion. What about that possibility?"

"Then you crash!" I told her.

My client did not look comforted by my flip answer.

"So, to make sure you don't crash," I went on, "we have a special Funding Crash Analysis—it tells you *in advance* whether your plans are likely to get you into hot water."

The concept of funding—and its ability to "monthly-ize" erratic expenditure patterns—is extremely powerful and is the cornerstone of the Financial Sanity system. But we leave this chapter on an ominous note. We already saw what happened to me when I tried to open up seven savings accounts: I didn't make it past the first month! What's to prevent the same fate from happening to you?

Fortunately, the solution is not far away. In Chapter 17 I will show you safeguards the Financial Sanity system has built in to make sure you don't crash.

Every man is the architect of his own fortune.
  —*Latin proverb*

14

Major Purchases and Scheduled Expenditures

In Chapter 12, I identified four kinds of expenditures I think should be handled through the funding system:

- Major Purchases, the amount and timing of which you can often *control*
- Scheduled Expenditures, the amount and timing of which you usually *know*

These first two kinds of expenditures are both handled with a special funding timeline we'll begin discussing in this chapter.

- Annual Control Expenditures, those you want to control on an annual basis even though you don't care about fluctuations from month to month
- Unscheduled Contingencies, which you know may occur, but you usually don't know when (and often don't know how much)

These latter two classes of expenditures can't—or shouldn't—be put on a timeline. They get handled on a simple monthly allocation basis, which we'll cover in the next two chapters.

The critical first task of funding is to decide which kinds of expenses you are going to fund for. In my experience, most first-time funders are too timid in this area. As you develop your experience with funding, you will start to want to fund almost everything. So, if you can't decide whether something is appropriate for funding—fund for it!

A Question of Spikiness

Funded items almost always have one key characteristic: They're spiky. "Spiky" (obviously a highly technical term) refers to the shape of a graph of the expenditure pattern. It is precisely the spikiness of the expenditure pattern that makes these kinds of expenses so troublesome.

Let's look at three classes of expenses and decide which have the characteristic of being spiky—and therefore are prime candidates for funding:

Figure 14-1 shows Auto Insurance, paid, in this case, once a year. Obviously spiky. The problem with a spiky expense (like annual auto insurance premiums) is that it can be a little difficult to find an extra $1,100 to $1,200 in your checking account when May rolls around.

Less spiky, but still spiky enough to be a problem for most people, is auto repairs. A sudden $450 repair bill can poke a giant hole in your monthly paycheck. There's usually not anywhere near enough slack in your budget to withstand that. As a result, a repair bill like February's in Figure 14-2 is likely to go on a credit card—and that starts a cycle of debt that, for many people, just doesn't seem to go away.

Gasoline expenditures, too, experience peaks and valleys, but they are less severe and not really spiky. In the example in Figure 14-3, monthly gasoline expense for April, the highest peak, was only $17 more than the monthly average. Recurring variable expenses, like gasoline, then, are usually not put into funding. You wouldn't ruin your funding by including it, but it wouldn't serve much purpose.

I hope these examples have given you a good idea of what to include on your Funding Schedule as spiky expenses. Here is a more complete list of expenses that commonly show up on people's funding schedules:

- property tax
- income tax (balance due April 15)
- various kinds of insurance premiums

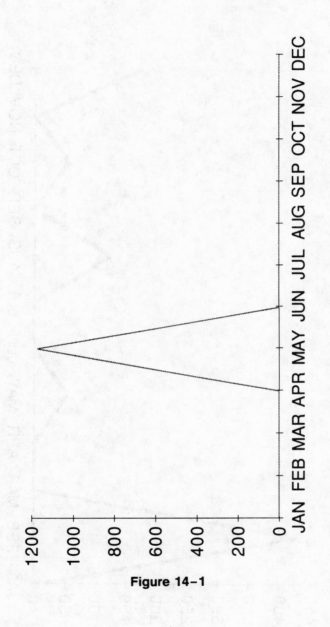

Figure 14-1

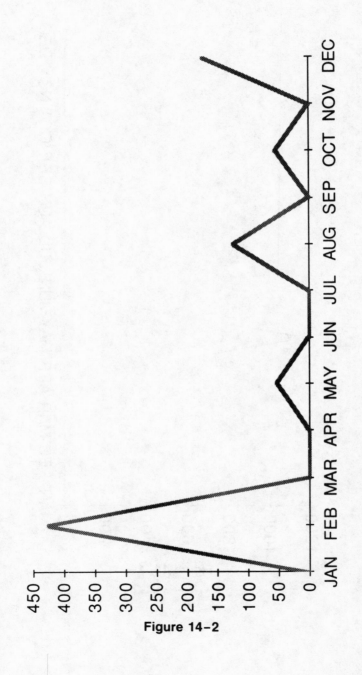

Figure 14-2

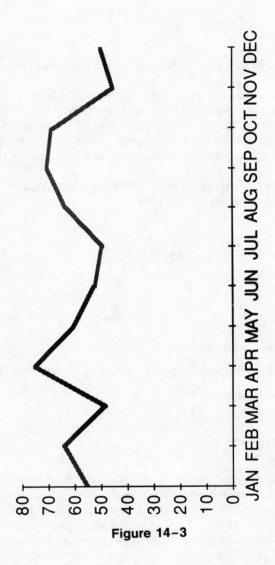

Figure 14-3

- auto, home and other repairs
- medical bills
- veterinary bills
- tuition
- dues
- IRA contributions
- clothes

Major Purchases and Scheduled Expenditures

It's easy for most of us to understand why Major Purchases and Scheduled Expenditures are more appropriately handled through funding. Anyone can figure out that putting a down payment on a house, buying a car or, for most people, purchasing a major appliance can't come out of what's left of one paycheck after paying the monthly bills.

Some of the typical major purchases I see people planning for in the Financial Sanity Workshop include

- vacation
- remodeling projects
- starting an investment program
- buying a house
- car
- vacation home
- major appliances
- home computer
- expensive sports equipment

Some of the Scheduled Expenditures commonly funded for include

- property (and other) taxes
- Christmas
- education
- maternity expenses
- annual insurance premiums

Keep in mind, as you review this list, that a major expense to one family may be another's pocket change. The real criterion for being on this list is whether the item is large enough to be a problem if you were to forget all about it until the day you had to pay it.

Most of us are used to the concept of saving something each month in order to make a big purchase. It's a concept we learned back when we were kids and wanted a new bike.

And saving for a major purchase can be extremely motivating— especially if the goal is a really important one.

Jill—Pizza or Pisa?

Jill was a bookkeeper for one of my clients, and one of the most important early influences on me in the area of budgeting. It was Jill who encouraged me when I was trying to save money to buy my first house.

Jill had done what many of our generation had only dreamed about. In her early twenties she and her boyfriend had traveled all over Europe for three months, driving a brand-new Volvo they bought over there and then brought back home. They were not highly paid professionals—Jill was a waitress and wouldn't finish college until years later. And they didn't do it with their parents' money. They did it on what they had saved.

For two and a half years, Jill and her boyfriend saved money for this trip. If they were going, they said, they were going to do it right. They figured out what it would cost them and they saved. To save that much, they carefully held themselves to a tight budget.

"That takes a lot of discipline," I congratulated her.

"Not really," Jill said. "This trip was the most important thing in our lives for that two and a half years. Every time we were tempted to blow our budget on something like pizza, we asked ourselves: 'What's more important—this pizza or our trip to Europe?'" Put in that context, budgeting, saving and controlling expenses were, if not easy, at least natural.

When I ask participants in the Financial Sanity Workshop about their *successful* budgeting experiences of the past, they invariably cite a time when they were saving for something important—more important than practically anything else in their life.

The trouble with saving for major purchases is that we are often trying to save for something that is *not* the most important thing in our life. And there's not just *one* thing we want to save for, but several.

And we hardly ever really have much of a plan for how much we need to save each month and precisely when we're going to have the money ready. We're very likely to engage in "Mindless Saving" (see Chapter 2), or unconsciously earmarking whatever we are saving to more than one expense. We likely don't have a clear vision of what we're saving money for. Our murky images of budgeting, saving and discipline try to compete with the clear, immediate picture of the thick crust, melting cheese and spicy sausage of an unauthorized pizza.

As a result, we seem to go nowhere when we save for big purchases and, after a while, give up, preferring to depend on getting things "the old-fashioned way"—we borrow.

Major Purchases List

Figure 14-4 is the beginning of a quick list similar to one I suggest you prepare for yourself. It simply lists all the major purchases you can think of on a timeline.

The Major Purchases List may look a lot like the Goals Planning Timeline you prepared in Chapter 3. Indeed, many of the items on your Goals Planning Timeline will probably qualify for the Major Purchases List. I only ask you to prepare this list now because some of the Major Purchases you are planning to make may not have been considered Goals when you made your Goals Planning Timeline.

You may, if you like, use the Goals Planning Timeline form for your Major Purchases List.

Exercise: Major Purchases List

1. Label a worksheet similar to Figure 14-4, with appropriate monthly time periods across the top line. You may want to use a copy of the Goals Planning Timeline from Appendix B, or you may even prefer just to add the items of this exercise onto the Goals Planning Timeline you have already prepared in Chapter 3.

2. Down the left side of the page write every expenditure you contemplate making in the Major Purchases category. (Partners should make separate lists, then compare and combine.) *Don't be overly realistic.* Write down things that you aren't sure you'll be able to afford. You'll get a chance to make the "final cut" later.

Be sure to refer to the Goals Planning Timeline you made back in Chapter 3.

3. In the monthly columns, drop the dollar amount the item will cost in the appropriate month or months. When you've completed the exercise, you'll have a schedule of the major expenditures your checkbook might be experiencing over the next several months.

4. Don't worry.

5. If what you've just mapped out looks like a financial roller coaster, in the coming chapters we'll see what we can do to make sure that your checkbook never feels the ups and downs.

Description	Jan 89	Feb 89	Mar 89	Apr 89	May 89	Jun 89
Ski Trip	650					
Frank's Wedding					400	
Living Room Carpet		1000				
Mountain Bikes					350	

Figure 14–4

Exercise: Scheduled Expenditures

The fundamental difference between a Major Purchase and a Scheduled Expenditure is that:

- A Major Purchase can often be scheduled at your discretion; Scheduled Expenditures are usually "due."
- Major Purchases are often fun, whereas Scheduled Expenditures include items like insurance and taxes—need I say more?

Get the same sheet of paper you titled "Major Purchases." Add to the list by writing down all the spiky expenditures you can think of. Don't include expenses that are too small to worry about. Include things like property taxes, insurance premiums—anything that happens at a particular time but is not monthly.

You have now completed work on your Major Purchases and Scheduled Expenditures such that you have a timeline of cash outlays. This will become a crucial planning tool in the coming chapters, as we work to "monthly-ize" the ups and downs of this erratic expenditure pattern.

My problem lies in reconciling my gross habits with my net income.
—*Errol Flynn*

15

Annual Control Expenditures

A CPA I know bought new clothes only twice in the five years I worked for him. Both times the store's president personally wrote my friend a letter of thanks, inviting him to come back and shop any time—as well he should: Each time, my friend had rung up a tab of several thousand dollars.

How do you control an erratic expenditure pattern like that? How do you know if you're spending too much? When you're not buying clothes (whole years went by for this guy!), how do you keep from using your clothes money for other expenditures?

The dilemma posed by precisely this spending pattern is the basis for the inclusion of Annual Control Expenditures in the funding program. And not only does Annual Control Expenditure Funding handle perplexing erratic spending patterns, it is also an easy and automatic way to—finally—control monthly discretionary expenditures that just always seem to be over budget.

Jerry and Monica

Take Jerry and Monica Bledsoe, for example. The Bledsoes like to throw three or four major parties a year. It's their major form of entertainment, and they are known for their imaginative theme parties.

Using good funding and budgeting technique, the Bledsoes sat down at the end of 1987 and calculated that they had spent about $1,400 on three parties that year. In 1988, Jerry and Monica hoped to have four parties, but they were very serious about staying within a budget of $1,500 for the whole year.

The Bledsoes planned four parties that they expected to cost right around $1,500:

Spring	$ 300
Summer	500
Jerry's 40th Birthday	400
Christmas	300
Total	$ 1,500

By November, the Bledsoes had spent $1,350 on parties. (It doesn't matter how much they spent on each, nor even how many they had thrown.) They had $150 left in their Party Fund, and they were left with a few choices:

· skip the Christmas party and apply the money to next year's party schedule
· have a Christmas party (or some comparable alternative) but spend only $150 on it
· find $100 to 200 in some other fund that wasn't spent this year or that could stand to be shorted

This last alternative is what Jerry and Monica did. They reallocated $50 from the veterinary account—Rags hadn't gotten into any fights that year—and Jerry sacrificed $100 from his clothes account.

No matter which alternative they had selected, however, any of the three would have kept the Bledsoes on target and within their budget.

This kind of erratic, nonmonthly expense is best controlled annually, rather than monthly, but we do need a specific mechanism for control.

Annual Control Expenditures

Think of Annual Control Expenditures as spending that you want to control over a lengthy period—say, a year—although you're not particular about how much you spend in any given month.

Men's clothing purchases are a classic example. Most men I know spend exactly $0 on clothes most months. Then, once or twice a year, either voluntarily or dragged by the women in their lives, they buy clothes—and they buy as if they won't see another men's store for at least six months. Because they won't.

Now, suppose you shop that way and you plan to spend about $2,400 a year on clothes. That's $200 a month. If you used conventional budgeting techniques, your monthly budget would show:

Budgeted	Actual	Under Budget
$ 200.00	$ 0.00	$ 200.00

What are you supposed to do? Pat yourself on the back? Take the money and treat your wife to the most expensive French restaurant in town?

And how about that fateful month when (after several months of expensive French dinners) you need new suits (with just a little more room at the waist)?

Budgeted	Actual	Over Budget
$ 200.00	$1,400.00	$1,200.00

Now what are you supposed to do? What can you do? You have to buy clothes sometime, you rationalize. Besides, you haven't bought clothes in over six months, you rationalize further. Scrambling, you put it all on a credit card.

Let's go back to what you were originally trying to do when you made your budget. You said you wanted to spend $2,400 a year. You never said anything about wanting to spend $200 a month. That was just an artificial piece of nonsense you were forced into because you were trying to make a monthly budget.

Using the Financial Sanity funding method, you'll concentrate on what you originally set out to do: spend $2,400 a year. You won't care how much you spend each month——as long as, at the end of a year, all the months only added up to $2,400.

The concept is very simple. Let's look at a classic man's wardrobe buying pattern, using an annual budget of $2,400:

Month	Allocation	Expenditure	Left to Spend	Comments
Jan.	$200.00	$ 0.00	$200.00	
Feb.	$200.00	$ 0.00	$400.00	
Mar.	$200.00	$ 0.00	$600.00	⎧Dragged
Apr.	$200.00	$ 0.00	$800.00	⎨shopping
May	$200.00	$850.00	$150.00	⎩by girlfriend
June	$200.00	$ 20.00	$330.00	Tie for May's suit
July	$200.00	$ 0.00	$530.00	
Aug.	$200.00	$ 0.00	$730.00	
Sept.	$200.00	$ 0.00	$930.00	⎧Dragged
Oct.	$200.00	$ 0.00	$1,130.00	⎨shopping
Nov.	$200.00	$1,400.00	–$ 70.00	⎩by fiancèe
Dec.	$200.00	$100.00	$ 30.00	Left over

This is picture-perfect Annual Control Spending. The spending pattern has nothing to do with $200 a month. In fact, in no month does this guy spend $200. But, at the end of it all, he's spent just under $2,400—just as he had planned.

Exercise: Annual Control Expenditures List

1. Make a list of all the expenses you would like to control on an annual, rather than a monthly, basis. Write down everything you can think of, then consult the Inflow-Outflow Information Sheet you prepared in Chapter 6.

2. Review all the outflow items on the Inflow-Outflow Information Sheet, and identify which ones you would like to treat as Annual Control Expenditures. If they were listed as an expense before ("E" code), change their coding now to "F" for funding.

3. Add the items from the list you prepared in Step 1 to your Inflow-Outflow Information Sheet, marking each of them with an "F" and assigning monthly or annual budget allotments to each.

At the completion of this exercise, your Inflow-Outflow Information Sheet should include all of your Annual Control funding candidates.

When you selected expenses for your Annual Control funding, you might have skipped over such expenses as entertainment as not being spiky enough. You may have reasoned that you tend to spend the same amount of money each month on this type of expense, so you don't need the monthly-izing that funding tends to bring to erratic expenditures.

Funding can still be very effectively used, however, for nonerratic expenses that are largely discretionary. The attribute of funding that is so useful in such cases is the automatic paying back that funding demands after you've overspent in any particular area.

Stan and Rhonda—Are We Having Fund Yet?

Stan and Rhonda had a problem with what they were spending on entertainment—eating out, going to movies and the theater and just generally having fun. About every other month they would go overboard on that part of their budget. The next month they would try to be good and keep to their budget; they were usually successful. But then, a month or two down the road, they were over-budget again.

"The problem is," as Stan pointed out, "we never make up for the over-budget months. If we overspend in Month A by $100, we really ought to be underspending in Month B by $100. You know, to make up for it."

"Yeah," said Rhonda. "We feel like we're really being good and responsible if we just spend the $150 a month we had budgeted." She looked at Stan. "We never really tried to make up for the times we overspent."

"And it really fouled up the rest of our budget," Stan said.

We looked at Stan and Rhonda's spending pattern for entertainment over a twelve-month period:

Month	Allocation	Expenditure
September	$ 150	$ 155
October	150	232
November	150	162
December	150	421
January	150	149
February	150	157
March	150	194
April	150	161
May	150	199
June	150	160
July	150	239
August	150	147
TOTAL	$1,800	$2,376

I recommended that Stan and Rhonda put entertainment into their Funding Schedule. "Let's look at what might have happened if you had had entertainment in your Funding Schedule from the beginning:"

Month	Allocation	Expenditure	Left to Spend
September	$150	$155	−$ 5
October	150	232	− 87

"At this point," I said, "you should be saying to yourselves: 'Time to seriously cut back. Let's try to make up this negative.' In fact, let's say you did—you cut way back in November."

Month	Allocation	Expenditure	Left to Spend
November	$150	$50	$13

"Now you're back on track—you've made up for your sins in October. Hopefully, too, you have some idea of how difficult it is to underspend to catch back up—and you won't spend $421 in December, like you did last time."

People in the workshops have been interested in controlling nonmonthly expenses in such areas as:

- clothing
- weekend, leisure and short vacation expenses
- charitable contributions
- gifts
- entertainment (especially occasional large parties)
- toys for kids
- unspecified home improvements
- furniture purchases

Time and again, the expenditures that fall in this area have been the real villains in a family's budget. Even when we're trying to be good about nonmonthly expenditures, it's difficult to know where we really are, if we don't keep track.

If some appalling disaster befalls, there's
Always a way for the rich.
— *Euripides*

16

Risk Management Through Funding

As we discussed before, funding is useful for four major classes of expenditure:

· Major Purchases
· Scheduled Expenditures
· Annual Control Expenditures
· Unscheduled Contingencies

The last class of expenditures—Unscheduled Contingencies—is perhaps the most difficult to plan for. It is an area where you can almost never be "right." And, if you plan conservatively and protect yourself from various and sundry disasters, you don't even *want* to be right.

Nonetheless, making some provision for emergencies, both large and small, can go a long way toward making life a more enjoyable experience for both you and your family. This chapter deals briefly with two ways of providing for contingencies:

· funding and
· insurance

Each of these tools has its place in a well-structured financial plan—and each of these tools can be misused.

Funding for Contingencies

Funding for contingencies is best used to cover expenses that

· you know are going to happen or
· you know are likely to happen

even if you don't know

· when they might occur or
· how much they'll cost.

Contingencies you know are going to happen are much easier to work with, especially if you have a fair idea of the amount. A classic example of this kind of contingency are auto repairs and the uninsured portion of medical expenses. Let's take auto repairs as an example.

Based on prior history, you know that it costs you about $800 a year to keep your not-so-new car in good repair. Repair bills show no clear pattern—some are very inexpensive and some are in the $400 range—but you feel confident about the general annual costs.

Funding for this kind of expense is simply a matter of reducing the expected annual costs to a monthly amount—in this case about $67 a month—and putting that amount in the Auto Repair Fund each month, taking out whatever you need for the auto repairs you actually incur.

Now let's assume that you are also worried about an impending large auto repair that isn't included in that $800 annual estimate. It might be something simple—like tires you know are going to need replacement by the end of the year—or it might be something much more ominous and unknown—like a strange foreboding that the transmission's about to die on you.

Properly, this larger, one-shot contingency should have a separate funding account all its own. For one thing, its characteristics are different from the normal maintenance and repairs expenditures. This expense will look and act more like a major purchase or a scheduled expenditure. Although you may not know quite when the expense will occur, this item should appear on your Major Purchases or Scheduled

Expenditures list. If you are conservative, you should schedule it for the earliest possible month in which it could occur. The work we do in Chapter 17—to prevent funding "crashes"—will use that information to make sure that your funding system doesn't run out of money because your clutch went out a month before you had hoped it would.

Other kinds of contingencies are much more nebulous and, as a result, more troublesome. Suppose, for instance, that you are worried that your employer may shut down its operation in your city, leaving you and fellow employees out of work for what could be months. You expect severance benefits to carry you through the first month, but after that there will be only unemployment insurance benefits, which will be $2,000 per month less than you need to support your family, until you get a new job. You calculate the difference between the benefits you will receive from unemployment and the after-tax income you need to support your family, then multiply that difference times the maximum number of months you expect to be out of work. If, in this example, you expected to be out as much as nine months, your funding requirement would be $18,000.

Suppose this event occurred as early as six months from now. Under the most conservative funding scenario, you would fund $3,000 per month for six months in order to have the funds available in full. It's highly unlikely that a financial event of this size could be adequately funded for in a short period of time. On the other hand, the risk involved is not an insurable risk, so the contingency can't be covered by insurance. How could you sleep at night, knowing that there was this big hole in your contingency planning?

There are a variety of ways a contingency can be covered in your planning so that you can avoid the preferable, but impossible, solution of funding the entire amount in cash. One alternative is borrowing. Let's say that you have or can get a preapproved line of credit for $12,000. This leaves $6,000 still to be funded* over six months—then a period of time unemployed, then the restoration of a regular income, at which point funding would resume (in this case for debt reduction of the line of credit) until the entire event had been fully paid for.

Of course, funding even $1,000 a month ($6,000 ÷ 6 months) may be too great a monthly burden, in which case still further creative remedies would have to be explored, including

---

*Additionally, you'd probably need to set aside some of the $12,000 for making payments on the $12,000 loan, since there is no room in your unemployment period budget for this extra expense. Therefore, the amount to fund in six months is probably greater than $6,000, a fact we will ignore, for simplicity, in this example.

- selling an asset
- earmarking long-range funding (see Chapter 19) that could be "borrowed"—to be paid back later
- diverting money from other funding accounts, representing things you are giving up due to the occurrence of the event

In general, Contingency Funding can be very troublesome, even in a mature budget that has years of funding under its belt. A combination of

- high dollar amounts
- significant uncertainty over when or whether the event will occur
- the great number of potential contingencies

all serve to muddy up the waters and generally make successful planning look difficult, if not impossible. However, in addition to the creative remedies we discussed above, when a contingent need does arise, you may be able to simply combine the money in various contingency funds to meet the needs of the actual contingency that occurs. This is really a form of self-insurance that makes use of the concept of pooling risks; but instead of pooling risks between different people, you are pooling risks of different events—a concept that assumes that only one or two of these unfortunate events will happen to you, and not all.

Finally, a conservative approach to contingency planning may eventually produce a rather large fund of money that is larger than needed to cover remaining contingencies. At this point, it is perfectly reasonable to reduce your bloated Contingency Fund and make a windfall available for more enjoyable expenditures. When you decide to create this windfall, treat it like (tax-free) bonus income. The technique—called Yellow-Pad Mini-Budgeting—for intelligently planning for windfall income is described in Chapter 21.

Funding for contingencies is problematic and only rarely a great deal of fun. Most contingencies aren't fun events. (Although there are exceptions: If your teenage son is an Olympic hopeful, you might feel compelled to plan for the contingency of spending thousands of dollars for travel to the 1992 Olympics so the whole family can watch him compete.)

In addition to the somewhat dismal nature of most contingencies (unemployment, disability, death, sickness, loss or destruction of property, etc.), contingencies tend to be very gray and foggy. Very often you do not really know whether the contingency will ever occur (you typically hope it doesn't) and, if it does occur, how much it will cost.

Some contingencies are impossible to fund for and should be handled another way, perhaps through insurance. But for those contingencies you can and want to fund for, puzzling issues remain:

- How much should I set aside?
- What happens to the money if the contingency never occurs?
- I can't possibly set aside enough money to completely cover *all* contingencies.

Here are some guidelines for your planning for contingencies. How you respond to these suggestions will reflect your attitudes about risk:

- How likely do you feel the occurrence of an emergency is?
- How great an impact on your way of life are you willing to allow the emergency to have?
- How well protected do you need to feel to sleep well at night?

Since these issues are personal and psychological, you'll probably be better off if you and your spouse (and perhaps other important members of your family) discuss your preferences.

Options in Contingency Funding

One concept that can ease the financial strain of funding for contingencies is *pooling.* Just as insurance is essentially a pooling of the individual risks of many people (resulting in a lower cost to protect each individual than had they fully funded for the contingency on their own), so contingency pooling assumes that not all of the contingencies you are planning for will occur. Perhaps only one or two could conceivably occur—certainly not all five or six. This will allow you to plan for only the most expensive of risks, reasoning that, if some other contingency occurs, the money used to fund the expensive risk will be available for the more moderate contingency.

Fund raiding is another option available to you. You may, for instance, be perfectly willing to give up your expensive annual vacation (for which you are funding monthly) if you found yourself unemployed for a time. This makes the funds set aside for vacation available to you to finance the contingency of unemployment.

Restructuring your budget is another very obvious response to a contingency. It simply calls for adjusting portions of your budget, including any funding you feel you can dispense with, to get by on less income—if the contingency occurs.

Selling of assets could also be included in your comprehensive contingency planning, as could *borrowing.* Both, however, require more planning than might appear at first blush. If you plan to sell assets, you should have a list of the assets you might sell and the proceeds you might realistically expect (net of selling costs). You should be aware of the time it will take to liquidate the assets, and the work that will be involved.

Similarly, with regard to borrowing, you should have your ducks in a row well prior to the emergence of the contingency. (Remember that the First Law of Borrowing is that nobody wants to lend you money if you really need it.) Open lines of credit, for instance, can be preestablished; you should leave enough borrowing power on the line to supply the money you plan to borrow in case of the contingency. Finally, keep in mind that the home equity loan or mortgage refinancing that you could qualify for right now may not be as available to you if you have been recently laid off.

There is probably no right answer to the questions raised by contingency planning. Without dwelling on the morbid possibilities of the future, look at the contingencies you might face in your life and plan your financial response to them. Out of this planning will come a need for funding—at least a few months of income set aside for emergencies. If you haven't been good about saving in the past, accumulating your Contingency Fund may take an uncomfortably long couple of years, but you may start sleeping better right away just knowing you've got a plan.

Funding vs. Insurance

When we think about protecting ourselves financially, it's often insurance that first pops into our head. But insurance is incredibly complex and makes for a very confusing "playing field" when making decisions about financial protection. And it's not made any less complex by the companies that sell insurance. Insurance protects against the unknown; the unknown is the breeding ground of fear. There's no way an insurance company or agent can give you enough information to help you make a rational insurance decision when there are so many variables in the insurance products available. So it's easier for them to appeal to you emotionally—to play on your irrational instinctual fears—than it is to carefully lay out your options and their associated costs.

I would suggest that, instead of thinking of insurance as your first line of defense against financial emergency, you think of funding as the cornerstone of your disaster planning. This is not to suggest that insurance won't be a part—a very big part—of how you protect yourself against unforeseen contingencies. But I think that an initial knee-jerk reaction to look first to funding to provide that peace of mind will keep you out of the irrationality trap. It will tell you when to buy insurance, how much and of what type much better than your friendly neighborhood insurance agent. It most likely will help you avoid buying insurance protection you neither want nor need. And it might very possibly lead you to acquire insurance protection that you otherwise might not have thought of buying.

Financial risks might broadly be categorized into two classes:

· income risks (where the danger is loss of income)
· expenditure risks (where you'll be required to pay something)

I've listed some possible events below, identified the loss at stake and indicated whether the risk is generally an insurable risk—that is, whether you can commonly get insurance coverage for it.

Event	Risk	Insurability
Someone sues you.	Expenditure	Insurable
You hurt yourself or get sick so you can't work.	Income loss	Insurable
You die or your spouse dies.	Income loss for your family or extra expenditure for care of children, etc.	Insurable
Your child dies.	No financial loss	Insurable
Your house is badly damaged.	Expenditure	Insurable
You lose your job.	Loss of income	Partially insured
You burn out on your job, lose the will to work and change careers.	Loss of income	Insurable for diagnosed stress; otherwise, not
Your fuel pump goes out.	Expenditure	Often insurable via maintenance contract

Not all unscheduled contingencies are bad news.

Event	Risk	Insurability
Your daughter gets engaged and you start planning the huge wedding you and she have always dreamed of.	Expenditure	Not insurable
You win a sales contest to Hawaii (all expenses paid for two) and want to take the kids.	Expenditure	Not insurable
Your parents' next-door neighbor finally consents to sell you the classic MG you've admired and wanted since you were fifteen.	Expenditure	Not insurable

As you review this list, you begin to realize that there are many contingencies that insurance just can't cover; and, on the other hand, sometimes insurance is available to cover contingencies that don't generally carry financial burdens (like the death of a child). In addition to contingencies for which insurance is unavailable, there are other contingencies that are better handled through funding.

Theoretically, insurance has two characteristics that allow it to provide you money when an emergency arises. The first characteristic is funding. Insurance, to a great extent, takes your money, skims off a commission for the broker and a profit for the insurance company, invests the remainder for you and makes it available when you need it later. Some policies, such as single-premium life insurance policies (where the entire policy is prepaid, and the insurance company is 100 percent certain you will collect—the only question is when), are almost completely funding by nature. Tax consequences aside, you could generally accomplish the same end by investing your funding money yourself rather than making the single lump-sum premium payment to the insurance company.

The second characteristic of insurance—and, to my mind, the more important aspect—is pooling of risk. Homeowner's insurance reflects this characteristic. Not everyone who carries homeowner's coverage is going to have a walnut tree crash through their living room next year. However, some will. And when this disastrous event occurs, the insurance company will pay for it. The insurance might cost $1,000 a year, and the repairs from the walnut tree incident might run $10,000. How does the insurance company make a profit on this particular customer? The answer is that the insurance company doesn't make any money on the walnut-tree people. But it also collects premiums from thousands of people who don't have walnut trees crashing into their living rooms. Those of us who won't be having a claim this coming year will also pay $1,000 for our insurance. Our "leftover" money is used by the insurance company to pay the walnut-tree people.

Risk pooling allows us to protect against disastrous contingencies without having to amass huge fortunes in funding. What we give up in exchange is that:

- Some of our money goes to compensation and profits for the insurance companies and their agents, as well as other selling expenses.
- We don't get to keep our leftover money if we don't have a disaster.
- We can't divert funding for one contingency to cover another contingency.
- We have to deal with insurance companies—which may not agree that the contingency has occurred—when we have a claim.

Most people, however, will find that insurance has a place in the scheme of their contingency planning. The purpose of the discussion of insurance that follows is not to be a comprehensive study of how to buy insurance. Instead, it is presented only to help you decide which contingencies might best be covered with insurance and which through funding.

Why Income Continuance Is Important to Us

Someone once made the observation that the Financial Sanity system is income-oriented, rather than wealth- or asset-oriented. The system assumes that there will be a steady flow of income to support ambitious funding and debt reduction plans. This observation is, I believe, generally correct. In addressing the needs of my generation, income is all I have to work with to help people improve their financial situation. When you're dealing with a group of people whose assets are generally scant and debts a little on the heavy side, it makes sense to look at income to solve those problems.

This generational dependence on income to straighten out our collective balance sheets makes it all the more important that our incomes be protected. Generally speaking, the only insurable risks having to do with loss of income are disability insurance and (in the case of families) life insurance. These two coverages should receive serious attention as part of the comprehensive system you are producing to provide financial peace for yourself and your family.

Disability Insurance

We, as a generation, depend more heavily on our income than past generations. For a variety of reasons—some of them economic and some of them having to do with the "personality" of our generation— our rate of saving is considerably lower than that of previous generations. Our incomes, on the other hand, are often high enough to make minor emergencies (the fuel pump, for instance) mere annoyances— sometimes more for the time they take than the money they cost. Our incomes, in fact, are so important for bailing us out of one jam or another that one of the most severe financial losses can be the loss of the income itself. And even if you had saved (or funded) religiously for just such a contingency, it would take years to have enough money to last you just a few months. Let's take an example.

Suppose you have a gross income of $5,000 per month, which nets out, after taxes, to about $3,000 per month. And suppose you funded $300—a healthy 10 percent of your after-tax income of $3,000— solely for income continuation in case you can't work. Assuming you get a 6 percent return on your money and assuming no inflation (all of my assumptions are generous on the side of funding, because I'm trying to argue against funding here), it would take you twenty months of funding to accumulate enough money to tide you over for just two months of disability. It would take more than five years to have seven months' protection. It would take several years of funding before you could feel comfortable about what you had accumulated to meet this emergency. In the meantime, you'd know that even half a year (some disabilities are permanent, you know) of income loss would mean a wrenching adjustment in the lifestyle of you and your family.

Disability, then, becomes one of those insurable risks that can't effectively be self-insured (funded) except by those of very substantial means. Shopping for disability insurance is no picnic. There are more options in the higher-grade disability policies (partial disability, own-occupation coverages) than are available on a new car—and they're harder to understand. I encourage you to look into it, however. It provides an important protection for people who are heavily dependent upon their incomes.

Life Insurance

Life insurance is another coverage which basically replaces income —in this case, the income that would have been earned by the deceased family member had he or she lived. Life insurance can be considerably easier to analyze and evaluate as long as you stick to buying term insurance only.†

Your basic question will be how much coverage to buy. Buying more coverage than needed moves insurance away from the protection function and makes it more like gambling. (Similarly, buying a policy on the life of a dependent who provides no income or expensive-to-replace services to the family is gambling. For instance, with rare exceptions it makes no sense to insure the life of your toddler.)

How Much Insurance Should You Buy?

The usual technique for determining how much insurance to buy, which I call Perpetual Monthly Benefit Analysis, requires you to estimate your family's monthly needs after your death, then make sure that there is enough coverage so that the invested proceeds of the policy will produce that much income each year—virtually forever, because the principal (the lump-sum proceeds of the policy) would never be touched.

For example, assume that your family's after-tax income needs are $3,300 per month. You are the sole income provider and you want to provide coverage so that your family would not have to suffer a degradation of its standard of living if you died.

Assuming that the insurance proceeds could be invested at 8 percent, how much insurance should you buy? Let's look at how you'd figure that:

Monthly Income Requirement	$ 3,300
Months per Year	× 12
Annual Income Requirement	39,600
Interest Rate	÷ 8%
Insurance Coverage Needed	$ 495,000

---

†I believe simple term insurance to be the best, if not the only, life insurance to buy. Other insurance products are basically combinations of term insurance and some investment. Because the two are lumped together, it is very difficult to analyze whether this other "investment" is worth your money. It is analogous to being offered insurance bundled with a certificate of deposit, except that the insurance company doesn't tell you the amount of the CD or the rate of interest. Favorable tax treatment of some insurance products adds to the confusion as much as it provides tax planning opportunities. Claims made by insurance salesmen are notoriously misleading, false or confusing. Life insurance generally pays agents and brokers large commissions (as does disability insurance), although the commissions on term insurance are generally much lower than on policies with an investment aspect to them. *Consumer Reports* produced an excellent and extensive report on all types of life insurance in its June, July and August issues of 1986.

As you can see, it would take nearly half a million dollars of coverage to provide $3,300 in perpetual monthly benefits.‡

Exercise: Contingency Planning

1. Make a "worry list" of as many of the things that could go wrong as you can without working yourself up into a fit of anxiety.

2. To the right of each item, make some notes as to how you might reasonably protect yourself and your family against this contingency. Especially try to specify whether you feel it should be handled with

- insurance
- funding
- other measure (such as sale of assets) or a combination of these three strategies.

3. Based on the solutions listed on the right side of your list, draw up your ideal "contingency portfolio"—a wish list of insurance and funding solutions that you would like to have, even if you're not sure you could afford them all.

Life's emergencies—big and little, good and bad—can be effectively managed through a combination of funding and insurance. Each tool has its place in your planning, and neither tool can effectively replace the other in all situations.

Planning for contingencies is typically the hallmark of a more mature budget; when you're starting to pay off debt and establish funding for the first time, it can be very difficult to make room in the budget for contingencies that might never happen. While not being prepared for disasters might properly make you feel nervous, you needn't feel inadequate as a financial adult because you haven't got all your bases covered. Even using the Financial Sanity system, it takes people a few years to move from a debt-ridden, overspending state to a position of having contingencies covered. Have patience: As you use the system, you will add more and more protection.

---

‡You may argue that perpetual benefits are really not necessary—that your family could eat through the principal of your life insurance proceeds, as long as it lasts long enough (say, thirty years)—to provide for them. In this case, you would tend to buy somewhat less insurance, based on the annuity (part interest, part principal) that would flow from such a lump sum. However, unless you only want to provide for a few years—perhaps five or so—the difference in insurance coverage is so small (about 10 percent for a thirty-year annuity) it seems to me not worthy of the calculation, especially since income needs at your death are only an estimate in the first place.

We learn geology the morning after the earthquake.
—*Ralph Waldo Emerson*

17

Funding Crash Analysis

Funding is an almost-magical technique for maintaining control of your financial future. But if you simply decide what you want to spend this year and divide by twelve, you may be in for a rude shock. Your life will not merely divide itself by twelve just to accommodate your budget. If funding was that simplistic, you would have thought of it yourself and been using it for the last five years.

The Funding Crash Analysis I introduce in this chapter is designed specifically to allow you to plan your funding so that it will survive the ups and downs of real life. The analysis, therefore, becomes the crucial element of the Financial Sanity program that allows for peace of mind about cash flow. Once you've "read the book" on your Crash Analysis, "seeing the movie" isn't nearly so suspenseful—and cash flow is an area in which we'd just as soon not have any suspense.

How Much Funding Can You Afford?

The Funding Crash Analysis is also where you will end up wrestling with priorities—deciding to fund for this item, postpone that goal and eliminate another. So, before we start the analysis, we need to have a pretty good idea of how much money we're talking about committing to funding each month.

Fortunately, you've probably already done most of the work you need to do to know how much money you can afford to devote to funding. It comes from two main sources:

· your Spending Power, as calculated back in Chapter 8
· what you're already normally spending on items that will be included in your funding program

Let's revisit Sam and Wendy, who, back in Chapter 7, calculated their estimated Spending Power for the coming year at $655 a year—about $55 a month.

Sam and Wendy actually planned their funding with $582—not $55—per month. Let's see how they determined that they could support so large a monthly funding contribution. Figure 17-1 shows how the Sheridans calculated how much money they had available for funding.

Figure 17-1: How Much Sam and Wendy Can Afford to Fund

Spending Power	$ 655	(from Spending Power Analysis [Figure 7-2])
Personal Assets	2,500	(minimum from Spending Power Analysis)
Christmas	800	(based on last year's expenditure)
Gifts	350	(based on last year's expenditure)
Clothes	950	(based on last year's expenditure)
Auto Repairs	450	(based on last year's expenditure)
Medical	280	(based on last year's expenditure)
Other Funding categories	1,000	(based on last year's expenditure)
Reduction in commuting costs being made available for funding	580	(calculated)
Less: Mortgage debt reduction	−700	(from Spending Power Analysis)
Total Available for Funding	$ 6,865	

Sam and Wendy had $6,865 annually to devote to funding—about $572 a month. Of course, they have the option of changing the amounts of money devoted to each individual category. They could, for instance, cut back on the purchase of Personal Assets and apply those funds to one of the other categories on the list, or to a new funding category altogether. Funding isn't the only available target for Spending Power. It can just as well be devoted to debt repayment. Nonetheless, $582 per month is, essentially, what the Sheridans have to play with.

Now let's find out how much you have to play with.

Exercise: Calculating Affordable Funding Level

If you've completed the Spending Power Analysis

1. Add your annual estimated available Spending Power to

- money that was included in the adjustments section of the Spending Power Analysis as baseline levels of expenditure *only if* those expenditures are going to be included in your funding
- money spent in the past year on any items that will be included in your funding schedule
- funds that you intend to divert from other parts of your last-year's spending pattern to make available to funding

2. Subtract from the figure derived in Step 1 the following:

- any portion of your calculated Spending Power that was based on debt reduction which it will be necessary or desirable to repeat this year
- the portion (if any) of the Spending Power estimated for the coming year which you intend to devote to anything else other than funding—debt reduction and living expenses, for instance

3. The resulting number is the amount you currently have available for funding and should be used in your planning as you do your Funding Crash Analysis.

If you haven't done the Spending Power Analysis

You can still get very close to an appropriate amount of monthly funding—even without the Spending Power Analysis—by using this shortcut method:

Add the amount of savings you accumulated last year, together with any major onetime purchases and extraordinary debt reduction. Subtract from that result any additional debt you incurred last year.

Use this number as your estimated Spending Power and follow the Steps 1 through 3 above.

Funding Crash Analysis

When I was recounting Denise's story (Chapter 13), I mentioned that your funds can borrow from one another. Indeed, it may be impossible for most of us to even get started in funding unless we can do some convenient interfund borrowing in the first several months.

Because of this borrowing provision, it's possible to run out of money in your funding account. This funding cash shortfall has nothing to do with whether you can afford how much you're funding monthly—the question we just addressed in the exercise above. A funding shortfall—or "crash," as we call it—is merely a timing problem.

The purpose of the Funding Crash Analysis is to determine whether or not, given your funding plans, your funding account will run out of money. Obviously, if your analysis shows that you will run out of money, then you need to change your funding plans.

You've already made four lists of items you want to include in your funding.

In Chapter 14 you made a combined Major Purchases List and a Scheduled Expenditures List, which you may or may not have merely incorporated into your Goals Planning Timeline. Together, these lists will provide you the raw material for the timeline portion of your Funding Crash Analysis.

In Chapter 15 you made an Annual Control Expenditures List, which was incorporated into your Inflow-Outflow Information Sheet. You also did an exercise in Contingency Planning in Chapter 16. These lists will generally provide information you need to complete the Control and Contingency portion of the Crash Analysis.

Review your four lists and see if there is anything you'd like to add to it before we start you on the path to your first Funding Crash Analysis.

Figure 17-2 is an example of the Funding Crash Analysis. Because this analysis is easily the most complex form in this book, I suggest you review its parts with me now.

The entire top half is the *Timeline* section. It's where Major Purchases and Scheduled Expenditures are plotted out. Expenditures that cannot be put on a timeline are listed in the bottom half, the *Control & Contingency* section.

There are five totals lines, labeled A through F, which you'll use to calculate whether or not your funding plans will cause a crash.

Description	Monthly Allocation	Timeline Mos.	Timeline Total	Funding To Date	JUL	AUG	SEP	OCT
Property Taxes	100	12	1,200	0				
New Car	300	14	4,200	0				
Total Allocation — Timeline Expenditures	400		5,400	**A**	0	0	0	0
Cumulative Timeline Expenditures (Add Total from Line A to Prior Month's Line B.)				**B**	0	0	0	0

Description	Monthly Allocation	Mos.	Period Total	Funding To Date	Period Description
Control & Contingency:					
Clothes	150	12	1,800		year

					1	2	3	4
Control & Contingency Monthly Allocation	150	Cumulative Allocation — Avg. Control & Contingency		**C**	150	300	450	600
Monthly Allocation — All Expenditures	550	Cum. Allocation — All Exps. Plus Total Funding To Date		**D**	550	1,100	1,650	2,200
First Degree Funding Surplus/(Shortfall) (Subtract Line B from Line D)				**E**	550	1,100	1,650	2,200
Total Funding To Date »			0					
Second Degree Funding Surplus/(Shortfall) (Subtract Line C from Line E)				**F**	400	800	1,200	1,600

Figure 17-2

Timeline

NOV	DEC	JAN	FEB	MAR	APR	MAY	JUN		JUL	AUG	SEP
	600				600						
										4,200	
0	600	0	0	0	600	0	0		0	4,200	0
0	600	600	600	600	1,200	1,200	1,200		1,200	5,400	5,400

750	900	1,050	1,200	1,350	1,500	1,650	1,800		1,950	2,100	2,250
5	6	7	8	9	10	11	12		13	14	15
2,750	3,300	3,850	4,400	4,950	5,500	6,050	6,600		7,150	7,700	8,250
2,750	2,700	3,250	3,800	4,350	4,300	4,850	5,400		5,950	2,300	2,850
2,000	1,800	2,200	2,600	3,000	2,800	3,200	3,600		4,000	200	600

Getting Started on Crash Analysis

Let's look in detail at Figure 17-2 before we move on to your own personal Funding Crash Analysis.

As you recall, the three items we were worried about in our simplified example in Chapter 13 were

- Property Taxes, due twice a year—$600 each installment
- Clothes, which we are trying to limit to $1,800 per year
- the down payment on a New Car, to be made fourteen months from now, for $4,200

Let's take the car first. Obviously a Major Purchase, it appears on a line in the top half of the analysis. We simply enter $4,200 on that line out in the fourteenth month—August of next year—which is when we said we wanted to buy the car. The Timeline Total column of that same line, which also shows $4,200, is the total of all the boxes on the New Car line to the right of it—July through the following September. In this case, there's just the one entry (for August) of $4,200, so the total is $4,200.

We want to save (ooops!—"fund") for this expenditure over fourteen months, so we put 14 in the Timeline Months column. Then we divide the $4,200 by the fourteen months to get the Monthly Allocation of $300.

Let's try Property Taxes next. Again, this expense is in the Timeline section because it is spiky and its expenditure dates are plannable. Six hundred dollars will be due in both December and April, so each of those boxes has $600 entered in it. The total $1,200 goes in the Timeline Total box. In this example, I selected a twelve-month period over which to fund these property tax payments, requiring a $100-a-month allocation, because I know that in the thirteenth month I'll begin funding for the next year's property tax payments.

Finally, our example shows Clothes in the bottom half of the Funding Crash Analysis. It's not in the Timeline half because we don't know which months we plan to buy clothes. We had said we wanted to spend $1,800 over the year, so the Period Total is $1,800 and the Months in the Period are 12. Eighteen hundred dollars divided by twelve months gives us the Monthly Allocation of $150.

Crash Calculations

Now that we know how to fill in the raw data of the Funding Crash Analysis, let's see how its calculations are made and what they can tell us.

Line A is for Total Allocation—Timeline Expenditures. You simply total all the entries in the Monthly Allocation column, then bring down the total for each of the months in the Timeline to the box below. The monthly totals are interesting, because that is the amount of money that the fund is going to be required to come up with—in addition to whatever is spent on items in the bottom half—in each of those particular months.

Line B is a cumulation of the monthly totals in Line A. In other words, Line A tells us that we need to come up with $600 in April, while Line B tells us that, since the beginning of the Timeline, we have had to come up with $1,200 as of the end of April.

Down below, on Line C in the Monthly Allocation column, we total the Monthly Allocations for Control & Contingency Expenditures. Then in the box right below that total (labeled "Monthly Allocation—All Expenditures") we add together the totals from the top and bottom half of the analysis—Lines A and C of the Monthly Allocation column. In the example in Figure 17-2 the Monthly Allocation—All Expenditures is $550 ($400 + 150). This is a very important number, because it is the amount of money you will be required to deposit into your funding account each month. It is the number you must work into the rest of your budget. The $550 due to your funding account should be considered like rent—you wouldn't think of not paying it unless you were willing to end up sleeping on a friend's couch.

Can We Afford to Be Having This Much Fund?

As one CPA commented after I showed her this system, "Your funding concept is great. My only concern is how do you really convince people that they can do this? The response I get from friends/clients is 'I don't have any money left over at the end of the month to fund.' "

Well, *of course* you don't have any money left over. Whoever heard of "leftover money"? The answer lies in the fact that you are already spending your income on funding-type items—just not in an organized way. Property taxes, car insurance and various emergencies are getting paid for under your current system. Funding just takes the trauma and anxiety out of paying bills that, for the most part, would get paid even if you didn't have any system. So don't panic when you see how big that monthly funding allocation is. I think you'll be surprised at just how much funding you can handle each month.

Line C merely reflects the spending pattern that would result if you spent an average amount each month for all the items in the bottom (Control & Contingency) half of your analysis. To calculate it, just take the Monthly Allocation for Control & Contingency Expenditures

($150 in our example) and multiply that number by the little numbers I have supplied for you between the boxes on Lines C and D on the Funding Crash Analysis. (The $150 Control & Contingency Monthly Allocation multiplied by 1 equals $150 for July, by 2 becomes $300 for August and so on.)

Line D reflects the cumulative contributions to the funding account —for both the top and bottom halves. To calculate it, simply multiply the number for Monthly Allocation—All Expenditures ($550 in our example) by the number between Lines C and D.

Now you know, month by month, exactly how much money is going to flow into the funding account and you know something about how much will flow out. Next, we'll make two calculations to see how much chance there is that the money will flow out faster than it is scheduled to flow in.

Avoiding Crashing and Burning

The first calculation is called the First-Degree Funding Surplus (or Shortfall, if it is negative). This number must be positive every month or you know—for certain—that you will "crash." That's because this number consists of the following equation:

· the cumulative amount of money that has gone into your funding account, for any given month
· less the cumulative amount that has been *scheduled* to go out (in the Timeline portion of the Funding Crash Analysis).

In other words, this calculation says: Assume we don't spend *anything* on *any* of the items in the bottom half of the analysis, but we use that money, as needed, for items in the top half (Timeline portion) of the analysis only. Would we *still* run out of money? Obviously, it's highly unlikely that we'd go for very long without spending any money on annual Control & Contingency items. So, if the First-Degree Funding calculation comes up with a shortfall in any month, we know that our plan is in serious trouble—it will not work. Too many of our planned expenditures are occurring too early in the schedule. We must move some of our Timeline Expenditures out to later dates, to give the funds time to build up.

To calculate First-Degree Funding Surplus/(Shortfall), simply take Line B (Cumulative Timeline Expenditures) and subtract it from Line D (Cumulative Allocation). Enter your calculation on Line E. As you can see, nowhere in Figure 17-2 is there a negative number on Line E. That means there's a First-Degree Funding Surplus, or, to put it another way, no shortfall.

Figure 17-3 is a continuation of the example we looked at in Figure 17-2. Our mythical couple has added a classic complement of baby boomer spending intentions: buying furniture, having a baby, buying a boat, contributing to an Individual Retirement Account, paying a hefty balance due at tax time and taking a ski trip—all entered in the Timeline section of the Crash Analysis because each is planned for a particular time.

Additionally, provision is made in the Control & Contingency section for medical and dental expenses, car repairs, various educational courses, parties, home improvements (planned over the next five years) and vacations (not including the ski trip).

It's not at all uncommon for first-time funders (and even veterans!) to be overly optimistic in their planning for expenditures. After all, as long as we have a generational reputation for being people who "want it all and want it now," we might as well play the part. In fact, because the funding techniques you're learning now are designed to force you to make proper priority decisions about the timing of expenditures, there's no reason to censor yourself as you make your initial plans. (Did I remember to tell you to do this in pencil?)

Our example, then, is not unusual: it features a First-Degree Funding Shortfall from August through January. You'll remember that a First-Degree Funding Shortfall means that there is no possibility of having enough money in the funding account to accommodate the Timeline spending as planned. And any spending in the Control & Contingency area would only add to the deficit. Let's see how we fix this problem.

There are basically two ways to solve any shortfall problem (without borrowing). You may decide to reduce or eliminate the expenditure that is causing the shortfall. For instance, in the example in Figure 17-3, if you eliminated the boat purchase entirely, you would eliminate the First-Degree Funding Shortfall. Elimination and reduction of expenditures is not usually your first choice for fixing a shortfall problem. For one thing, anything that's on the Funding Analysis is likely to be something you want very much. You've already eliminated things that weren't that important to you when you chose among priorities in order to drive down the cost of your monthly Funding Allocation to an affordable level.

Since you've already decided you *can* afford the monthly tab required to buy everything on your Funding Analysis, you probably don't need to eliminate the item from your funding program. You can probably solve your problem by just deferring the expenditure. Deferral is simply delaying an expenditure until a later month, when the monthly allocations to your funding account have had a chance to build up sufficiently.

Description	Monthly Allocation	Timeline Mos.	Total	Funding To Date		JUL	AUG	SEP	OCT
Property Taxes	100	12	1,200	0					
New Car	300	14	4,200	0					
Furniture	375	14	5,250	0					5,250
Maternity Expense	179	14	2,500	0			2,500		
Boat	393	14	5,500	0			5,500		
IRA Contributions	286	14	4,000	0					
Taxes	232	14	3,250	0					
Ski Trip	86	14	1,200	0					
Total Allocation — Timeline Expenditures	1,951		27,100		A	0	8,000	0	5,250
Cumulative Timeline Expenditures (Add Total from Line A to Prior Month's Line B.)					B	0	8,000	8,000	13,250

Description Control & Contingency	Monthly Allocation	Period Mos.	Total	Funding To Date	Period Description
Clothes	150	12	1,800		year
Medical/Dental	60	1	60		month (estimate of average)
Car Repairs	167	12	2,000		year
Courses	30	15	450		next 15 months
Parties	75	12	900		year
Home Improvements	83	60	5,000		coming 5 years
Vacations	117	12	1,400		year

					JUL	AUG	SEP	OCT
Control & Contingency Monthly Allocation	682	Cumulative Allocation — Avg. Control & Contingency		C	150	1,363	2,045	2,727
					1	2	3	4
Monthly Allocation — All Expenditures	2,633	Cum. Allocation — All Exps. Plus Total Funding To Date		D	2,633	5,265	7,898	10,531
First Degree Funding Surplus/(Shortfall) (Subtract Line B from Line D)				E	2,633	-2,735	-102	-2,719
Total Funding To Date »»»			0					
Second Degree Funding Surplus/(Shortfall) (Subtract Line C from Line E)				F	2,483	-4,098	-2,147	-5,446

Figure 17–3

Timeline

NOV	DEC	JAN	FEB	MAR	APR	MAY	JUN	JUL	AUG	SEP
	600				600					
									4,200	
	4,000									
					3,250					
		1,200								

NOV	DEC	JAN	FEB	MAR	APR	MAY	JUN	JUL	AUG	SEP
0	4,600	1,200	0	0	3,850	0	0	0	4,200	0

13,250	17,850	19,050	19,050	19,050	22,900	22,900	22,900	22,900	27,100	27,100

3,408	4,090	4,772	5,453	6,135	6,817	7,498	8,180	8,862	9,543	10,225
5	6	7	8	9	10	11	12	13	14	15

13,163	15,796	18,429	21,061	23,694	26,327	28,959	31,592	34,225	36,857	39,490

-87	-2,054	-621	2,011	4,644	3,427	6,059	8,692	11,325	9,757	12,390

-3,495	-6,144	-5,393	-3,442	-1,491	-3,390	-1,439	512	2,463	214	2,165

The Funding Crash Analysis I have shown you is designed to be an especially efficient analytical tool for planning the deferral of expenditures. Here's how it's done.

Scan across Line E until you get to the last negative number on the whole analysis. Remember that the shortfall calculations are based on *cumulative* numbers. In Figure 17-3 the last negative month is January. February shows a positive surplus of $2,014. This means that were you to move all the expenditures that are currently scheduled from July to February and put them *all* in February, the First-Degree Funding Surplus would still be $2,014. Conceptually, it's a little hard to keep this dynamic in mind; but it's an important concept, so take a few minutes to study Figure 17-3.

Obviously, deferring all your Timeline Expenditures until February is a simplistic approach. It's usually not necessary. That's fortunate, because usually it is also not possible.

Let's just take Figure 17-3 again. If you're planning in June to incur maternity expenses in August, I'll just bet that delaying that birth is an option no longer available to you. Likewise, paying property taxes in February instead of December, when they're due, is not the kind of behavior people expect from someone who has his or her finances under control.

Most of us would agree that Property Taxes and Maternity Expenses are not deferrable, while the Furniture, Boat, IRA Contribution and Ski Trip are. However, we might also note that the Ski Trip can't be delayed past ski season and the IRA Contribution can't be made any later than April 15, the statutory deadline.

Now that we've identified the movable expenditures, the next important shortcut is to identify the month with the biggest shortfall. Again, because we're working with cumulative numbers, solving the worst month will probably solve all the months with shortfalls.

In Figure 17-3, the worst shortfall occurs in August ($2,734), but October ($2,718) is almost equally large, and December ($2,052) is not far behind. Based on such a scenario, our plans for deferral should be aimed at delaying about $2,750 or more of August-or-earlier expenditure; and that delay must take us past December, except for maybe about $700.

Figure 17-4 shows what our example looks like after correcting First-Degree Funding Shortfalls. On examination, first notice that all the numbers in Row E are positive—that's how we know we've handled First-Degree Shortfalls. This is what we did to solve our First-Degree Shortfall problems:

· We postponed the IRA contribution from December to April.

• We postponed the Boat purchase and, along the way, decided on a smaller boat.

Important factors to notice include:

• We could have postponed the Furniture purchase, say, instead of the Boat. Notice that we didn't have to postpone every purchase in the months that had shortfalls—only enough to avoid the shortfalls.
• The decision to purchase a smaller boat was probably unrelated to trying to solve the shortfall problem.

Avoiding Smaller Crashes

Assuming we've made whatever corrections required to make First-Degree Funding Surplus positive in every month, we next turn our attention to Second-Degree Funding (Line F).

Second-Degree Funding Surplus/(Shortfall) makes an assumption about our spending in the Control & Contingency category: It assumes that spending in this area—the bottom half of the analysis—will average out each month. There's no particular reason to expect this spending to average out, especially on a Crash Analysis with only a few items. But the calculation using an average spending rate will at least give us an idea about how aggressive our planned spending pattern is—and what we might do to accommodate it and avoid a crash.

Although not at all exact, the Second-Degree Funding Surplus/(Shortfall) is probably your most accurate prediction available of how much money you'll have in your Funding Account each month.

Unlike a First-Degree Funding Shortfall—an obvious instant and unquestioned failure in the spending pattern as planned—a Second-Degree Funding Shortfall is more, well, *negotiable.*

Although Figure 17-4 has no First-Degree Funding Shortfalls, it does have three Second-Degree Funding Shortfalls. Let's examine each of those shortfalls and see what, if anything, we should do about them.

The first shortfall occurs in October—four months into the funding program. The analysis predicts that there will be a $802 shortage in the funding account if spending on Clothes, Medical/Dental, Car Repairs, Courses, Parties, Home Improvements and Vacations matches the average for each of those expenditures. (Again, we all know that it's highly unlikely that exactly what is funded will be spent in each category. But it's not so unlikely that $2,728 in total spending —$682 times 4 months—will be spread over all these categories.) So, the solution lies not in scrimping on planned-for Control & Contingency items, but looking to some "negotiable" Timeline Expenditures instead.

Description	Monthly Allocation	Timeline Mos.	Timeline Total	Funding To Date	JUL	AUG	SEP	OCT
Property Taxes	100	12	1,200	0				
New Car	300	14	4,200	0				
Furniture	375	14	5,250	0				5,250
Maternity Expense	179	14	2,500	0		2,500		
Boat	179	14	2,500	0				
IRA Contributions	286	14	4,000	0				
Taxes	232	14	3,250	0				
Ski Trip	86	14	1,200	0				
Total Allocation — Timeline Expenditures	1,736		24,100	**A**	0	2,500	0	5,250
Cumulative Timeline Expenditures (Add Total from Line A to Prior Month's Line B.)				**B**	0	2,500	2,500	7,750

Description Control & Contingency	Monthly Allocation	Period Mos.	Period Total	Funding To Date	Period Description			
Clothes	150	12	1,800		year			
Medical/Dental	60	1	60		month (estimate of average)			
Car Repairs	167	12	2,000		year			
Courses	30	15	450		next 15 months			
Parties	75	12	900		year			
Home Improvements	83	60	5,000		coming 5 years			
Vacations	117	12	1,400		year			
Control & Contingency Monthly Allocation	682	Cumulative Allocation — Avg. Control & Contingency	**C**		150	1,363	2,045	2,727
					1	2	3	4
Monthly Allocation — All Expenditures	2,417	Cum. Allocation — All Exps. Plus Total Funding To Date	**D**		2,417	4,835	7,252	9,670
First Degree Funding Surplus/(Shortfall) (Subtract Line B from Line D)		Total Funding To Date »»» 0	**E**		2,417	2,335	4,752	1,920
Second Degree Funding Surplus/(Shortfall) (Subtract Line C from Line E)			**F**		2,267	971	2,707	-807

Figure 17–4

Timeline

NOV	DEC	JAN	FEB	MAR	APR	MAY	JUN	JUL	AUG	SEP
	600				600					
									4,200	
						2,500				
					4,000					
					3,250					
		1,200								

NOV	DEC	JAN	FEB	MAR	APR	MAY	JUN	JUL	AUG	SEP
0	600	1,200	0	0	7,850	2,500	0	0	4,200	0

NOV	DEC	JAN	FEB	MAR	APR	MAY	JUN	JUL	AUG	SEP
7,750	8,350	9,550	9,550	9,550	17,400	19,900	19,900	19,900	24,100	24,100

3,408	4,090	4,772	5,453	6,135	6,817	7,498	8,180	8,862	9,543	10,225
5	6	7	8	9	10	11	12	13	14	15
12,087	14,504	16,922	19,339	21,756	24,174	26,591	29,009	31,426	33,843	36,261

4,337	6,154	7,372	9,789	12,206	6,774	6,691	9,109	11,526	9,743	12,161

929	2,064	2,600	4,336	6,071	-43	-807	929	2,664	200	1,936

October's shortfall can be avoided if we can move one of the Timeline Expenditures occurring in or prior to October to a month after October, where there are months and months of Second-Degree Funding Surpluses. Again, the timing of Maternity Expenses is not negotiable, so we look to Furniture.

This kind of expenditure is very easily rescheduled. Out of $5,250 of furniture purchases, it might be fairly easy to delay $1,000 or so to cover the October shortfall. Of course, rescheduling the entire purchase for November would also do the trick.

Next let's analyze April's shortfall of $30. This is such a small amount that appropriate planning might consist merely of allowing this money to be covered out of surplus cash floating around in one's checking account, or borrowing a little on a credit card (by not paying the entire balance due, as we usually advise). It would be prudent, however, to keep a watchful eye on Control & Contingency expenditures: If they are running significantly ahead of the average, some greater attention may have to be focused on this supposedly tiny shortfall.

May's shortfall of $793 is too serious to be almost ignored like April's. Again, we look first to events in and shortly before May—expenditures that could perhaps be moved to after May.

All the events of April are tax-related. There's no bending of due dates here. January's ski trip could perhaps be moved a bit—but not past May! Only the May purchase—$2,500 for a boat—looks reasonably postponable. Much as that poor boat keeps getting pushed around the calendar, holding off until June would probably not foul up the summer boating plans too badly.

Borrowing to Cover Funding Shortfalls

For many people—especially those with lines of credit with reasonable interest rates and ready access—scheduled shortfalls like the ones in this analysis might be easily handled with short-term borrowing and no rescheduling of purchases at all. In fact, after charting out your expenditure pattern with the Funding Crash Analysis, you might feel considerably more comfortable borrowing a quick thousand dollars for furniture or a boat than you would have before. The Crash Analysis shows that you will be able to pay back those loans in a month. Without the analysis you might wonder: Is this going to be another one of those debts that just sits there forever and is never paid back?

Ultimately, a lot of postponing and forsaking of expenditures goes on while you try to pare down your monthly allocation to something you can afford, then plan the timing of purchases to avoid funding shortfalls. As annoying as it may be at the time, it is probably some of the best priority planning you have ever done. Far more accurate and sophisticated than merely numbering a list of priorities, it pits alternative against alternative, choice against choice, in a real environment of time and limited resources. The planning done while you analyze your funding is as close as you can get to a real-world model of spending limited resources.

Exercise: Funding Crash Analysis

1. List each of your funding items in the Description column of the top or bottom half of the Crash Analysis, as appropriate. As we go, refer to Figure 17-2 as a simplified example. It uses the data you're familiar with from the example I used during my consultation with Denise.

2. List the time periods (usually months) across the top of the Timeline. Don't be bound up in the old twelve-month trap. You can do your planning for seven months—or twenty-seven. The Crash Analysis reproduced in Appendix B has fifteen spaces on its timeline.

That's a hint.

3. You've already done about half the work involved in the Crash Analysis: you've already collected the items you think you'd like to include in your funding program. Gather together your Major Purchases List, Scheduled Expenditures List, Annual Control Expenditures List, Contingency Planning notes, and Goals Planning Timeline.

Most of the items on these five lists will go onto your Funding Crash Analysis and, eventually, on your Funding Tracking Ledger. Your first task with each item is to figure out whether it goes on the top (Timeline) half or the bottom half of the Crash Analysis.

Items on your Major Purchases and on your Goals Planning Timeline will almost invariably end up on the top (Timeline) half of the Crash Analysis. So will expenditures for which you can answer "yes" to one of the following questions:

· Is the timing of this expenditure known to me now?
· Can I control the timing of this expenditure?

If you can't answer "yes" to one of the above questions, you won't be able to place the expenditure on your Timeline, and the expenditure properly belongs in the bottom half of the analysis. (Please note: If you have an expenditure that falls off the end of the Crash Analysis Timeline that you're using—like your kids' college educations, for instance—you'll need to use the long-range funding concepts outlined in Chapter 19.)

For Timeline Expenditures:

4. List the expenditure categories in the Description column.

5. For each expenditure, write the amounts to be spent in the column representing the month the money will be spent. (Err on the side of sooner, rather than later. For instance, if you plan to buy your next car in May, June or July, write the expenditure down for May.)

Only worry about actual cash flow (or credit card charges, which we treat the same as writing a check). Don't worry just yet about the financed portion of purchases. Therefore, if you're buying a $15,000 new car and you're putting $4,000 down, the $4,000 is the amount that is put on the schedule.

6. You may very well have some savings stashed away somewhere. Convinced as you are now (after reading Chapter 2) that savings without a cause is folly, you are now in the mood to assign your existing savings to various of the funds you are now setting up. Place the amount of your savings that you are assigning to each fund in the Funding to Date column for the appropriate line. Obviously, you should make sure that the total of all your Funding to Date entries does not exceed the amount you actually have set aside in savings (or are willing and able to set aside immediately).

7. Add up the entries for each line and put the total in the box under the column marked Timeline Total. If you have anything entered in the Funding to Date column, subtract that from your total of Timeline total.

8. Next—and this is a little tricky—decide for how many months you will fund this item. At first, you may think this an unnecessary question: "Of course, there are fifteen columns (or twelve or whatever you're using) on my analysis, I'm obviously funding for fifteen months." But this isn't necessarily true. If, for instance, an annual expense falls once during the fifteen months, you'll be underfunding if you divide that expenditure by fifteen. A twelve-month recurring expense should be funded one twelfth each month—not one fifteenth. Put the number of months you plan to fund for in the Timeline Months column.

9. Divide the Timeline Total by the Timeline Months. Round off to the nearest dollar and put the answer in the Monthly Allocation column.

10. Total each column of the Timeline section at Line A. Accumulate the Timeline columns at Line B. (That is, take the Line A total for the column you're working on plus the Line B total from the previous column.)

For Expenditures in the bottom half of the Crash Analysis:

11. Keep in mind that the goal is to arrive at an amount to be entered in the Monthly Allocation column. If you already know the Monthly Allocation desired, enter that number on the appropriate line for each Control or Contingency Expenditure.

12. For some expenditures, however, you may know your spending goals by some period of time other than a month (for instance, you may want to spend $2,000 *a year* on clothes or $1,800 on vacation activities *between now and June of next year).* In these cases, enter the total amount in the Period Total column and describe the period in the Period Description column. Determine how many months that period covers and put that number in the Period Months column.

13. For each line, divide the Period Total column (less anything you have put in the Funding to Date column) by the Period Months column and enter in the Monthly Allocation column.

14. Total the Monthly Allocation column (for Control & Contingency Expenditures) at Line C, and (for all expenditures, including Timeline Expenditures) at Line D. This Line D amount will be your monthly funding allocation. This is the amount of your income you'll need to allocate each month to funding items.

15. Stop here and decide whether the number you come up with for Monthly Allocation—All Expenditures is a monthly number you can deal with. If you have been following all the steps in this book, you already know how much funding you can afford: You calculated it earlier in this chapter. But if you have launched into funding "cold," you'll have to assess how much you can afford using the trial-and-error method. If your cash flow won't allow the size of the amount in the Monthly Allocation—All Expenditures box, go back and scale down some of your spending plans.

Once you've come to some peace with your calculated monthly funding allocation, you're ready to complete the Crash Analysis to see if your spending plans are headed for disaster.

First-Degree Funding Shortfall

16. As you'll recall, a First-Degree Funding Shortfall occurs when the money set aside to date for *all* funding does not even cover the planned expenditures in the Timeline (much less any Control or Contingency Expenditures). To calculate First-Degree Funding Shortfall, for each month you need to know:

• cumulative planned Timeline Expenditures
• cumulative funding money set aside

so that you can subtract the first from the second. If planned expenditures exceed money set aside—well, we don't call it *Crash Analysis* for nothing!

You already have calculated the Cumulative Timeline Expenditures on Line B. Now you need to calculate Line D. While you're at it, you may as well figure Line C, too, since they're both calculated in the same manner.

17. Line C is simple multiplication. You know how much the monthly allocation for Control & Contingency Expenditures is: It's in the Monthly Allocation column of Line C. Simply multiply that monthly number times the number of months for each column of the Timeline. I have put the number of months in small numerals between Lines C and D, for your convenience.

18. Now add up all the amounts in the Funding to Date column (both the top and bottom sections) and enter the total at the bottom of the page in the box labeled Total Funding to Date. This amount, remember, should represent an amount of money you already have set aside for these funding items.

19. Line D is figured in a similar fashion to Line C. Multiply the Monthly Allocation—All Expenditures amount by the appropriate number of months, from those little numbers between Lines C and D. Each month, after multiplying these two numbers, add in the amount in the Total Funding to Date box and write the sum in Line D. (The Total Funding to Date box amount gets added in *each* month.)

20. Now you're ready to calculate First-Degree Funding Surplus or (heaven forbid) Shortfall. All you need do, for each month in the Timeline, is subtract Line B from Line D: Cumulative Allocation—All Expenditures minus Cumulative Timeline Expenditures.

21. If you have a Funding Shortfall—don't despair. Just fix it! You may feel that this is the low point of your budgeting experience, but it's actually budgeting at its best. Why? Because you are making financial decisions—choices. And that's exactly what you're supposed to be doing when you budget.

The most effective way to cure a First-Degree Funding Shortfall is to identify discretionary Timeline Expenditures and merely move them farther to the right on the Timeline. The cumulative totals you calculated are especially helpful now, because they allow you to move expenditures around and know the consequences of your rescheduling without lengthy recalculations of your analysis.

If you're feeling miserable as you delay, on paper, the purchase of your new car by a few months, just think how much better you feel doing that now, in the privacy of your own kitchen table, instead of discovering this disappointing reality on the showroom floor.

22. After fixing your First-Degree Funding Shortfall, the next step, of course, is to check your Second-Degree Funding Surplus/ (Shortfall). To do that, you need to calculate Line F.

Line F is simply Line E minus Line C. Line E is the First-Degree Funding Surplus/(Shortfall) (which, you'll recall, did not take into account spending on Control & Contingency items). And Line C is our best guess at what we anticipate those Control & Contingency Expenditures to be, on a cumulative basis. The difference between the two lines, then, is an estimation of what we might expect to have, in cash, in the entire funding account, month by month.

23. Just as with the First-Degree Funding calculations, there may be Second-Degree Funding Shortfalls you find unacceptable. You will want to adjust the timing of Timeline Expenditures—or make notes to yourself about what your Control & Contingency spending pattern should be—before finally accepting your completed Funding Crash Analysis.

Ready to Fund

Congratulations! You have completed—successfully, I hope—the most useful and most mathematically intensive analysis in my whole program. Although doing your first Funding Crash Analysis may have seemed like a big deal, you will actually come back to this analysis over and over in your personal financial planning. It, more than anything else, tells you what you're capable of pulling off. When a new idea hits you ("Hey! Let's put a skylight in the darkroom!"), the Funding Crash Analysis will tell you whether and when you can achieve your new idea for spending money.

In the meantime, however, having done your first Crash Analysis, you are now ready to actually be a funder and not just talk about it! Celebrate a little, and when you come back I will outline for you the much simpler process of actually maintaining your funding, month by month.

We must master our good fortune, or it will master us.
—*Publilius Syrus*

18

Keeping Track of Your Funding

The work you did in creating the Funding Crash Analysis will feed into the ledger you will keep monthly to track your contributions to and withdrawals from your funding account. You're already familiar with the Funding Tracking Ledger from Chapter 13, but you couldn't make your own Tracking Ledger until you had done the Crash Analysis we just completed. Now you're ready to launch into the nitty-gritty of funding.

Exercise: Setting Up Your Funding Tracking Ledger

1. Format a worksheet with column headings and captions like Figures 13-2, 13-3 and 13-4.

2. List the time periods (usually months) in the boxes across the top of the ledger.

3. List the various items you're funding for in the boxes down the left side of the page. These categories will correspond exactly to those you defined on your Funding Crash Analysis. At this point, it is no longer important to keep the Timeline Expenditures separated from Control & Contingency Expenditures. Once you've completed your Crash Analysis, those distinctions are no longer important. You can list funding categories in any order you find useful: alphabetically or by frequency of expenditure are two appropriate possibilities.

While you're listing your funding categories using your Crash Analysis as a source, you might as well be efficient and copy two numbers off the Crash Analysis for each funding category.

The first is the Monthly Allocation figure. Put that on the line marked Allocation on your Funding Tracking Ledger. The other number you'll want to record is the amount in the Funding to Date column on the Crash Analysis. It goes in the Balance Forward box in the first column of each funding item. (If you have no Funding to Date—which is often the case in first-time funding—nothing, or zero, should be entered in the first Balance Forward box.)

4. At the bottom of your Funding Tracking Ledger, put "Total—All Funds" in the Fund label box and add up all the Allocations and all the beginning Balances Forward from all the other funds.

At this point, check to see that the totals made on your Funding Tracking Ledger agree with the numbers on your Crash Analysis. Figure 18-1 gives an example of the two checkpoints:

• The Allocation box for the Total—All Funds section of the Tracking Ledger equals the Monthly Allocation—All Expenditures on the Crash Analysis.
• If applicable, the first Balance Forward column of the Total—All Funds section of the Funding Tracking Ledger equals the Total Funding to Date box at the bottom of the Crash Analysis.

5. Believe it or not—you're done! At least for now. The next time you need to work with this ledger will be at the end of the month.

Funding Crash Analysis   Funding Tracking Ledger

Figure 18-1

At End of Month:

6. At the end of your first month, add up all the expenditures you made in each of your funding categories. Include purchases you made:

- from your checking account
- with cash
- on credit cards
- any other way

(For suggestions of ways to set up your personal accounting system to provide these numbers efficiently, see Appendix A.)

7. With your month's expenditures in hand, you're now ready to calculate how much money you need to send off to your funding account. At the end of the month, deposit the month's Allocation into your funding account, after having deducted anything spent on funding-related items during the month. (There are other methods of managing the funding account, discussed later in this chapter.)

Merely subtract the amount you spent on funding items from the Monthly Allocation and write your fund a check and deposit it! If the month's fund-related expenditures exceeded the Monthly Allocation, make a withdrawal from your funding account for the difference and use the money to replenish your checking account—weary, at this point, from making so many funding-type purchases.

8. Next, put the expenditures you made in the Funding Tracking Ledger on the Expenditure line for each fund category. Remember to round to the nearest dollar.

9. Now that the Expenditure part of the column has been filled in, calculate the math for the entire column. The math is very simple. Merely add the Balance Forward and Allocation together, and subtract out the Expenditure amount to obtain New Balance. (The use of the Adjustments +/− line is discussed later in this chapter.)

The calculator key guide for the calculation is as follows:

+	Balance Forward
+	Allocation
−	Expenditure
+/−	Adjustments
=	New Balance

10. Add each line item into the Total—All Funds section at the bottom of the Ledger. This will tell you what the New Balance of the entire fund should be. Check this number against what's actually in the funding account. They should be equal, except for the addition of interest income, which we'll discuss below.

Setting Up for Next Month:

11. Now's a good time to fill in what you can of next month's column in the Tracking Ledger. The Balance Forward line is equal to the New Balance from the prior month's column. The Allocation is likely to be identical to last month's Allocation, unless you have prepared a new Crash Analysis and changed something.

The Mechanics of Maintaining a Funding Account

I mentioned before that it's crucial to have a funding account that is separated from all your other accounts. Unless the amount found festering in your funding account tends to remain rather low, it's preferable for the account to be an interest-bearing one. These are the basics.

The remaining questions about how to set up and manage a funding account center on personal style and preference. A principal issue is whether you'll make funding expenditures directly from the funding account (in which case it needs to provide check-writing capability) or through your personal checking account, credit cards and cash, and merely replenish your regular checking account from the funding account.

You'll also need to decide when you'll make deposits to your funding account. Options include:

- at the beginning of the month
- during the month
- shortly after the end of the month (to give you time to subtract out your funding-related expenditures before making that month's contribution)
- by direct deposit from paychecks

You might eventually have more than one funding account—one for short-term needs and one or more for longer-term funding objectives, perhaps with higher yields.

As your funding account continues to grow, you'll want to begin investing your funds in different investments, consistent with the timing and liquidity needs, as well as the risk tolerances, of your various funding objectives.

Even if you are, at that point, a first-time investor, you will be approaching the investment community armed with what every investor should know before he invests: timing, liquidity and risk preferences. You'll then be able to concentrate on investment issues such as diversification, portfolio balance and yield within a well-defined context of what you need from your investment portfolio. You will, after all, know about as much as any investor can know about precisely when you'll need how much.

Accounting for Funding Interest

When we talk about long-range funding in the next chapter, interest will be a crucial part of the program and will have to be credited to each of your individual long-range funds in order for you to reach your long-range funding objectives.

In your short-range funding (which perhaps dominates the funding program you have set up thus far) interest is much more of a "freebie"—an added bonus of money that can be put into a slush fund and/or applied to various funding accounts at your will.

I usually recommend setting up a Miscellaneous Fund within your funding, and I usually suggest some moderate amount of monthly funding allocated to this account. The purpose of the account is to cover bad estimates about how much should be funded for all the other funded expenditures, so that when medical bills are running way ahead of schedule, for instance, money can be taken out of the Miscellaneous Fund and applied to the beleaguered Medical Fund.

The Miscellaneous account, therefore, is an ideal account in which to direct interest income. You may wish, instead, to apply it to another pet fund—perhaps one to which you were not able to allocate as much as you wished—or merely use the interest for some whimsical funding purpose.

Interest income should be entered into the fund via the Adjustments +/− line and be treated as a plus (+) entry—that is, an addition to the New Balance of the fund.

Adjustments to Funding Accounts

From time to time—usually in connection with a revision of your Funding Crash Analysis—you'll want to move some money around. For instance, you might find your Auto Repairs Fund might be seriously negative after an unexpected onetime breakdown. Since it's likely you won't have money just sitting available outside your funding account, you're likely to need to look to your funding accounts to make up the negative balance. You might have a Miscellaneous Fund to partially come to the rescue, and you may also have to "steal" (not borrow) money out of other funds more discretionary in nature than Auto Repairs to make up the difference.

Let's illustrate precisely that example. Figure 18-2 shows an abbreviated Funding Tracking Ledger in which an adjustment is made to the Miscellaneous & Interest Fund as well as the Vacation Fund in

Funding Tracking Ledger

Month	January	February	March	April	May
Fund					
Vacation					
Balance Forward	1,200	1,500	1,800	1,800	2,100
Allocation	300	300	300	300	300
Expenditure					
Adjustments +/-			—300		
New Balance	1,500	1,800	1,800	2,100	2,400
Auto Repairs					
Balance Forward	329	399	—776	34	104
Allocation	70	70	70	70	70
Expenditure		1,245			
Adjustments +/-			+ 740		
New Balance	399	—776	34	104	174
Misc. & Interest					
Balance Forward	64	340	390		259
Allocation	50	50	50	50	50
Expenditure					
Adjustments +/-	+ 226	(qtly int)	—440	+ 209	(qtly int)
New Balance	340	390		259	309
Total - All Funds					
Balance Forward	13,938	14,062	11,501	12,853	14,009
Allocation	1,898	1,898	1,898	1,898	1,898
Expenditure	2,000	4,459	546	951	1,595
Adjustments +/-	+ 226	(qtly int)		+ 209	(qtly int)
New Balance	14,062	11,501	12,853	14,009	14,312

Figure 18-2

order to make up an unexpected but unavoidable overdraft against the Auto Repairs Fund.

The Price of Tranquillity Is Payable Monthly

The maintenance program for funding is really quite minimal from here on out. All you do is follow the monthly procedures for maintaining the Funding Tracking Ledger. It's true that the Tracking Ledger is basically accounting (and you *know* how I feel about wasting time doing accounting), but I think you'll have to agree that it is a very minimal commitment to accounting. Most readers should be able to maintain their Tracking Ledger monthly with somewhere between five and twenty minutes of work each month—not a high price to pay for financial tranquility.

While many readers will take this new system as an opportunity to organize their entire personal financial domain—and make a greater commitment to organized bookkeeping and recordkeeping—many of you will find that the maintenance of the Tracking Ledger will be the only additional bookkeeping requirement this system places on you. It is a burden well worth the effort.

Again—and I can't stress this enough—what you've just learned is "it." This is the biggest, most powerful secret for staying in control that you've ever been taught. As I've told countless Financial Sanity Workshop participants: *"If you do only one part of the Financial Sanity system, do funding."*

Future, n. That period of time in which our affairs prosper, our friends are true and our happiness is assured.
—*Ambrose Bierce*

19

Long-Range Funding

If, by using a funding program, all you accomplish is making sure you have enough money to fix your car and pay your property taxes, that is a worthy financial management achievement. But financial management is only a part of what this book is all about. Mostly, Financial Sanity is concerned with dreams.

No doubt, many of the dreams you recorded on your Goals Planning Timeline are off in the future. Whether responsible dreams, like providing for a comfortable retirement or sending kids to college; dramatic, romantic dreams involving foreign travel and adventure; or fun dreams of boats and ski cabins, it's the mission of long-range funding to make sure you can attain those which are most important to you.

Long-Range Funding

Long-range funding differs from short-term funding in two important and related respects: interest and inflation.

You may have noticed, in the Funding Crash Analysis, that I didn't ask you to take into account any interest you might be earning in your funding account. For instance, if you were funding for the planned purchase of a stereo a year from now at the estimated cost of $1,200, the funding techniques would ask you simply to divide $1,200 by twelve months, for a monthly contribution of $100. Assuming you did this, and assuming your monthly deposits of $100 earned interest at 8 percent, you would have not merely $1,200 at the end of a year, but about $1,245. Put another way, to get $1,200 in a year, you don't really need to put aside $100 monthly; $96.40 would do the trick.

Reasons for excluding interest from your funding plans include:

· The effect of interest over such a short period is fairly minor: A $3.60 difference in the monthly funding amount is not worth the trouble to calculate.
· The cost of the stereo was an estimate anyway. An extra 4 percent of savings is hardly a critical error.
· Financial Sanity provides a unique facility for allowing you to borrow money from one fund to speed up spending from another fund—without getting into trouble. But while your Car Fund is borrowing money from your Stereo Fund, less interest is being earned in the Stereo Fund.
· Interest earned in the funding account might be absorbed by price increases in the targeted expenditure—either because of inflation or other factors.

In spite of many good reasons to ignore the effect of interest in *short*-term funding, in *long*-term funding ignoring interest will significantly overstate the amount you need to fund monthly. Although inflationary price increases are every bit as much a factor in long-term funding, interest rates historically trend higher than inflation, so you should, over the life of a well-managed, long-range funding project, be able to maintain an edge on inflation. How to calculate and manage that edge is what this section is about.

Financial Sanity's Unique Approach to Long-Range Funding

In the Financial Sanity system, long-range funding is based on three premises:

· Interest (or other investment return) accumulation is taken into account at "real" interest rates rather than nominal or stated interest rates.

• No attempt is made to predict inflation. Funding is targeted to provide funds at today's prices.

The two premises above are intended to be approximately self-balancing. Interest will, of course, accumulate at nominal (stated) interest rates, not at real interest rates; and inflation will push up the cost of the planned expenditure beyond today's cost. Ideally, the extra money earned in interest will match the extra money required by price increases. But in case it doesn't, long-range funding still protects you from underfunding: From time to time, you will recalculate the monthly funding amount, taking into account:

• the number of months left to fund and
• the new current cost of the funded expenditure
• less the amount of accumulated funding (including interest earned) to date.

This recalculation feature is the ultimate fail-safe protection of this funding system. It guards against errors you may make in estimating costs; it forgives your errors in estimating the real rate of return; it protects you against price increases that exceed the rate of inflation; and it even offers some limited protection against any failure to make all of your anticipated funding contributions.

Real Interest

If the concept of real interest rates is foreign to you, here's a quick example. You have a dollar at the beginning of the year, which you *could* use to buy a loaf of bread that costs exactly a dollar. Instead, you elect to invest the dollar in a savings account which pays 11 percent interest. At the end of the year, you withdraw your $1.11 from your savings and go to the store to buy bread. But inflation has increased the price of bread to $1.05. You were hoping to have 11 cents left over after buying your bread, but instead you have only 6 cents. The 6 cents you have represents the real interest. It is (almost) the same as if bread had stayed priced at a dollar and you had invested your money in a savings account paying 6 percent.

Figure 19-1 charts the recent historical relationship between interest rates (as represented by Treasury Bill yields) and inflation. The difference between interest rates and inflation is known as "real" interest. Throughout most of the 1980s, as Figure 19-1 illustrates, real interest rates hovered around 4 percent. In short, regardless of the stated interest rate (which topped 14 percent at its peak), the difference between interest rates and the level of inflation was reliably about

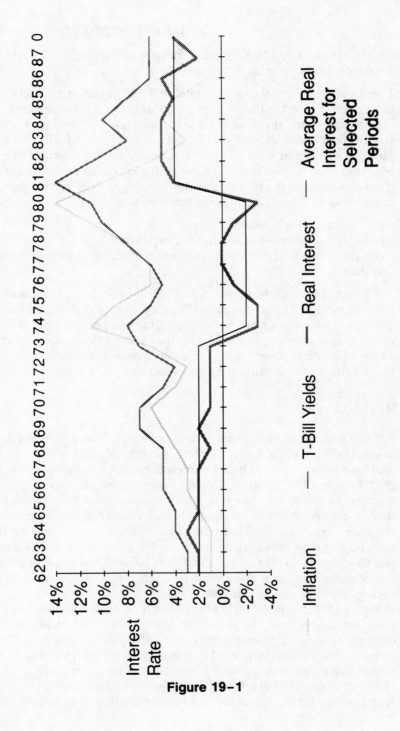

Figure 19-1

4 percent. (Four percent is actually fairly high, historically speaking; 2 percent might represent a better working number for the long haul; and during inflationary times, you might want to assume that your return will be 0 percent if you are in debt-type instruments, such as certificates of deposit and money market funds.)

This pattern suggests that perhaps we don't need to pay quite so much attention to what's happening with inflation. After all, predicting inflation is beyond the reasonable capacity of our finest economists—why should *we* expect to be any good at it? Even without predicting inflation, however—no matter what happens to the price of bread—we can pretty well count on having a loaf plus 6 cents at the end of the year. So does it really matter much that the price of bread went up 10 cents or 5 cents or 15 cents?

The concept of planning savings (or funding) buildup by taking into account only the real interest rate is radical and liberating—and it's the foundation of Financial Sanity's Long-Range Funding theory.*

Calculating Long-Range Funding

Figure 19-2 helps you to quickly calculate the monthly payment required to fund an expense fifteen months to thirty years away. It shows the amount you should set aside each month, given:

• the number of months until your target expenditure
• the real interest rate you select

"What rate should I use?" you may well ask. Believe it or not, it doesn't make all that much difference. Pick a lower rate and you'll experience less volatility in the monthly payments you recalculate from time to time. You also may reach your goal a little early. Pick a higher rate, on the other hand, and you'll effectively be rigging your payments so that they are more affordable in the early years and more expensive later on. (This may be a desirable planning strategy.)

Generally, I would recommend the 2 percent rate on the chart. Use 0 percent (straight funding—the way you fund for shorter-range expenditures) if you want to be conservative or if you feel that interest rates are not keeping pace with the general rate of inflation. Use higher percentages for relatively inflation-proof planned expenditures, or if you want to pay less now and more later.

*Care should be taken in applying the real interest rule. For instance, real interest rates were low or negative during much of the 1970s, when inflation was rampant. Generally speaking, real interest rates will be high when inflation is dropping, lower when it is heating up. As your funding account grows larger, a diversified portfolio of investments should provide better long-term stability than strictly debt-instrument investments, like certificates of deposit.

Monthly Payment Required to Fund $1,000 in Today's Dollars over a Given Period at Selected "Real" Interest Rates

Real Interest Rates (Interest less Inflation)

Months	0%	2%	4%	6%	8%	10%
15	66.67	65.78	64.91	64.04	63.19	62.34
16	62.50	61.62	60.75	59.89	59.04	58.20
17	58.82	57.95	57.08	56.22	55.38	54.55
18	55.56	54.68	53.82	52.97	52.13	51.30
19	52.63	51.76	50.90	50.05	49.22	48.39
20	50.00	49.13	48.27	47.43	46.60	45.78
21	47.62	46.75	45.90	45.06	44.23	43.41
22	45.45	44.59	43.74	42.90	42.07	41.26
23	43.48	42.62	41.77	40.93	40.11	39.30
24	41.67	40.81	39.96	39.12	38.31	37.50
25	40.00	39.14	38.30	37.46	36.65	35.85
26	38.46	37.60	36.76	35.93	35.12	34.32
27	37.04	36.18	35.34	34.51	33.70	32.91
28	35.71	34.86	34.02	33.20	32.39	31.59
29	34.48	33.63	32.79	31.97	31.16	30.37
30	33.33	32.48	31.64	30.82	30.02	29.23
31	32.26	31.41	30.57	29.75	28.95	28.17
32	31.25	30.40	29.57	28.75	27.95	27.17
33	30.30	29.45	28.62	27.81	27.01	26.23
34	29.41	28.56	27.73	26.92	26.13	25.35
35	28.57	27.72	26.90	26.09	25.29	24.52
40	25.00	24.16	23.33	22.53	21.75	20.99
45	22.22	21.38	20.57	19.77	19.00	18.25
50	20.00	19.16	18.35	17.57	16.81	16.07
55	18.18	17.35	16.54	15.76	15.01	14.29
60	16.67	15.83	15.03	14.26	13.52	12.81
65	15.38	14.55	13.76	12.99	12.26	11.56
70	14.29	13.46	12.67	11.91	11.18	10.49
75	13.33	12.51	11.72	10.97	10.25	9.57

Real Interest Rates (Interest less Inflation)

Months	0%	2%	4%	6%	8%	10%
80	12.50	11.68	10.89	10.15	9.44	8.77
85	11.76	10.94	10.16	9.42	8.72	8.07
90	11.11	10.29	9.51	8.78	8.09	7.44
95	10.53	9.71	8.94	8.21	7.53	6.89
100	10.00	9.18	8.41	7.69	7.02	6.39
105	9.52	8.71	7.94	7.23	6.56	5.94
110	9.09	8.28	7.52	6.81	6.15	5.54
115	8.70	7.88	7.13	6.42	5.77	5.17
120	8.33	7.52	6.77	6.07	5.43	4.84
125	8.00	7.19	6.44	5.75	5.12	4.54
130	7.69	6.88	6.14	5.45	4.83	4.26
135	7.41	6.60	5.86	5.18	4.56	4.00
140	7.14	6.34	5.60	4.92	4.31	3.76
145	6.90	6.09	5.36	4.69	4.09	3.55
150	6.67	5.86	5.13	4.47	3.87	3.34
155	6.45	5.65	4.92	4.27	3.68	3.16
160	6.25	5.45	4.73	4.07	3.49	2.98
165	6.06	5.26	4.54	3.90	3.32	2.82
170	5.88	5.08	4.37	3.73	3.16	2.67
175	5.71	4.92	4.20	3.57	3.01	2.53
180	5.56	4.76	4.05	3.42	2.87	2.39
185	5.41	4.61	3.90	3.28	2.74	2.27
190	5.26	4.47	3.77	3.15	2.61	2.15
195	5.13	4.34	3.64	3.02	2.50	2.04
200	5.00	4.21	3.51	2.91	2.38	1.94
205	4.88	4.09	3.40	2.80	2.28	1.84
210	4.76	3.97	3.28	2.69	2.18	1.75
215	4.65	3.86	3.18	2.59	2.09	1.67
220	4.55	3.76	3.08	2.49	2.00	1.59

Real Interest Rates (Interest less Inflation)

Months	0%	2%	4%	6%	8%	10%
225	4.44	3.66	2.98	2.40	1.91	1.51
230	4.35	3.57	2.89	2.31	1.83	1.44
235	4.26	3.47	2.80	2.23	1.76	1.37
240	4.17	3.39	2.72	2.15	1.69	1.31
245	4.08	3.30	2.64	2.08	1.62	1.24
250	4.00	3.22	2.56	2.01	1.55	1.19
255	3.92	3.15	2.49	1.94	1.49	1.13
260	3.85	3.07	2.42	1.87	1.43	1.08
265	3.77	3.00	2.35	1.81	1.37	1.03
270	3.70	2.93	2.28	1.75	1.32	0.98
275	3.64	2.86	2.22	1.69	1.27	0.94
280	3.57	2.80	2.16	1.64	1.22	0.90
285	3.51	2.74	2.10	1.58	1.17	0.86
290	3.45	2.68	2.04	1.53	1.13	0.82
295	3.39	2.62	1.99	1.48	1.09	0.78
300	3.33	2.57	1.94	1.44	1.04	0.75
305	3.28	2.51	1.89	1.39	1.01	0.71
310	3.23	2.46	1.84	1.35	0.97	0.68
315	3.17	2.41	1.79	1.31	0.93	0.65
320	3.13	2.36	1.75	1.26	0.90	0.62
325	3.08	2.32	1.70	1.23	0.86	0.60
330	3.03	2.27	1.66	1.19	0.83	0.57
335	2.99	2.23	1.62	1.15	0.80	0.55
340	2.94	2.18	1.58	1.12	0.77	0.52
345	2.90	2.14	1.54	1.08	0.74	0.50
350	2.86	2.10	1.51	1.05	0.72	0.48
355	2.82	2.06	1.47	1.02	0.69	0.46
360	2.78	2.03	1.44	0.99	0.67	0.44

Figure 19-2

Suzanne and Ted's Fund for Christine's College Education

You'll recall that in Chapter 3 Suzanne and Ted, on their Goals Planning Timeline (Figure 3-1), targeted sending their daughter Christine to college in the year 2000. They figured that college costs were currently $12,000 per year—in 1988 dollars. They want to have funds available for up to five years of college for Christine.

Each year of college funding will be a separate funding goal:

Year	Cost in 1988 Dollars	Years to Fund
2000	$12,000	12
2001	$12,000	13
2002	$12,000	14
2003	$12,000	15
2004	$12,000	16

Suzanne's first step is to calculate the monthly funding allocation required to reach each of these goals. She selects a real interest rate of 2 percent and uses the table in Figure 19-2 to calculate the following monthly amounts:

			(For $1,000)	(For $12,000)
	To Fund		Table	Monthly
Year	Years	Months	Amount	Allocation
2000	12	144	$6.09	$73
2001	13	156	$5.65	$68
2002	14	168	$5.08	$61
2003	15	180	$4.76	$57
2004	16	192	$4.47	$54

Whenever the "Months to Fund" was not on the chart, Suzanne merely took the table amount for the number of months nearest what she was looking for. Interpolation between lines on the table is not required.

Taking only the $73 monthly funding for the year 2000, let's imagine that we can see into the future[†] as Suzanne and Ted track the buildup of this fund for Christine's first year of college. Their Long-Range Funding Recalculation Worksheet is in Figure 19-3.

They began funding $73 a month for this first year of college in August 1988. They look at their progress three years later, in September 1991, when college costs have risen to $16,600 a year and their

---

[†]The prospective history in this example was borrowed from the actual history of cost increases at an Ivy League university from 1975 to 1986. The buildup of funding in the Funding to Date column reflects the interest obtainable at that time from money market accounts and 180-day bank certificates of deposit, after deducting 30 percent for taxes.

Description of Funding Objective

Christine's First Year at College

Estimated (or earliest) anticipated date of expenditure (Month-Year): *August 2000*

Current Date (Month-Year)	Currrent Cost	Funded To Date	Needed To Fund	Time Left To Fund	Real Rate	Table Payment	New Monthly Allocation
August 1988	12,000	0	12,000	144 mos.	2%	6.09	73
September 1991	16,600	3,088	13,512	106 mos.	2%	8.71	118
November 1994	22,800	8,621	14,179	69 mos.	2%	13.46	191
August 1996	25,800	14,106	11,694	48 mos.	2%	19.16	224
May 1998	28,800	21,089	7,711	27 mos.	2%	36.18	279
September 1998	31,800	23,012	8,788	22 mos.	2%	44.59	392
February 1999	34,700	25,041	9,659	18 mos.	2%	54.68	528
-				mos.	%		

Figure 19–3

fund has grown to $3,088, leaving $13,512 left to fund (in 1991 dollars) over the remaining 106 months.

Still using a conservative 2 percent real interest rate, Suzanne and Ted consult the table in Figure 19-2 to determine that—for the 106 months remaining to fund—a $8.71 payment will be sufficient for each $1,000 they are trying to accumulate. The remaining amount needed to fund is $13,512, so they calculate the monthly payment as follows:

$$\$13,512 \times \$8.71 \div \$1,000 = \$117.69,$$

which they round to $118. This becomes their new monthly funding allocation.

Suzanne and Ted continue to check the progress of their fund, as stories about rapidly escalating college costs appear in newsmagazines every year. Every few years, they research the new cost of sending Christine to the "benchmark" college they had selected (as being as expensive as they intended to provide). They compare this new cost to what they have accumulated in their fund, and, consulting Figure 19-2 of their well-worn copy of *Financial Sanity,* set a New Monthly Calculation.

As you can see from Figure 19-3, the recalculated monthly payment tends to rise smoothly over the years. If college costs follow inflation, then the changes in monthly allocations would tend to follow inflation, too. In that kind of scenario, the $118 allocated in 1991 would be as affordable as the $73 allocated in 1988.

This system—like just about any other funding, saving or investment program—does not protect you against dramatic price increases at the last minute. It does, however, provide exceptionally good protection from the ravages of inflation and even protects against dramatic price increases, as long as they occur early enough in the funding timetable.

Exercise: Long-Range Funding Calculation

Do this exercise separately for each long-range funding item you have. Each item will have a different funding period and perhaps even a different real interest rate from the other items. You may want to document your funding calculations on a worksheet like Figure 19-3. The Long-Range Funding Recalculation Worksheet will let you keep track of the assumptions you made at the time you calculated the monthly funding amount for each item and will let you document changes as you make them.

1. Describe the objective of your funding project at the top of the page—"Beach House," for instance, or "Archaeological Expedition to Central America."

2. Select the month and year by which you want to have funded for this item. You may not know exactly when funding will be needed, and therefore will have to estimate. If you're conservative, you might pick the earliest possible date the funding might be needed, although this will be less important if there is other long-range funding accumulating sufficient to cover any shortfall and if the money in other long-range funds won't be needed until after the shortfall has been made up.

3. Enter the Current Date in the first line of the first column.

4. Enter the Current Cost of the expenditure in the second column.

5. If you have already accumulated funds for this expenditure, you can give your funding account a kick start by entering the amount in the Funding to Date column. The amount you enter will have to be deposited into your funding account and allocated to this fund.

6. Subtract the Funding to Date amount from the Current Cost amount and enter that result in the Needed to Fund column.

7. Based on the current date and the targeted date, calculate the number of months left to fund for this expenditure.

8. Pick a (real) interest rate that you think is appropriate for this period of time. You can change the real interest rate any time you use the Recalculation Worksheet.

9. Use the table in Figure 19-2 to calculate the monthly payment required to fund a $1,000 target. Select the column that represents the interest rate you have selected; then look down that column until you get to the line that represents the number of months from your Time Left to Fund column. The resulting number is the monthly amount necessary to fund for a $1,000 expenditure. Enter that amount in the Table Payment column.

10. Multiply the Table Payment by the Needed to Fund amount and divide by $1,000. Enter the result in the last column.

Keep your Long-Range Funding Worksheet (one for each long-range funding item in your budget) in your Financial Sanity workbook. After you have several months (or even a few years) of experience with funding, you will want to revisit the Long-Range Funding Recalculation Worksheet and recalculate your required monthly payment. To do so, simply follow the above procedures, starting with step 3.

Incorporating Long-Range Funding into Your Regular Funding

Long-range funding fits neatly into your Funding Crash Analysis and Funding Tracking worksheets. Simply treat the long-range items as a single unit and enter it in the Control & Contingency section of your Funding Crash Analysis. Put the total of all the monthly funding contribution amounts in the Monthly Allocation box for that line. Or, if you prefer, you can enter each long-range funding account individually in the Control & Contingency section and keep separate accounts for each fund in your Funding Tracking Ledger. If you do show them separately on your Funding Crash Analysis, be sure to mark them specially as long-range funding items.

You'll want to exclude all long-range items from Line C of your Funding Crash Analysis. This will effectively leave long-range funding expenditures out of your second-degree funding shortfall calculation. This makes sense because it can safely be assumed that you will not be making any expenditures for long-range funding items, yet the contributions for long-range funding items are available to cushion temporary shortfalls of funding cash. Excluding the long-range items from Line C will make any second-degree shortfall smaller.

Accounting for Interest on Long-Range Funding Money

One of the premises of long-range funding is that there will be interest (or other investment income) to more than offset inflation-driven price increases in the targeted expenditure.

How, then, does the interest get handled on your Funding Tracking Ledger?

One method is to set up a "zero-target" funding account designed to collect interest income. The zero-target interest account does not have a monthly contribution amount, but every month on the Funding Tracking Ledger it will receive a positive adjustment on the Adjustments +/− line for the amount of interest earned. Periodically, the interest account can be cleared out by making a negative adjustment that is balanced by positive adjustments in the long-range funding accounts. A reasonable way of allocating this would be to assign interest in proportion to the balances in the accounts.

Let's say, for instance, that $160 in interest has accumulated over the last three months in the Interest Fund. The long-range funds are as follows:

Retirement	$ 4,000
Education	$ 3,000
Sabbatical	$ 1,000

The interest would be allocated as follows:

Retirement	$ 80
Education	$ 60
Sabbatical	$ 20
Total	$ 160

What About Taxes on the Interest?

If you're earning interest on your long-range funding (or other kind of return on invested capital, such as dividends or capital gains), it most likely will be taxed. How does that affect your funding plan?

The easiest way to keep taxes from fouling up your well-laid funding plans is to simply pay the taxes out of the rest of your budget and leave your funding essentially unaffected by taxes. Another alternative, of course, is to invest in a tax-free vehicle, such as municipal bonds. But this ploy may impact your funding plans, since the yield on tax-free investments is usually somewhat lower than that of taxable vehicles.

Borrowing from Your Long-Range Funds

Although borrowing from one fund to finance the ambitious spending of another is one of the unique advantages of the funding program, it can cause some treacherous problems if that borrowing is from long-range funding accounts. Long-range funding accounts depend on earned interest to meet their targeted expenditure goals. If you are borrowing the money yourself for some speeded-up funding expenditure, you'll have to pay the interest back out of the rest of your budget.

As always with the Financial Sanity system, you have complete freedom in the management of your financial affairs. I would just warn you, however, that heavy, chronic or long-outstanding borrowing from long-range funding accounts is probably indicative of overspending and should be viewed as a warning sign.

Growing Up: Funding Beyond a Year or Two

Although first-time Financial Sanity funders are often quite happy just to be funding for property taxes and wardrobe expenses, we all have to grow up eventually, and funding for longer-range spending targets marks a critical step in our financial maturity. However, you really know you're being financially responsible when you're funding for the financial independence of retirement. In Chapter 23 we'll discuss what goes into retirement planning and how you can start on that road to financial independence.

We will either find a way, or make one.
—*Hannibal*

20

Balancing the Budget

At this point in your work with the Financial Sanity system, you may feel as if you have purchased an allegedly miraculous electronic appliance (some assembly required). You've been putting Tab A into Slot B for hours now, and you're eager to plug the damned thing in and see if it runs. That's essentially what we're about to do.

If this new budget of yours were an electronic appliance, the first thing you'd look for upon plugging it in would be whether the ready light went on (generally a good sign) and whether smoke started coming out the back (usually considered a bad sign).

In a budget, what you're looking for is whether the whole thing balances (there's enough income to cover all your planned expenses) and whether it's realistic (it won't "blow up" on you by setting spending guidelines that you can't maintain).

If you've followed the Financial Sanity program step-by-step thus far, there's a good chance that the overall budget you create in this chapter will come pretty close to balancing the first time through. That's because you've addressed issues of affordability in earlier chapters, especially Chapter 7, where you calculated your Spending Power, and Chapter 17, where you estimated how much of your Spending Power you could afford to devote to funding.

However, a large negative number at the bottom of your Master Budget is a distinct possibility—especially if you've skipped a few chapters to get here. Fortunately, such a shortfall is repairable—and with tools found in the average home.

When you calculated your Spending Power in Chapter 7, you were answering, in *macro* terms, the question "How much can I afford?" In this chapter, you will make sure that the budget planning you have done so far is realistic in *micro* terms—right down to a matter of $10 to $100.

The reward for completing this section is that, in doing so, you

· complete your budget, and
· know that it works!

I can't overestimate the value of this latter point. In all the previous chapters the emphasis has been on making a plan that *we know will work*. We're tired of would be, could be, should be. If you've come this far, I know you're willing to work on your finances. But I'm betting that you're unwilling to do all the work and not have your finances "handled."

Other people will continue to live in hazes of uncertainty punctuated by occasional flashes of anxiety. But if I'm right about your level of commitment, you will go through life in quiet comfort, knowing you're in control of money and that money is not in control of you. And, even better, in six months, two years, ten years—when your financial situation has changed entirely—you will have this trusty, dusty old book on your shelf, ready to be pulled down so you can do your planning all over again. You have all you need to create financial peace for yourself—whenever you want it.

Never sell this book.

The Budget Monitoring Analysis and Master Budget Summary

The mechanisms for seeing whether your budget will work are

· the Budget Monitoring Analysis
· the Master Budget Summary
· the Cash Flow Planner

The Budget Monitoring Analysis is used to budget and monitor your Income and your Expenses, both Fixed and Variable. The Master Budget Summary puts that Income and Expense information together with your earlier work on funding and debt planning to bring the entire budget together on one piece of paper. The Cash Flow Planner predicts your cash position and explains why your checking account might have a balance different from what you predicted.

Figure 20-1 shows portions of both the Budget Monitoring Analysis and Master Budget Summary used by clients Sandy and Terry to file down the rough edges of their first budget.

First Attempt		Second Attempt	
Budget Monitoring Analysis		**Budget Monitoring Analysis**	
Month	Month 1	Month	Month 1
	Budget		Budget
Income		*Income*	
Sandy's Salary	2,200	Sandy's Salary	2,200
Terry's Business	2,750	Terry's Business	3,000
Total Income	4,950	**Total Income**	5,200
Fixed & Variable Expenses		*Fixed & Variable Expenses*	
Bank Service Charges	4	Bank Service Charges	4
Church	20	Church	20
Cleaners and Laundry	50	Cleaners and Laundry	50
Telephone	40	Telephone	40
Gas and Electric	100	Gas and Electric	100
Cable TV	31	Cable TV	31
Water and Garbage	30	Water and Garbage	30
Auto Insurance	100	Auto Insurance	100
Bottled Water	15	Bottled Water	15
Medical Insurance	150	Medical Insurance	150
Health Club	10	Health Club	10
Gardener	20	Gardener	20
Sandy's Miscellaneous Cash	100	Sandy's Miscellaneous Cash	86
Terry's Miscellaneous Cash	100	Terry's Miscellaneous Cash	86
Groceries	300	Groceries	300
Entertainment	150	Entertainment	100
Gasoline	100	Gasoline	100
		Miscellaneous	100
Total Fixed & Variable Expenses	1,320	**Total Fixed & Variable Expenses**	1,342

Master Budget Summary		**Master Budget Summary**	
Month	Month 1	Month	Month 1
Income (Total from Budget Monitoring Analysis)	+ 4,950	Income (Total from Budget Monitoring Analysis)	+ 5,200
Funding (Monthly Allocation — All Expenditures from Funding Crash Analysis)	- 1,121	Funding (Monthly Allocation — All Expenditures from Funding Crash Analysis)	- 1,121
Debt (Payment for Total — All Debts from Debt Reduction Planner)	- 2,704	Debt (Payment for Total — All Debts from Debt Reduction Planner)	- 2,704
Fixed & Variable Expenses (Total from Budget Monitoring Analysis)	- 1,320.	Fixed & Variable Expenses (Total from Budget Monitoring Analysis)	- 1,342
Budgeted Increase/<Decrease> in Checking Account Balance	= —195	Budgeted Increase/<Decrease> in Checking Account Balance	= 33

Figure 20-1

Sandy and Terry, of course, had figured their funding and set their debt reduction goals before they started work on their Master Budget Summary. And, taking information about their Income and Fixed and Variable Expenses from their Inflow-Outflow Information Sheet (Chapter 6), they proposed a budget that is reproduced on the left-hand side of Figure 20-1. The detail of Sandy and Terry's Income and Expenses (both Fixed and Variable) appear in the Budget Monitoring Analysis, which is in the top part of Figure 20-1. Below that is an excerpt from their Master Budget Summary, which brings together information from three separate sources:

· Income and Expenses from the Budget Monitoring Analysis
· Funding Monthly Allocation from the Funding Crash Analysis
· Total Debt retirement payments from the Debt Reduction Planner

The result of their first attempt produced a budget that showed an obviously unsatisfactory deficit of $195 a month.

Sandy and Terry hacked away at their budget to make it balance. The right side of Figure 20-1 shows the results of their work. They decided that an extra $250 per month could be squeezed out of Terry's business if they both pitched in and worked two evenings a week. They also worried that they would inevitably forget something important in their budget, so they allocated $100 to Miscellaneous. To balance, they still needed to cut back, so they chopped $50 off their monthly Entertainment allotment and dropped each of their walking-around-money (Miscellaneous Cash on their budget) allocations to $86 from $100.

The bottom half of Figure 20-1 shows their Master Budget Summary for Month 1. Their revised budget shows Total Income of $5,200. Their outflows for Funding, Debt and Expenses suggest an anticipated cushion of $33 being added to their checking account each month.

(Ideally, Sandy and Terry might rig their budget to equal $0. The extra $33 can be reallocated to some funding account. If they want a cushion for minor overspending in the Expense portion of their budget, then they can simply open a fund called "Cushion" and allocate $33 to it each month.

But budgeting down to $0 each month is strictly a theoretical concept. There will always be some ebb and flow in your unfunded monthly expenses, and the natural cushion is the money in your checking account. There is absolutely no harm in building in a small cushion as Terry and Sandy have done. A large cushion, however, would more appropriately be made into a funding account, so that its use could be more carefully monitored.)

Now we're ready to get you started on your own Budget Monitoring

Analysis and Master Budget Summary—and to find out how well your budget will balance.

Exercise: Budgeting Your Income and Expenses
—the Budget Monitoring Analysis

1. Using your Inflow-Outflow Information Sheet as a guide, list your sources of income in the boxes labeled Income and put the amount for each source in the first Budget box.

2. Add up all your budgeted Income and put that number in the Total Income box.

3. List all your Fixed and Variable Expenses—which include everything not covered by funding or debt repayment. Your basic source for this list is the Inflow-Outflow analysis in Chapter 6, but that list hasn't yet been carved in stone—you may want to add to or subtract from the amounts and categories on that list.

4. Add up the list of Fixed & Variable Expenses and enter that sum in the Total Fixed & Variable Expenses box.

Now you're ready to find out whether this budget of yours really works—you're ready to "plug it in." For this you'll need the Master Budget Summary.

Exercise: Making Sure Your Budget Works
—the Master Budget Summary

1. Enter your Total Income and Total Fixed & Variable Expenses from the Budget Monitoring Analysis you just completed.

2. Next, put in the amount of your intended monthly contribution to funding. This number is the amount of money you plan to send to your funding account each month, and comes from the Monthly Allocation—All Expenditures box on your Funding Crash Analysis in Chapter 17. Notice that, for the purposes of this analysis, it makes no difference what the various components of funding are. Funding has become another one of the bills you pay, like rent, and never experiences any unplanned ups or downs. The overspending and underspending of funded accounts is all contained within the fund and doesn't have an effect on your budget.

3. Next, enter the amount you are allocating for Debt service payments. This number comes from your Debt Reduction Planner—the amount in the Payment box from the Total—All Debts section.

The plus and minus symbols between the description column and the Budget column are calculator keys to help you calculate the "bottom line" which, in this worksheet, is Increase/(Decrease) in Checking Account Balance. Use the plus and minus symbols to tell you whether to add the number in the box to its right or subtract it.

Basically, you're adding in the Income and subtracting everything else from it to determine whether you expect to see your checking account go up, go down, or stay the same.

4. The moment of truth has arrived. The bottom line—which predicts whether your checking account will go up or go down each month—will be either positive, negative or zero. If it's negative, you'll probably have to take action, as Sandy and Terry did, by either

- cutting expenses
- slowing down debt repayment
- planning less-ambitious funding (or—my personal favorite)
- raising income

You now have—after making a few adjustments—a budget that at least *looks* as if it will work. This brings to a close the purely planning portion of the Financial Sanity system. This moment is cause for celebration. Take some time off to enjoy the milestone you've reached. Maybe take about a month. Then we'll see you for the next exercise to examine what happened in that month with your newly minted budget.

Monitoring the Budget

Now that you have a month's worth of actual earning and spending performance under your belt, you're ready to see whether the balanced budget you've outlined is something you can actually live with— something you can maintain in the real world. This process, realistically, will take a few months of trial, error and adjustment before you can get a budget that works as well "in the field" as it does on paper. You should plan on comparing your Budget amounts to Actual amounts—making adjustments to both your spending behavior and your budget—every month for at least three months.

The monitoring process—which is performed on the Master Budget Summary sheet you just prepared—is your way of checking yourself to see how well you are implementing the plan you have designed.

Terry and Sandy—Cracking Down on Runaway Expenditures

The pretty little budget Terry and Sandy had concocted in Figure 20-1 didn't work out *quite* so smoothly in real life. Figure 20-2 shows that the couple overspent a net of $54 for the month, mostly made up for by the $190 they earned in excess of budget.

Budgeting, as I hope I've made clear already, is a decision-making

Budget Monitoring Analysis

Month	Month 1			
	Budget	**Actual**	**Difference**	**Budget**
Income				
Sandy's Salary	2,200	2,190	—10	2,200
Terry's Business	3,000	3,200	200	3,100
Total Income	5,200	5,390	190	5,300
Fixed & Variable Expenses				
Bank Service Charges	4	6	—2	4
Church	20	20		20
Cleaners and Laundry	50	41	9	50
Telephone	40	62	—22	40
Gas and Electric	100	98	2	100
Cable TV	31	31		31
Water and Garbage	30	30		30
Auto Insurance	100	100		100
Bottled Water	15	7	8	15
Medical Insurance	150	150		150
Health Club	10	10		10
Gardener	20	20		20
Sandy's Miscellaneous Cash	86	144	—58	100
Terry's Miscellaneous Cash	86	97	—11	100
Groceries	300	287	13	300
Entertainment	100	342	—242	200
Gasoline	100	129	—29	100
Miscellaneous	100	12	88	100
Total Fixed & Variable Expenses	1,342	1,586	—244	1,470
Better Than / <Worse Than> Budget			—54	

Master Budget Summary

Month	Month 1		Month 2
Income (Total from Budget Monitoring Analysis)	+ 5,200		5,300
Funding (Monthly Allocation — All Expenditures from Funding Crash Analysis)	- 1,121		1,121
Debt (Payment for Total — All Debts from Debt Reduction Planner)	- 2,704		2,704
Fixed & Variable Expenses (Total from Budget Monitoring Analysis)	- 1,342		1,470
Budgeted Increase/<Decrease> in Checking Account Balance	= 33		5

Figure 20-2

tool, not an instrument of self-torture. So, rather than sit around and mope about their failure to keep within their Entertainment budget, Sandy and Terry used the information from their monitoring to make some decisions. They looked at the Budget Monitoring Analysis and asked themselves: "What does this tell us? What can we learn from these results?"

They looked, for instance, at the $242 of overspending they did in Entertainment. They had spent almost three and a half times their budget. They couldn't just blithely say "We'll do better next time." It was obvious that an entertainment budget of $100 a month had been just wishful thinking. It was just as obvious they couldn't go on spending the way they were used to.

Sandy and Terry adjusted their budget for Month 2 to allow $200 a month for Entertainment; at the same time, they told themselves that even $200 would require severe belt-tightening.

This kind of reality check and decision-making is the essential value of monitoring a budget. As valuable as it is, however, it usually isn't painless.

Sandy and Terry made other adjustments to their budget for Month 2:

· Their experiment in double-teaming Terry's business was far more successful than they had hoped. Although they had budgeted for a $250 monthly increase in earnings (from $2,750), they achieved a $450 increase. Based on their first-month results, they felt that they could sustain a $350 after-tax increase, leaving their budgeted income target at $3,100.
· They left alone many of the budget categories that experienced only minor variances.
· They decided that it was unrealistic to keep their Miscellaneous Cash budget so low, and restored it to the $100 levels they had originally wanted before they made the cuts in Figure 20-1.
· They could have—but fortunately didn't have to—make cuts in their funding and debt reduction plans.

Terry and Sandy have a brand-new budget for Month 2. It leaves a surplus of just $5.

Notice that Sandy and Terry didn't track Budget amounts versus Actual amounts for funding and debt. That's because the contributions to funding are preset, and not affected by the spending that occurs from within the funding account. Any failure to make the required funding contribution is a complete breakdown in your budgeting system and should cause you to sit down immediately and reassess.

The monthly cash devoted to debt can be a little more variable because of the interplay of monthly purchases on credit cards. But these variances are timing differences only—they don't represent a failure to stick to your budget—and are accounted for in the Cash Flow Planner, which we'll discuss later this chapter.

Exercise: Monitoring Your Budget

1. Determine* the actual amounts of income earned in each of the categories in the Income section of your Budget Monitoring Analysis and enter them in the Actual column. Total the Actual Income in the Total Income box.

2. Enter all the fixed and variable actual expenses for the month—from both your checking account and your credit card charges (using the credit card accounting method you chose from Appendix A). Total the Actual Expenses in the Total Fixed & Variable Expenses box.

3. Now you're ready to see how your Actual Income and Expenses differed from your Budgeted. This is the crucial piece of information that will allow (and encourage) you to make decisions—decisions to alter your spending (or earning) behavior, and decisions to change the budget itself.

For each line of Income, simply take what's in the Actual column and subtract what's in the Budget column. This is the opposite of what you'll do for all the other lines on the summary. For Fixed & Variable Expenses you'll start with the Budgeted amount and subtract the Actual. This will result in a Difference column that produces positive numbers when your Actual is turning out better than your Budget, and negative numbers when you go over your Budget.

4. Next—and this is the most important part of the process—analyze the Difference column. Here are some detailed suggestions for each area:

· Income: If your difference is significant, you should know why. Were you too optimistic? If so, plan for less income and Mini-Budget (see Chapter 21) the pleasant surprises. If you did significantly better than Budget (and didn't blow it all somewhere else in your budget), consider a Mini-Budget to apply all the extra cash you have floating around.

· Fixed and variable expenses will tend to show numerous small variances and perhaps one or two large ones. The small variances can be safely ignored; the larger ones require some thinking. Is your budget merely unrealistic? Should you simply allocate more to this expense and cut back (or earn more) somewhere else? Or is it time to make a concerted effort to economize in the errant area? Maybe

*See Appendix A for tips on keeping efficient books and records.

this expense needs to be put into funding as an Annual Control Expense. Repeated spending over budget in any single account should be cause for serious financial soul-searching.

Planning Cash Flow

The Cash Flow Planner helps you understand why your checking account balance might sometimes behave differently from the way your budget had suggested. The Planner therefore starts with the very simple, three-line Cash Flow Budget at the top of Figure 20-3. Here, Sandy and Terry have noted that they have $360 already in their

Cash Flow Planner

Month of [Month 1]

Cash Flow Budget

Checking Account Balance at Beginning   + [360]

Budgeted Increase/<Decrease> in Checking Account Balance
(From Master Budget Summary)   + [33]

Projected Ending Checking Account Balance   = [393]

Actual Cash Flow Summary

Projected Ending Checking Account Balance   + [393]

Better Than / <Worse Than> Budget
(From Master Budget Summary)   + [—54]

Funding:
Budgeted Monthly Funding Allocation
(From Funding Crash Analysis)   + [1,121]
Direct Spending
(From Funding Tracking Ledger)   - [850]
Due To / <Due From> Funding Account
(This amount should be deposited in the Funding Account) +/- [271]

Deposits Actually Made to Funding Account   - [ ]

Withdrawals from Funding Account   + [ ]

Debt Reduction:
Purchases Charged to Credit Cards   + [285]
Payments:
Payments Budgeted
(From Debt Reduction Planner)   + [2,704]
Payments Made
(From Debt Reduction Planner)   - [2,861]

        +/- [—157]

Checking Account Balance at End   = [738]

Figure 20-3

checking account; they expect an additional $33 (from their Master Budget Summary), to end up with $393. So much for the fantasy portion of this worksheet.

Next the Cash Flow Planner will explain to Sandy and Terry why there is not $393 in their checking account at the end of the month, but $738. Unexplained, it's mysteries like these that drive people to financial insanity.

The explanation offered by the Cash Flow Planner centers on three basic elements:

- the difference between Actual and Budget
- Funding
- Debt

The first of these—the difference between the Actual Income and Expense and the Budgeted amount—is easily understood as an explanation for why cash didn't end up as originally budgeted. This factor is handled first in the Actual Cash Flow Summary portion of the Cash Flow Planner. Sandy and Terry merely took the −$54 Better Than/(Worse Than) Budget total from the bottom of the Budget Monitoring Analysis.

The next factor—Funding—occurs because of the method and timing of making funding contributions. If Sandy and Terry merely wrote a check for their entire monthly funding allocation sometime during the month—*and* if they made all their funding purchases out of the funding account and not out of their regular checkbook—there would be no need for a funding adjustment.

But there are many ways of handling the mechanics of moving money back and forth between the funding account and your regular cash account (see Chapter 18). In this case, Sandy and Terry made funding purchases out of their regular checking account, or charged them. Then, *after* the end of the month, they made a deposit to their funding account for their monthly allocation, less whatever they had spent during the month on funding items.

In Month 1, Sandy and Terry spent $850 on funding items. Their Budgeted Monthly Funding Allocation is $1,121. As you can see in Figure 20-3, the Cash Flow Planner calculates for them that they need to send their funding account an additional $271. In the Cash Flow Planner, this $271 increases the amount one would expect to see in the checking account, because the Cash Flow Budget assumed that the entire $1,121 funding allocation would have been made by now. The fact that $271 is still owed means that the $271 is still floating around in the checking account.

Had Sandy and Terry made any contributions to their funding account—whether for this period or for a previous or future period—

that amount would have been entered in the Deposits Actually Made to Funding Account box.

Debt works in somewhat the same way. While many programs aimed at getting debt under control just tell people to rip up their credit cards, the rule in Financial Sanity is that you can use your cards—you just have to pay them back right away. But, while "right away" means that you'll pay off new charges on your credit card as soon as you get billed for them, it doesn't necessarily mean that you have to write a check for your purchase in the same month you charge it.

Making credit card purchases, therefore, is a way to increase the amount of cash you have in your checking account without decreasing the amount of spending you do. Sandy and Terry charged up $285 on their VISA card during the month.

Next they logged their payments. Payments made are hardly ever exactly as budgeted, because you're always paying off New Charges on the cards. That's what happened to Sandy and Terry: They budgeted payments of $2,704, but paid $2,861. The net "overpayment" of $157 served to reduce the amount of cash left in the checking account.

Now that Sandy and Terry have seen how their checking account ended up where it did, let's make the same calculation for you.

Exercise: Cash Flow Planner

1. Using a format like the Cash Flow Planner in Figure 20-3 (or the blank form in Appendix B), predict your end-of-the-month cash position by taking your beginning-of-the-month Checking Account Balance and adding the Budgeted Increase (or subtracting the Decrease) in Checking Account Balance from the Master Budget Summary. The resulting number is the Projected Ending Checking Account Balance.

2. After the end of the month, enter the Better Than/(Worse Than) Budget result from the bottom of the Budget Monitoring Analysis for that month, using whatever sign (plus or minus) that appears on the Monitoring Analysis.

3. Calculate how much you owe your funding account by taking the Budgeted Monthly Funding Allocation and subtracting from it the Direct Spending that you did. The result—called the Due to/(Due from) Funding Account—is the amount you should deposit in your funding account if you haven't already done so.

In the next two boxes, enter the amount actually deposited in the funding account (it makes absolutely no difference what month the deposit is for) and any amounts withdrawn from the funding account during the month.

4. Enter Purchases Charged to Credit Cards. It does not matter whether these purchases were for funded or nonfunded expenditures, or cash advances.

5. Enter the Payments Budgeted and the Payments Made on their respective lines.

6. Use the pluses and minuses to the left of the boxes to do the math on the Cash Flow Planner. If a negative number is entered in any box, change the sign otherwise associated with the box. The "bottom line" of this analysis will tell you what your checking account balance should be. If it doesn't agree with the actual balance in your account, check your math, then check to make sure that everything in your checking account (and credit cards) is finding its way through your accounting system.

Fortune brings in some boats that are not steered.
— *William Shakespeare*

21

Bonuses and Erratic Income

Carl was a construction contractor who, with a partner, had a business building custom homes. Carl and his partner took regular salaries from their corporation, but from time to time there were additional funds in the corporation available for distribution.

During an early consultation with Carl, he mentioned that he planned to renovate a bathroom in his house with a bonus he had coming in a few months. Over the years, I have trained myself to start asking questions whenever I hear that a client plans to get a lump-sum distribution of any kind.

Carl—Spending the Same Money Three Times

"How much do you expect the bonus to be, Carl?" I asked.

"About $10,000. We take a ten- or twelve-thousand-dollar bonus twice each year, usually when we sell a spec house," Carl explained.

"Okay," I said. "Must be nice." I took out a yellow pad and scrawled "BONUS—$10,000" and double-underlined the dollar amount. "You said you were going to remodel the bathroom. How much will that cost?" I asked, already writing "BATHROOM" on my yellow pad.

Carl told me how he was going to do most of the work himself and gave me a few details, but the bottom line was that the bathroom was going to cost $5,000.

"BATHROOM—$5,000."

"That's pretty much all we have this bonus earmarked for." Carl paused. "Except"—he grinned—"for the bike."

"BIKE—"

Carl worked very hard in his business. There wouldn't be a $10,000 bonus if he hadn't. Summer was coming up, and Carl was looking forward to spending some cool evenings and warm weekends with his favorite sport—bicycling. But rather than ride the old ten-speed he bought in college, Carl was ready to treat himself to a beautiful new racing bike. Bicycling is my favorite sport, too. Carl easily convinced me of the necessity of a new $800 bicycle.

"BIKE—$800."

Since there was $4,200 left over, Carl thought it best that that money be put aside in savings, which he and his wife Beth hadn't done a lot of.

I did write down "SAVINGS—$4,200," but I did not draw off the total. And I left a lot of room at the bottom of the legal pad.

I'd had a little experience in this area. Over the years, I had begun to observe a phenomenon I call the Rule of Three. I noticed, to both my amusement and distress, that whenever people talked of large sums of "extra" money flowing in—bonuses, big commissions, loan proceeds and the like—they almost invariably had spent it in their mind— three times.

Mind you, they didn't just come right out and tell me "Bob, I'm going to spend 100 percent of it here, 100 percent of it there and another 100 percent someplace else." Instead, they plan the way Carl does.

Carl had already planned to allocate his $10,000 to a bathroom, a bicycle and a savings account. The Rule of Three in the back of my mind, I was interested in seeing how much Carl *really* had planned for this bonus.

The first thing most people forget is taxes. This is reasonable. Taxes are one of those things that everyone wants to forget. We talked a little about his tax situation and decided that Carl was looking at a combined marginal tax rate of about 35 percent.

"TAXES—$3,500."

"Shoot," said Carl. "I forgot about that. That shoots most of that $4,200 for our savings."

"Cheer up!" I said, ever the optimist. "It'll probably get worse."

I talked fairly extensively with Carl about the conversations he'd had with Beth, with his friends, his kids, his partner, his parents and so forth.

"What did you do with the last bonus?" I asked.

"Well, it seemed like it just sort of evaporated. We deposited the check and just a couple of weeks later it was spent—all on necessary things, of course. It's not like we went out and squandered it on a sports car or something. But the next month we were back to normal—short of money. I couldn't believe how fast it disappeared."

"Did you have a plan for the money?"

"Yeah, we did. We were going to use some of it to pay off our credit card debt—it was about $6,500 at the time. As a matter of fact, Beth and I sort of promised ourselves that we would pay off that debt with this bonus coming up." Carl looked a little disturbed. The conversation wasn't going the way he had planned.

"How much do you owe now?"

"About $7,500."

"CREDIT CARDS—$7,500."

We talked about the fact that he hadn't set aside money for taxes from his bonuses last year, and I found out he still owed that money on tax returns he hadn't filed yet.

"LAST YEAR'S TAXES—$2,200."

Carl had allocated the entire $10,000 to three items—a bathroom, a bicycle and a savings account. With my cheery assistance, Carl had spent another $13,200 on taxes and debt reduction in a matter of minutes. But we hadn't even talked yet about a more insidious use of funds.

Carl and Beth's most sinister cash drain came with permanent changes in their standard of living, particularly the ones they don't consciously decide on. Carl and Beth—together and separately—took the bonuses into account when they decided what they could afford. The mental dialogue went something like this: "I got (or I'll be getting) a big bonus in June. We can afford to eat out a little more often," or "Including bonuses, we pull in $60,000 a year—we ought to be able to afford . . ."

All that kind of thinking can add up. After brutal interrogation, I helped Carl identify these fairly permanent increases in their cost of living:

- son Billy's piano lessons—$500 a year
- eating out more often—$700 a year
- more expensive lunches for Carl—7 pounds and $750 a year
- an annual trip with the family to see relatives—$1,500

These annual expenses totaled just under $3,500, and you could safely assume that there were more—I rounded the total up to $4,000. But bonuses come twice a year, so the amount to be covered by this bonus would be about $2,000.

"STD. OF LIVING—$2,000," I wrote.

A couple of other purchases were destined for the list. Making some quick mental calculations as Carl spoke, I jotted down "CAR—$2,500" and "FURNITURE—$1,000." And without even consulting Carl, I penciled in "ALLOWANCE FOR OVERRUNS—$800," which I feared may have been too optimistic.

I totaled up my list:

Bathroom	$5,000
Bike	800
Savings	4,200
Taxes	3,500
Credit Cards	7,500
Last Year's Taxes	2,200
Standard of Living	2,000
Car	2,500
Furniture	1,000
Allowance for Overruns	800
TOTAL	$ 29,500

Not quite $30,000, I noticed, but I decided against telling Carl he should consider himself lucky. I had made my point, but I hadn't made any points with Carl.

"I've never had less fun with $10,000 in my life," he noted wryly. "You're a hell of a lot of fun, Bob. We'll have to get together again sometime, just for laughs."

But Carl was beginning to see the dynamics of the way he and Beth handled his bonuses. "You know," he said, "the more money I make in bonuses, the further behind I get. I'd be better off not getting them!"

Well, that wasn't quite true. However, the taxes were pretty much out the window, and the heavy lunches weren't doing anything to improve Carl's waistline. But everything else on his list was positive stuff. He and Beth just had to choose carefully what they wanted—and what they were willing to give up or postpone.

Trying the Yellow-Pad Mini-Budget Yourself

If you have any erratic or lump-sum income, try the Yellow-Pad Mini-Budget method for yourself. Try, too, to ask the tough questions that I asked Carl—to get to those unconscious extra expenditures that you make because you know you've got this particular source of income.

Exercise: Yellow-Pad Mini-Budget

1. Take out a sheet of paper. (Yellow is preferable but not absolutely essential.)

2. At the top of the page write what the source of your extra income will be and its amount.

3. Now start writing down all the things you want to do with the money, in the following order:

- spending you have no choice about (like taxes—but remember: Not all income is taxable; recipients pay no income tax, for instance, on gifts and inheritances)
- highest-priority spending
- less-important spending

4. When your spending plans equal the anticipated income, stop.

5. You now have a Mini-Budget for your extra income.

6. When the money shows up, spend it (or put it into funding) in accordance with your Mini-Budget.

The arrival of your windfall will not be quite the spectacular event it was back when you had no control, no planning. Instead of taking your spouse out to that expensive new Cajun restaurant to plot how you will spend the money, you will already know how you'll spend it. To a certain extent, the money will feel a little bit as if it were "already spent." (Of course, halfway through your blackened redfish, you'd have realized the same thing—that, even without planning, your windfall income was already all spent, perhaps more than once!)

Lest you feel that all this planning is a bit unromantic and takes all the fun and excitement about receiving extra money, let me assure you that the fun is still there. However, instead of saying "Good news, I'm bringing home $10,000!" you'll simply be saying "Good news, I'm bringing home our new bathroom!"

Let's take a look at Carl's Yellow-Pad Mini-Budget in Figure 21-1, just to see what one looks like:

Figure 21-1: Carl's Yellow-Pad Mini-Budget

Bonus		$ 10,000
Taxes	$ 3,500	$ 6,500
Standard of Living	2,000	4,500
Last Year's Taxes	2,200	2,300
Dinner Out	100	2,200
Debt Reduction—Credit Cards	2,200	0

Obviously, Carl was not able to do everything he had dreamed of doing. Notably missing are the bathroom, the savings and that necessity of life: his new ten-speed. Carl and Beth's lump-sum debt reduction plans also had to be cut back, perhaps suggesting that they should be doing more to reduce debt out of their regular monthly budget.

As you do this exercise, you might watch out for some special rules that I've developed as I work with people in this area.

You may anticipate a lump-sum payment but not know how much it will be. Don't despair. This is actually much easier to handle than you might expect.

First, determine the minimum amount that you're sure you'll receive (this amount may be zero) and do a Yellow-Pad Mini-Budget for that amount. Next, do a Mini-Budget for another chunk of additional money. Keep making Mini-Budgets until the sum of all the money in the budgets constitutes the maximum you're likely to receive.

Barbara—Ghostwriter Plans for Phantom Income

Barbara, a talented ghostwriter who took one of my early work-shops, did this for the contracts she anticipated getting one year. A certain number of assignments and income were assured her, and she based her normal, monthly budgeting on that "guaranteed" amount. She also had the possibility of two books she might work on during the year. One was worth $10,000 to her, the other $20,000. Her principal concern was $7,500 in short-term debt and her desire for a laser printer for her computer. Her Mini-Budgets looked like this:

First $10,000

Taxes	$ 2,500
Direct Expenses	750
Debt Repayment	5,750
For Fun	1,000
TOTAL	$10,000

Second $10,000

Taxes	$ 2,500
Direct Expenses	750
Debt Repayment	1,750
Contingency Fund	2,000
Laser Printer	3,000
TOTAL	$10,000

Third $10,000

Taxes	$ 2,500
Direct Expenses	750
House Fund	6,000
Fun	750
TOTAL	$10,000

"You know what I love about this the most," she said after doing her Mini-Budgets, "is that the minute I get a call about one of these contracts I will immediately know exactly what it will mean to me—not in money, but in reality. This system really puts money in its place."

Barbara was right, of course. As we discussed in an earlier chapter, money has no valid use other than getting material things. The Mini-Budget translates dollars, which are too easily misinterpreted, into the real things those dollars are—and are not—going to buy.

Big bonuses or other windfall lumps of money can cause so much havoc in our financial lives that some people who've been so "victimized" have actually claimed they'd have rather not gotten the money. Although most of us would opt to take the money and somehow deal with the resulting difficulties, Financial Sanity's simple scratch-pad technique for "mini-budgeting" windfall income is the surest way for us to make sure that we enjoy it when it arrives.

Erratic Income

Many people have erratic incomes, subject to extremely flush months and corresponding dry spells. The particular pattern of your earnings, together with your attitudes about risk, will determine what strategy you apply in your budgeting.

Some real estate agents with whom I've talked about this have decided to make their first priority the establishment of a fund with three or more months' average earnings set aside for lean months. The fund would be replenished with subsequent earnings after it was drawn down for low-earning periods.

One commission salesman client made so much money that he was able to take his first few months' earnings each year and put aside enough money to last him the entire rest of the year. Thereafter, his after-tax income—whatever it turned out to be—was available to him for whatever extra things he wanted to budget.

For people with erratic incomes, I offer the Erratic Income Technique, a system that combines two key elements:

• the establishment of a monthly Baseline Budget level—something less than your average anticipated (after-tax) monthly income;
• Yellow-Pad Mini-Budgeting;

and usually a third component:

• the quick availability of short-term credit

Baseline Budget

To illustrate how this system helps you stay in control in an environment of erratic income, let's look at an example.*

Figure 21-2: Erratic Income Example (Data)

	Monthly Income
January	$ 1,417
February	9,848
March	4,304
April	5,520
May	2,956
June	9,197
July	3,611
August	1,270
September	9,272
October	814
November	3,045
December	4,993
TOTAL	$ 56,247
Average Income	$ 4,687
Baseline Budget	$ 3,500

Figure 21-3 is a graphic representation of the same data. Notice that, although $4,687 is the average monthly income for the year, February, April, June, September and December are the only months in which at least $4,687 is coming in the door. If you tried to spend that average monthly income of $4,687 each and every month, you'd have to tap into funds other than income during those seven other "short" months. That requires an attention to the minute detail of our monthly spending that none of us should have to put up with. Besides,

*Unlike most of the examples in this book, the examples in this chapter of erratic income patterns were not drawn from experience and case histories but were created randomly by a simulation model.

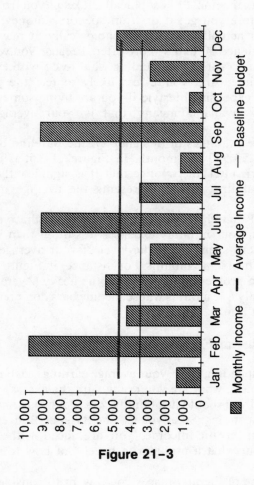

Figure 21-3

with erratic income streams you won't know that your average monthly income *is* $4,687 until you get to the end of the year.

To build some conservatism into the system and to avoid the need for minute management of our monthly spending, it's helpful to establish a Baseline Budget. A Baseline Budget is nothing more than a somewhat conservative, somewhat pessimistic estimation of your monthly after-tax income. Philosophically, it keeps you from spending your money before you get it or from spending money you hoped to get but never actually receive. Psychologically, it may allow you to feel the experience of luxury more often, because you will be faced with the delightful "chore" of deciding what to do with excess funds from time to time. And you're less likely to feel the pressure of maintaining an expensive lifestyle if you are living somewhat below your technically available means (that is, your average monthly income).

In most of the examples in this chapter, the Baseline Budget level has been set at $3,500 per month. In Figure 21-3 it is represented by the thin, horizontal line. Notice that it is significantly below the heavy horizontal line, which represents the average monthly income.

As a practical matter, a Baseline Budget means that your income will be less than your monthly expenses less often than if you were trying to maintain spending at the level of your average income—creating fewer "problem" months. For instance, in Figure 21-3, while there were seven problem months below the heavy (Average Income) line, there are only five months whose income bars don't reach the thin Baseline Budget line.

The Mechanics of Erratic Income Technique

If you aren't spending all of your average earnings each month, you might very well ask, what are you doing with the excess?

Heaven forbid you should just blindly *save* it! As you know by now, I believe only in spending. So, if you use the Baseline Budget technique to manage your erratic income, you are faced with a problem periodically—but what a problem to have!—of how to spend your extra money.

Obviously, one of the first places you'll want to consider spending extra money is contributing to a Contingency Fund to be used to replace income in those months when you earn less than the Baseline Budget amount.

Figures 21-4 and 21-5 reveal a classic scenario of the Erratic Income Technique successfully at work.

Figure 21-4: Erratic Income Technique at Work (Data)

Monthly Income		Average Income	
January	$ 6,763		$ 4,120
February	3,788		
March	1,011		
April	4,205	Baseline Budget	
May	8,295		$ 3,500
June	1,009		
July	3,388		
August	2,691		
September	4,792		
October	2,422		
November	5,080		
December	5,999		
TOTAL	$ 49,443		

The heavy line in Figure 21-5 labeled Funds Available represents the accumulation of money over and above the Baseline Budget outlays. Some of this accumulation, of course, must be available to cover the short months of March, June through August and October. The heavy black line drops down in those months, as some of the accumulated money is used up. The rest of the accumulation, however, is available for funding other expenses and purchases.

In Figure 21-5, March's pathetic showing was covered by funding left over from the extremely high income of January. But things don't always work out so conveniently. Figure 21-6 shows what happens when the income pattern isn't front-end loaded and borrowing options have to be exercised. The gray curve from February through May represents borrowing that had to occur to maintain spending at the Baseline Budget level.

With the earnings pattern exhibited in Figure 21-6, a borrowing facility (line of credit, credit card cash advance, etc.) of more than $4,000 would have to be available to take us through the shortfall months of February through April. Then cash would build up in May through August to such an extent that the tremendous shortfall of September (looks like a month-long vacation in the Caribbean to me) would be completely covered.†

Almost never will you know what the average income is turning out

---

†The total Funding Available for Yellow-Pad Mini-Budgeting will always be the monthly Average Income (straight heavy line) and the monthly Baseline Budget (straight thin line) times the number of months involved.

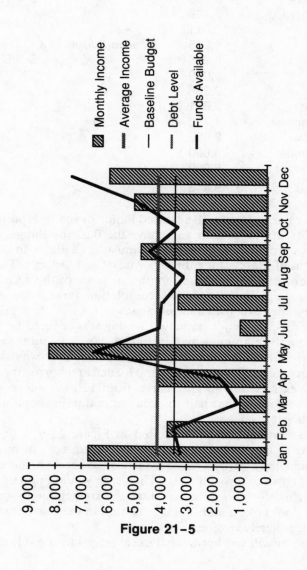

Figure 21–5

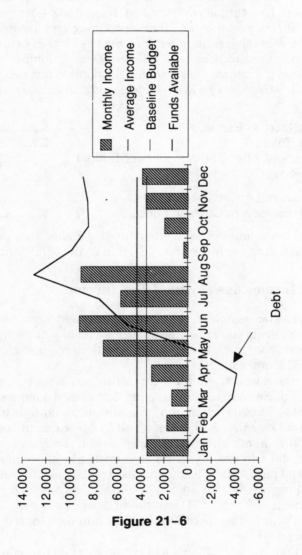

Figure 21–6

to be until you get well into the year. So, depending upon how erratic your income can get, you may want to keep some of your excess funds available for low-income months rather than having to borrow. For instance, a person with the income pattern demonstrated in Figure 21-6 might try (through Yellow-Pad Mini-Budgets) to accumulate about $4,000 in a reserve fund that serves no other purpose other than as a cushion in the lean months. This might effectively ensure that he would never need to borrow to get through any month.

Using this plan, then, your monthly (I would do this every month — it's more fun) Yellow-Pad Mini-Budget would invariably start out like this:

Total Income Earned	$_____
Less Taxes	$_____
Excess of After-Tax Income over Budget Baseline	$_____
Repayment of Short-Term Debt	$_____
Accumulation of Cushion Funds	$_____

and would continue on with other funding items that, presumably, would constitute the more "fun" portion of the Mini-Budget.

Erratic Income Isn't Always Big Income

"Your erratic income planning methods might work fine for these high-roller clients you're talking about," some of you might be saying, "but what about me? My income's erratic, too. Some months it's enough. The other months it isn't."

One woman who saw me for consulting was a sales representative for a large business machine company. She earned a modest but fairly comfortable $3,000 each month. In addition, about four times a year she received incentive bonuses of about $1,500 each. Instead of living off $3,000 a month and making special Mini-Budgets for her additional $1,500 bonuses, Doris became misled by those months when she was making $4,500. She built up her regular cost of living to match about 80 percent of that $4,500 "monthly" income. There was just one problem, of course: Doris didn't have a *monthly* income of $4,500. A year in the life of Doris's slide into debt looked something like Figure 21-7.

In less than two years, Doris had run up $10,000 in credit card debt. Even by the time she had recognized her problem enough to come talk to me, she still did not see how she had been tricked by her quarterly bonuses. She came to me hoping to find some way to continue her standard of living (without raising her income). And when we talked

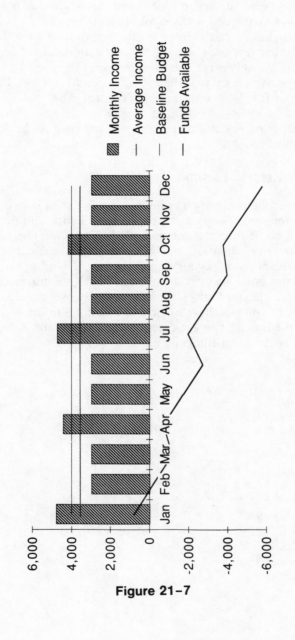

Figure 21-7

about ways to reduce her monthly living costs, she didn't feel like she could really give up much of anything—beyond her monthly manicure—and she complained loudly about that.

If you do have erratic income that's only sufficient in its high months, you are just simply living beyond your means. The months of high income are only serving to trick you into thinking you can afford your lifestyle. You need to reduce your expenditures (see Chapter 24) and pull your inflow and outflow into control. The "extra" income of the higher months—if reliable enough—can be used to fund nonmonthly expenses and thereby reduce the need for heavy monthly funding contributions.

Life with Erratic Income

Erratic income is clearly a complicating factor in budget planning, one that often leads people to throw up their hands and do no budget planning at all. But erratic income can be fun, too. The key is to set down a baseline standard of living that doesn't depend on the unguaranteed portion of your erratic income. Then use Mini-Budgets for the erratic portions of your income. That's the fun part—but it's fun only because you know your baseline expenses are taken care of.

For those of you who have no erratic income, I'm sorry you've been left out of the fun. Maybe you can create a little erratic income, just so you can play the Mini-Budget game.

Buy land. I hear they aren't making any more of it.
—*A paraphrase of Will Rogers*

22

The Essential Financial Guide to Buying a Home

The purchase of a home—the most significant and stressful financial transaction most of us ever make—is at once both complex and familiar. On one hand, it involves more money than almost any other financial decision we make. Our homes are very often the largest component of our Net Worth and often, too, a significant component of our retirement planning.

Adding to the complexity are the legalities of real estate transactions and the almost unfathomable varieties of mortgage loans. No modern home transaction can be made without an eye for inflation—but if our best economists can't predict inflation, what's a financial "civilian" to do? Finally, our real estate investments get us more involved in tax issues than most other parts of our financial lives.

On the other hand, residential real estate is fundamentally familiar to us. We've lived in it all of our lives—we literally know the product from the inside out. Further, owning our own homes is the corner-stone of the American Dream and has been for generations. Everybody gets into the real estate act. Everybody has an opinion, theory, warning or experience to share about real estate. And what you hear from your dental hygienist or the guy who owns the body shop may be every bit as instructive as what you hear from the lawyers, accountants and "financial experts" you may know.

The real estate business is essentially a cottage industry, with relatively easy entry. It's an area where instinct, taste and gut-level judgments can be as important as more technical aspects of analysis.

The complex-yet-familiar dichotomy of real estate adds up to one thing: A lot of people end up getting involved in an area more complex, perhaps, than all the rest of their financial dealings combined. That's why buying a home deserves its own chapter in Financial Sanity.

Getting Started

We've already talked about some of the planning considerations of buying a second house, and we've outlined some of the analytical tools. We tracked Sam and Wendy's four-year odyssey to build up their ability to afford the next house they wanted to buy—even in the face of escalating home values. That work we did in Chapter 9 is an important part of the technology of analyzing your real estate buying options.

In this chapter we will discuss an even earlier problem: how to buy your *first* house.

In Chapter 9, when Sam and Wendy were calculating how big a mortgage they could afford, they started their calculations already knowing how large a monthly mortgage payment they could afford. Unfortunately, however, that one little number is often difficult to estimate. It may be easy to estimate how much you can afford in car payments or how much you can afford to spend each month eating out. You have, by this time, mastered the basics of that kind of budgetary decision-making.

But how much you can afford in mortgage is complicated by one major factor—taxes. It is simplistic—and wrong—to say "I pay $1,000 a month in rent, so I guess I can afford $1,000 a month in mortgage payments." The tax advantage of deductible home mortgage interest will allow you to afford substantially more in tax-deductible mortgage payment than you were affording in nondeductible rent.

We approach the question of affordability of mortgage payments from two angles. The first approach will answer the question "How much can I afford in mortgage payments?" The second approach may be more useful to you when attempting to reach a goal of affording a particular class of home. It answers the questions "How far am I from affording the home I want? How much money do I need to free from the rest of my budget in order to afford this house?"

In both approaches, the complicating factor is taxes. The analyses you learn in this chapter, together with those presented in Chapter 9, should leave you quite competent a real estate buyer—knowing precisely what you can and can't afford and knowing what's required in order to make the purchase of what I hope is your dream home a reality.

Both approaches require that you know your tax rate, and calculating that rate is exactly what the Tax Multiplier Worksheet was designed for.

Anne and Daniel Ryan were both in the marketing department of the same company when they met, and they later married. For the first two years of their marriage they lived in a modern condominium they rented for $1,000 a month. Between them, they made $65,000 a year. They had, from the first, talked about buying a little house, and they kept up a fairly regular savings program to accumulate a down payment. They averaged about $150 a month and had saved about $4,000 in a little over two years.

Anne and Daniel came to me with what is probably the single most common question I get asked. Regardless of how the question is framed, people essentially want to know if they can afford to buy a house and, if so, how expensive a house.

Using the Tax Multiplier Worksheet

Figure 22-1 is an oversimplification of a potentially complex aspect of your financial life. If your tax profile is at all complex, I suggest that it will be worth your while to have a tax professional calculate your anticipated tax and tax rates.

But the vast majority of readers probably have tax situations that are not complex. The Tax Multiplier Worksheet is designed to let you estimate what your marginal tax bracket is without making any involved tax calculations. But, because it's a simplified method, it may yield misleading results if you

• have complicating factors that substantially affect your taxes;
• have an income that is close to the dividing line between the 15 and 28 percent bracket.

With these caveats in mind, let's see how the Ryans found out what their marginal tax bracket was using the Tax Multiplier Worksheet.*

---

*The Tax Multiplier Worksheet is based on tax rates for 1988 and should be usable until there is, inevitably, major change in the tax law.

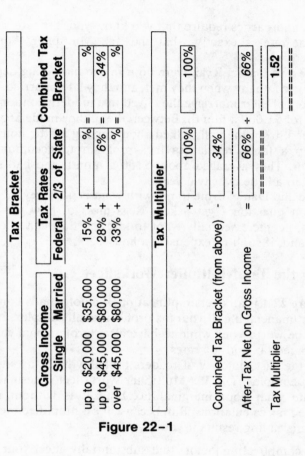

Tax Multiplier Worksheet

Tax Bracket

| Gross Income | | Tax Rates | | Combined Tax |
Single	Married	Federal	2/3 of State	Bracket
up to $20,000	$35,000	15% +	% =	%
up to $45,000	$80,000	28% +	6% =	34%
over $45,000	$80,000	33% +	% =	%

Tax Multiplier

	+	100%
Combined Tax Bracket (from above)	-	34%
After-Tax Net on Gross Income	=	66%
Tax Multiplier		1.52

Figure 22–1

The Ryans make $65,000 between them, so they land squarely in the "up to $80,000" (28 percent) bracket of Figure 22-1. Being California residents, they are subject to a top state tax rate of about 9 percent, two thirds of which is 6 percent. They added the 6 percent to the federal 28 percent to get an estimated combined tax bracket of 34 percent.

The rationale for using only two thirds of the state rate has to do with the fact that state taxes are deductible on the federal return. In all but the lowest tax bracket, federal tax rates are either 28 or 33 percent—close enough to one third for estimating purposes. Since one third of any state taxes paid, therefore, are "paid back" by the federal government in the form of reduced federal tax, it's equivalent to the state taxes being two thirds of their stated rate. The two-thirds rule works pretty well for the 15 percent federal bracket, too—not so much because of the federal deductibility but because, at those lower incomes, state taxes are probably at lower brackets than the maximum. Remember: This is all an estimate. If you want or need more accuracy, ask your tax advisor to prepare a tax projection for you.

Mortgage Affordability for First-Time Buyers

Next, I led the Ryans through the analysis in Figure 22-2. The Mortgage Affordability Worksheet for First-Time Buyers allows people new to the housing market to convert what they spend in rent and savings (neither of which are tax-deductible) into an equivalent dollar amount of tax-deductible mortgage and tax payments.

Daniel and Anne's $1,000 monthly rent plus their $150 monthly savings rate were both available to apply to house payments. They totaled $1,150. Balanced against this available cash, however, were some increased expenses (not tax-deductible) that the Ryans would also need to pay—cutting into their capacity to pay a monthly mortgage.

They already had renter's insurance, but their homeowner's insurance would be more. And, although their utilities were included in their condo rent, they wouldn't be when they moved into their own home. The $60 average utilities bill, added to the $75 per month increase in insurance costs, trims $135 off the $1,150 that would have been available for mortgage and property taxes. That leaves the Ryans with a disappointing $1,015.

But take heart! I advised Anne and Daniel. The tax multiplier of 1.52 that they had calculated magically converts their meager $1,015 to $1,543 available for both mortgage and tax payments.

"I understand that tax deductibility makes things less expensive,"

Mortgage Affordability Worksheet — For First-Time Buyers

Sources of Funds:

Monthly Rent
Monthly Amount You Currently Spend on Rent   + 1,000

Other Housing Costs
Include Any Associated Costs, Such as Garage Rental   +

Monthly Savings
How Much You've Been Able to Save Each Month
  That You Can Apply to Monthly Housing Costs
  *(Do not include savings that you intend to continue
  setting aside for other purposes.)*   + 150

Avoided Costs
Any Monthly Costs You Will No Longer Incur as a Result of Moving
  (An example might be a net reduction in commuting costs.)   +

Other Available Funds
*(This might include income from a rental unit on the purchased property
  or any expected funds inflow as a result of the move.)*   +

Total available cash   = 1,150 +

Nondeductible Costs:

	New		Old			
Insurance	+ 100	-	25	=	75	+
Utilities	+ 60	-		=	60	+

Other Increased Costs
*(Include increased commuting costs,
  gardening, cable TV, etc.)*   +   -   =   +

Total Nondeductible Increased Costs   = 135 -

Net Available for Mortgage and Taxes   1,015 =

Tax Multiplier   *(From Tax Multiplier Worksheet)*   x 1.52

Maximum Justifiable Monthly Payment for Mortgage and Taxes   1,543 =

Figure 22-3

Daniel said to me, "but I really don't quite grasp this Tax Multiplier thing."

It was inconceivable to Daniel that he could obligate himself for about $1,500 a month when he only had about $1,000 a month available.

"I think it will be clear to you," I said, "if we follow your numbers all the way through the preparation of your next tax return."

I penciled out what the Ryans would be facing in taxes as a result of their house purchase. Figure 22-3 shows that, after tax savings are factored in, the higher monthly payments after the house purchase are, effectively, almost equal to the lower monthly payments before.

Whether you are a first-time buyer or not, do the next exercise. It's very short, and it will tell you your combined federal and state tax

	Before		After
Rent	1000		0
Savings	150		0
Insurance	25		100
Utilities	0		60
Mortgage & Taxes	0		1,543
Total Outlay	1,175		1,703
Tax-Deductible Items from Outlays Above	0		1,543
Marginal Tax Rate	x 34%		x 34%
Tax Savings	0		525
Net Outlay, After Taxes	1,175		1,178
	========		========

Figure 22-4

bracket—a handy number to know in a variety of decision-making situations.

Exercise: The Tax Multiplier Worksheet

1. Make sure that your tax situation isn't highly unusual before using this worksheet.

2. Find the range into which your gross income falls, in either the Single or Married column as appropriate. (The Married column assumes joint income.)

3. Read across until you get to the ⅔ of State box, where you should enter ⅔ of your state's top income tax rate, rounded to the nearest percentage.

4. Add the ⅔ of State percentage to the Federal percentage for that line and enter the sum in the Combined Tax Bracket column. This result is your marginal tax bracket. Each new dollar you earn will cost you this percentage in taxes. Each new deduction you generate will save you taxes by this same percentage.

5. If you're going to be using the Mortgage Affordability Worksheet for First-Time Buyers, you'll need to complete the second part of the Tax Multiplier Worksheet. Subtract from 100 percent the Combined Tax Bracket percentage you calculated on the top half of the Tax Multiplier Worksheet. This yields the After-Tax Net on Gross Income, which is, effectively, how much you get to keep of every additional dollar you earn.

6. Divide 100 percent by the After-Tax Net on Gross Income percentage. This yields your Tax Multiplier, which should be a number greater than 1 but less than 2.

Having completed the Tax Multiplier Worksheet, you're ready to see how much in mortgage payments you could afford if you stopped renting and bought your own place. If you're already a homeowner, however, skip the Mortgage Affordability Worksheet for First-Time Buyers.

Exercise: Mortgage Affordability Worksheet for First-Time Buyers

1. The first part of the worksheet adds up all of the *monthly* funds you have available to be converted to housing payments after you buy a house. They include

· rent
· funding or savings that you've been able to reliably set aside each month and are willing to devote to housing costs
· any other housing or nonhousing costs that will disappear (or decrease) when you move

The total of all these costs becomes the Total Available (monthly) Cash that you can reliably devote to housing costs.

2. From the Total Available Cash we must subtract any nondeductible costs associated with owning and living in your new home. Typically these might include Insurance and Utilities, but any change in monthly costs that will occur when you move should be reflected here. If you are already incurring some Nondeductible Costs, be sure to enter them in the Old boxes. Since they will disappear when you begin incurring the new costs, the old costs are subtracted from the New costs to yield a net. The net costs are added and entered in the Total Nondeductible Increased Costs box.

3. Subtract the Total Nondeductible Increased Costs from the Total Available Cash. This yields the Net Available for Mortgage and Taxes.

4. Because tax payments and the vast majority of mortgage payments are tax-deductible, you can afford to spend more than the Net Available for Mortgage and Taxes. The Tax Multiplier tells you how much more. Enter the Tax Multiplier you derived in the Tax Multiplier Worksheet and multiply it by the Net Available for Mortgage and Taxes. The product—Maximum Justifiable Monthly Payment for Mortgage and Taxes—should be entered in the last box. This is the number you can use to do all your future house-buying planning.

The Great Down Payment Race

The Ryans were a classic case of being down-payment poor, monthly-payment rich.

The primary issues of affordability in buying a house are generally the interrelated issues of

- How much *down payment* do I need/can I afford?
- How large a *monthly payment* do I need/can I afford?

Ideally, these two affordability factors should move together: Before you buy the new house, the money you *could* use to make larger mortgage payments you instead save, resulting in a buildup of cash that is available for a down payment. This is essentially the pattern Sam and Wendy used in Chapter 9 to prepare themselves to buy a new house in three to four years.

In reality, however, we're rarely dealing with a carefully planned set of personal finances, and the pattern is rarely so neat.

Two-income professional couples, for instance, can often afford sizable monthly payments but may have very little available for a down payment. It's impossible to find a pleasant little two-bedroom bungalow in my area for $200,000, but even supposing it were possible, the down payment requirement on a conventional loan might typically be $40,000.

People I counsel—especially in overheated real estate markets— are sometimes frustrated that they can't buy a house they feel they can afford (if someone would just provide 100 percent financing). If they wait, they fear they'll lose ground in the Great Down Payment Race, which dictates: "I have to buy now, because if I save money to buy next year the prices will have gone up and I'll only be further behind."

Is the Great Down Payment Race fact or myth? In truth, it is partly both.

It *is* true that real estate prices (in most areas) will go up. It is also true that most of the clients and friends I observe are further behind after waiting a year. You can win the Great Down Payment Race, as I will demonstrate shortly, but without some heads-up planning you will probably lose it. The two main reasons are:

· Although you could be saving for a down payment because you have the income to afford it, you get discouraged or lazy or undisciplined. You keep hoping income alone will bail you out.
· Yes, you're saving for a down payment, but you're not saving enough. Inflation of housing prices is working faster than you are. Remember: Your savings will get a lower rate of return than the appreciation of the home you want to buy.

Two analyses I did for Daniel and Anne highlight the true economics we face when we think we're in the unwinnable Great Down Payment Race. Both use the same set of basic assumptions:

· The target home costs $160,000 at the beginning of the analysis.
· The purchase is to be financed with a 20 percent down payment. (For simplicity of illustration, extra cash for closing costs has not been provided for.)
· Real estate in the area is expected to appreciate at 15 percent.
· Money available for funding is estimated to increase by 10 percent each year.
· The Ryans had $4,000 saved up at the beginning of the analysis.

Figure 22-5 shows the Ryans losing the Great Down Payment Race. With monthly funding contributions of only $150, inflation of housing prices causes the Ryans to go backward instead of forward. The meager $150 funding rate is just too small for so ambitious an accumulation of money in such a short period of time.

The Ryans had thought they were doing pretty well to save $150 a month regularly. They felt a little cheated when I showed them that—at this rate—they would never get there.

"How much *would* we have to fund each month to buy in—I don't

	Beginning	Year 1	Year 2	Year 3	Year 4	Year 5
Cost of House	$160,000	$184,000	$211,600	$243,340	$279,841	$321,817
Conventional (80%) Mortgage	128,000	147,200	169,280	194,672	223,873	257,454
Down Payment	32,000	36,800	42,320	48,668	55,968	64,363
Accumulated for Down Payment	4,000	6,199	8,768	11,756	15,217	19,214
Monthly Funding for Down Payment		150	165	182	200	220
	Short $28,000	Short $30,601	Short $33,552	Short $36,912	Short $40,751	Short $45,149

Figure 22–5

know—say, four years?" Anne winced as she lowered her expectations even as she asked the question.

Daniel had been flopping around in his chair, making exaggerated demonstrations of his exasperation. "Forget it!" he said. "It's impossible. We could put aside 100 percent of our income every month and we'd still never have enough for a down payment. How can you win when they keep changing the rules?"

I sat down with the Ryans to come up with the answer to Anne's question—and to allay some of Daniel's despair. The analysis I did with them is in Figure 22-6, the Monthly Payment Required to Fund Down Payment in Inflationary Real Estate Market.

We used 23 percent of the $160,000 selling price of the home—20 percent being the loan-to-value cushion conventional lenders usually like to see and 3 percent covering loan origination fees, title insurance, escrow fees and so forth. That left us with a net down payment requirement (if the house were purchased today) of $36,800. The Ryans already had $4,000 saved, so that left them $32,800 short.

Next we divided that number by $1,000 in order to use the multiplier from the table at the bottom of the analysis. Figure 22-5 provides multipliers under various assumptions of housing appreciation rates and lengths of time you might be willing to spend accumulating funds. In this case, we were dealing with Anne's goal of four years, in a housing market that seemed to be enjoying 15 percent annual appreciation. This yielded a multiplier of 26.71, which was multiplied times 32.8 to yield a monthly payment of $876.

The $4,000 the Ryans had saved already helps reduce their need for a down payment, but not as much as the Ryans might have thought. The $4,000 will be losing money each month, in comparison to the down payment need. While the $4,000 earns only 8 percent, the down payment requirement grows each month by 15 percent. (The accumulation of monthly money Daniel and Anne set aside is similarly losing ground each month, but the multiplier table at the bottom of the analysis takes that into account.)

To estimate the amount of money the Ryans needed to make up for the loss of earning power of their $4,000 nest egg, I had them fill out the box in the middle of Figure 22-5. The difference between the 15 percent housing appreciation rate and the 8 percent they were earning was 7 percent, or $280 per year. One twelfth of that was $23, which we added to the calculated $876. The Ryans' "bottom line": If they set aside $899 a month for four years, Daniel and Anne could buy the $160,000 house they wanted four years from now, even though that same house will have become considerably more expensive at that point.

To see how the dynamics of this funding program put the Ryans closer and closer year by year, see Figure 22-7, which shows that at the end of Year 4, when the target house is now almost $280,000, the Ryans will have accumulated $63,724, slightly more than the $63,664 required for a down payment.

Monthly Payment Required to Fund Down Payment in Inflationary Real Estate Market

Current Purchase Price of Desired House	$160,000

Down Payment Percentage for Conventional Loan *(Usually 20%)*	+	20%	
Typical Closing Costs in Your Area *(Use 3-5% if you don't know.)*	+	3%	

Percentage of Purchase Price Needed in Up-Front Cash   x   23%

Total Down Payment Requirement for Conventional Mortgage   +   36,800

If Some Funding Money Has Already Been Accumulated:

Less Amount Funded to Date	4,000	-	4,000
Estimated Annual:			
Appreciation Rate of Housing +	15%		
Less Interest Rate on Invested Funds -	8% x		
=	7%		
Annual Inflation Differential	280		
	÷ 12		
Monthly Funding to Make up for Inflation Differential	23		

Amount Needed to Fund for Down Payment   = $32,800
÷ $1,000

32.8
x
Multiplier   *(from table below)* $ 26.71

+   876

Monthly Funding to Make Up for Inflation Differential   *(From Above)*   +   23

Monthly Funding Required to Reach Down Payment Goal   = $899
*(Note: Unlike regular long-range funding calculations,
this amount should be increased annually to reflect normal inflation.)*

**Monthly Payment Required to Accumulate a $1,000 Down Payment
(in Current Dollars)   in a Highly Inflationary Real Estate Market**

		Time to Build up Down Payment			
		2 Years	3 Years	4 Years	5 Years
Expected	10 %	44.18	29.69	22.44	18.09
Rate of					
Appreciation	15 %	48.13	33.81	26.71	22.51
in Cost					
of House	20 %	52.25	38.29	31.57	27.77

Figure 22-6

	Beginning	Year 1	Year 2	Year 3	Year 4
Cost of House	$160,000	$184,000	$211,600	$243,340	$279,841
Down Payment	36,800	41,860	48,139	55,360	63,664
Accumulated for Down Payment	4,000	15,524	29,125	45,085	63,724
Monthly Funding for Down Payment		899	989	1,088	1,197
	Short $32,800	Short $26,336	Short $19,014	Short $10,275	Over $60

Figure 22-7

Exercise: Monthly Payment Required to Fund Down Payment in Inflationary Real Estate Market

1. Using a format similar to that in Figure 22-6 (a blank form is available in Appendix B), enter the purchase price of the home you want to buy. Use today's cost.

2. Calculate the percentage of the Purchase Price you'll need in up-front cash by adding:

- the Down Payment Percentage (often 20 percent and generally between 5 percent and 25 percent) and
- estimate of the Closing Costs customary in your area and appropriate to the loan you'll be getting ("points," or origination fees, typically run from 0 to 2½ percent; escrow, title insurance and other fees will also apply)

3. Multiply the percentage obtained in Step 2 by the Current Purchase Price of the property. This results in the Total Down Payment Requirement (in today's dollars).

4. If you already have a running start on accumulating money for this down payment, enter it in both boxes of the line labeled Less Amount Funded to Date. In the right-hand column of the worksheet, subtract the Amount Funded to Date from the Total Down Payment Requirement to yield the Amount Needed to Fund for Down Payment.

5. If you have accumulated funds, complete the mini-worksheet inside the large box in the middle of the analysis. Subtract the interest rate you expect to receive on your invested funds from the appreciation rate you're expecting in the local housing market. The net percentage should be multiplied by the Amount Funded to Date. The result—the Annual Inflation Differential—is, in dollars, how much you expect to be "going backward" as your invested funds fail to keep up with inflation in the housing market.

Divide the Annual Inflation Differential by 12 to obtain a Monthly Funding to Make Up for Inflation Differential. This is the approximate amount of money that you'll need to contribute each month to make up for the loss of value of your already accumulated invested funds. Enter the same amount on the second-to-last line of the analysis.

6. The Amount Needed to Fund for Down Payment should be divided by $1,000, to yield a number that will work with the Multiplier we are about to derive.

7. From the table at the bottom of the analysis, find the expected rate of appreciation of real estate in your area. (The number you select—10, 15 or 20 percent—should correspond with the Appreciation Rate of Housing you used in the mini-analysis.) Read across the line appropriate to the appreciation rate you selected until you reach the column representing the number of years you plan to spend accumulating cash for the down payment. The number at the intersection is your Multiplier.

8. Enter the Multiplier and multiply it by the result you got when you divided the Amount Needed to Fund by $1,000. The resulting product is the amount you'd need to set aside each month if it weren't for the fact that you have to make up for the loss of purchasing power in your invested funds.

9. Add the result you got in Step 8 to the Monthly Funding to Make Up for Inflation Differential you got in Step 5. The result is the Monthly Funding Required to Reach Down Payment Goal.

10. At the beginning of each year, add 10 percent to the amount you have been funding for the twelve months of the previous year and use that amount as your funding amount for the course of the upcoming year.

If You're Not a First-Time Buyer

The exercise we just completed is primarily useful to first-time buyers. Homeowners (at least those in robust real estate markets) rarely have difficulty coming up with a minimum down payment if they are selling their old home and applying their equity in it to the sale of the new home. If you are hoping to keep your old place as a rental, however, you should do this analysis for the new house you'll buy.

If this is your second house purchase and you are using this analysis anyway, put the Net Realizable Value of your current home in the right-hand box of the Less Amount Funded to Date line, but don't perform the calculations in the large box in the middle of the page. Because your home will (presumably) rise in value at the same rate as the home you're planning to purchase, your net realizable value will not lag behind the value increase of the new house. (In fact, it will probably rise faster than the down payment requirement will, due to your leverage: 100 percent of the increase in the property value accrues to the net realizable value, even though you may only "own" 25 to 30 percent of the house, after mortgages.)

The Great Down Payment Race is winnable, but not easily. High-income people with no cash for a down payment can—even in a highly inflationary real estate market—buy their first house using conventional financing and without resorting to help from family members. But to accomplish this feat, substantial monthly funding will be required.

The classic 80 percent loan-to-value mortgage isn't the only alternative the high-income home buyer has. A substantial number of young (and even not so young) first-time buyers receive some help from their parents. Second mortgages—carried by family, private investors or the sellers of property—are another alternative especially appropriate for high-income buyers in escalating real estate markets. Finally, there are a wide variety of loans that don't require 20 percent down, available especially to buyers with high incomes in areas where real estate values are firm or escalating. Again, however, putting together a 10 percent down payment is likely to appear almost as difficult as putting together a 20 percent down payment. The techniques outlined in this chapter will work just as well for any down payment.

In Appendix A you will find another analysis format—the Mortgage Affordability Worksheet for Second-Time Buyers. It works in a manner similar to that for first-time buyers. It

- calculates the increase in tax-deductible expenses
- uses the Tax Multiplier Worksheet to convert the change in tax-deductible expenses to a nondeductible equivalent
- calculates the increase in nondeductible expenses
- adds all the increases to derive the total extra money needed per month
- subtracts all the known sources of extra money
- tells you how close you are to (or how far from) being prepared to afford the payments you will be required to make

Since the techniques of the analysis are similar to those we've discussed throughout this chapter, I will not go through detailed instructions here. Use the analysis to calculate how much juggling around you'll have to do in your budget to afford the house you want.

Knowing that it will work has been a recurring theme of this book. You don't want to make a tremendous budgetary sacrifice to save for a down payment, only to find yourself beaten in a race you really had no chance of winning. On the other hand, if you can *know* approximately what it will take to accomplish your goal, you can make an informed commitment to it—or an informed decision to pursue an alternative path.

For Age and Want save while you may;
No morning Sun Lasts a whole Day.
   —*Poor Richard's Almanack*

23

Achieving Financial Independence

Retirement planning is, fundamentally, just like any other funding project, except for two differences. First, retirement planning presents some limited opportunities for tax-advantaged funding that are not generally available for other long-term projects, such as funding for a child's college education. Second—and the focus of this chapter—is the difficulty in determining just how much money you'll need to attain financial independence.

How Much Do You Need for Retirement?

Retiring essentially involves achieving financial independence. Financial independence is defined as having enough money to support your lifestyle and living expenses without having to earn any more money (other than the earnings from investments). So what we're calling retirement planning is really planning for financial independence and has nothing to do with how old you might be or even whether or not you choose to stop working when your goals are met.

The obvious question then becomes: How much do I need every month to support my lifestyle? Figure 23-1, Calculation of Retirement Income Requirement, provides a worksheet for calculating the amount of monthly income you'll need. Some financial advisors, based on flawed reliance on a government study, suggest you target 80 percent of your preretirement income. It doesn't take much imagination, however, to see that people's retirement income requirements are likely to vary wildly. It's much safer and more prudent to actually calculate your needs, and that's why I've provided Figure 23-1.

Once you've estimated your monthly income requirements after

Calculation of Retirement Income Requirement

Current Monthly Income	*(after withholding)*	+	4,000

Subtract:
Eliminated Funding
Items currently being funded which won't need to be funded after retirement

Income Taxes *(Taxes after retirement will be added in below)*	
Retirement Funding	300
College Education Funding for Matt Jr.	250
Life Insurance	200

Total Eliminated Funding	-	750

Eliminated Expenses

Commuting	120
Mortgage Payments *(if your house will be paid off by then)*	1,100

Total Eliminated Expenses	-	1,220

Add:
New Funding

Travel	1,000
Sports/Leisure	
Medical	

Total New Funding	+	1,000

New Monthly Expenses

Medical Insurance *(increase over current costs paid by you)*	100
(Use today's rates for a person of your planned age of retirement.)	
Rent *(if selling residence)*	
Swim Club Dues	80

Total New Monthly Expenses	+	180

Total Monthly After-Tax Requirement	=	3,210

Tax Factor *(Use Tax Multiplier Worksheet.)*	x	1.50

Monthly Pretax Income Requirement		4,815

Figure 23-1

retirement, you next calculate the lump sum of money you need to have accumulated to provide this income. The worksheet in Figure 23-2, Capitalization of Monthly Retirement Income Requirement, leads you through this analysis.

Finally, you may want to balance what you can afford to fund each month against your aspirations for early retirement. The Retirement Planning Alternatives Worksheet in Figure 23-3 is designed to let you do that easily.

Let's walk through each of these worksheets. As we go, we'll follow along as Lisa and Matt Pettit, a small-town dentist and her working husband, plan for their own—preferably early—retirement.

Calculating Your Income Needs After Retirement

Essentially, the calculation of your postretirement monthly income starts with the income you're earning now and merely makes adjustments for changes in your spending patterns after you retire. Your funding needs will change—you won't need to fund for retirement, for one thing—as will your expense patterns. Some of the expenses you incur now (commuting costs, for instance) will disappear, while other expenses will go up.

Matt and Lisa begin their retirement planning by entering the $4,000 they take home each month on Figure 23-1 in the Current Monthly Income box.

Next, they look through their funding categories to determine which will have disappeared by the time they are retired. Retirement funding, of course, will be unnecessary after they achieve permanent financial independence. So, they feel, will be the need for life insurance. They are currently funding the premiums at the rate of $200 a month. Finally, Matt Jr. will be through college by then, so they won't still be putting aside $250 for that.

Their Total Eliminated Funding adds up to $750.

There are also some expenses in their current budget that will disappear or be substantially reduced. They won't be spending the $120 it costs them to commute to their jobs. And they plan to eliminate their $1,100-per-month mortgage. We'll discuss methods for "getting your mortgage to retire when you do" later on in this chapter.

These two eliminated expenses reduce by another $1,220 the amount of monthly income the Pettits will need when they retire.

There are, however, some expenses and new funding which will increase after retirement. Travel plans loom large for Matt and Lisa, who have found it difficult to get away from family and professional responsibilities and pursue their love of faraway people and places.

They expect to budget $1,000 a month (all the numbers on this analysis are in today's dollars) for travel after they stop working.

Matt and Lisa believe their medical insurance will be $100 more than they are currently spending, and they plan to join a local swim club. These expenses will add another $180 to their postretirement monthly budget, for a net after-tax income requirement of $3,210.

The Pettits use the Tax Multiplier Worksheet (like the one found in Figure 22-1) to calculate that their Tax Factor is 1.50, which they multiply by the net of $3,210 to obtain a Monthly Pretax Income Requirement of $4,815.

This amount is the Pettits' best guess at what they must have coming in each month—before taxes and expressed in today's dollars—after they stop earning income from their jobs.

Now, let's have you calculate your postretirement income needs.

Exercise: Calculation of Retirement Income Requirement

1. Enter your net monthly income (after withholding) on the first line. (If you pay your taxes through estimates, you can wait until the next step before removing taxes from your gross income.) We remove taxes at this point in the calculation, then add them back at the end.

2. Scan the list of the items you are funding for—you can look at your Funding Crash Analysis—and write down any funding you are currently doing that you won't need to do when you've retired. I've already put Retirement Funding on the list for you, as well as Income Taxes. If you're self-employed or otherwise required to make estimated payments or fund for an April 15 balance due, you should remove that amount of monthly funding from your postretirement budget. You'll add the taxes back in at the end.

3. Similarly, some of your current income goes toward expenses, such as commuting, that will be eliminated in your retirement years. Scan through your list of fixed and variable expenses for candidates. You should include mortgage as an expense that will disappear only if paying off your mortgage early is part of your retirement planning. (See the section on mortgages later in this chapter.)

4. Some of your expenses, both funded and unfunded, will increase during retirement. Funding items might include travel, sports and leisure and an increase in uninsured medical costs. Expenses will probably include medical insurance but may also include other new expenses that reflect a different lifestyle. Be sure to include rent if you own your home now but plan to sell.

5. After subtracting the eliminated expenses and funding and adding the new, your current monthly income has now been modified to reflect the income you'll need in retirement. This number is entered on the Total Monthly After-Tax Requirement line.

6. Since your earnings from investments will generally be taxable, you need to factor in some provision for taxes. You can use the Tax Multiplier Worksheet in Chapter 22 to determine a multiplier appropriate to the income you'll be making when you retire.

7. The "bottom line" of Figure 23-1—Monthly Pretax Income Requirement—represents the amount of earnings you'd like to be seeing from your investments when you retire. You'll be using this number on Figure 23-2, where you'll calculate how large a lump sum of investment assets you'll need to generate this level of income.

How Big Should Your Retirement Nest Egg Be?

We know how to calculate how much to set aside each month in order to build up a nest egg of a certain size. We covered that in Long-Range Funding (Chapter 19). In order to make that calculation, however, we need to know what lump sum of money we're shooting for.

Calculating a lump sum that can produce a desired stream of income is known as "capitalizing" the stream of income. The lump sum is the capital that produces the income. Matt and Lisa capitalized their monthly postretirement income needs in Figure 23-2, Capitalization of Monthly Retirement Income Requirement, the result of which is the Funding Target that Matt and Lisa can treat as one of their long-range funding goals.

They began with the bottom line of Figure 23-1: the $4,815 Monthly Pretax Income Requirement. From that they subtracted noninvestment income they expected each month. They made a wild guess that social security would provide $200 a month. (See a discussion later in this chapter of the likelihood of social security providing you benefits.) They added a $580 monthly annuity from Matt's defined benefit pension plan. The monthly annuity estimate came from documents Matt's employer distributes annually.

These two sources of income are subtracted from the Monthly Pretax Income Requirement to obtain a net amount—that is, the Monthly Income to Be Generated by Retirement Funds—of $4,035.

Next the Pettits capitalize this income number by multiplying it by a Capitalization Factor, determined by what rate of return they expect from their invested funds. They choose a conservative 6 percent, which, according to the chart provided in the middle of the capitalization worksheet, implies a capitalization factor of 200.

To help you understand how the capitalization factor works, let's follow it forward and backward. The Pettits multiply $4,035 by 200 to yield $807,000. When they invest that $807,000 at 6 percent, it will yield $48,420 a year, or $4,035 a month.

Capitalization of Monthly Retirement Income Requirement

Monthly Pretax Income Requirement   *(from Calculation of Retirement Income Requirement)*   + [4,815]

Less:
   Anticipated Other Sources of Income

Social Security *(if you are comfortable relying on its availability)*	0
Defined Benefit Pension Plan	580

                                                    Total Other Income   - [580]

Monthly Income to Be Generated by Retirement Funds   [4,235]

Capitalization Factor:

If you expect to earn investment returns of this:	*Multiply your monthly requirement by this:*
4%	300
6%	200
8%	150
10%	120
15%	80

                                                                    x [200]

Lump Sum Needed to Generate Retirement Income   [847,000]

Add:
   One-time Costs Associated with Retiring

Moving	
Pay Off Mortgage *(This is an analytical short-cut. For a more accurate answer, leave this box blank and complete the Retirement Planning Alternatives Worksheet.)*	

                                                    Total One-Time Costs   + [   ]

Subtract:
   Assets Already Devoted to Retirement

Current value of tax-advantaged retirement plans	28,000
Less taxes on withdrawal	10,000

                                                                      [18,000]

Current value of non-tax-advantaged retirement assets	
Home *(Count only if home is to be sold. Use current value less selling costs. Make sure mortgage is paid off. Use Retirement Planning Alternatives Worksheet.)*	
Anticipated Inheritance	200,000
Sale of Dental Practice	100,000

                                                    Total Other Assets   - [318,000]

Total Retirement Funding Target in Current Dollars $ [529,000]
   (Fund with rest of long-range funding or use Retirement Planning Alternatives Worksheet)

Figure 23-2

Now showing that they need a nest egg of $807,000, Matt and Lisa next would add any onetime costs they anticipate incurring around the time they retire. Such costs may include moving costs—except Matt and Lisa don't plan to move. Some users of this analysis may also choose to show the payoff of their mortgages here; it will shortcut one of the later analyses.

Finally, the Pettits subtract all the assets they have (or will have) already available for funding their monthly retirement needs. They start with their modest efforts so far at retirement funding—annual IRA contributions that have accumulated to about $28,000. Since this money will be taxed when it emerges from the IRA account after retirement, the Pettits reduce it by an estimated $10,000 in taxes, based on the marginal tax bracket they calculated they were subject to on the Tax Multiplier Worksheet.

In addition to the $18,000 net IRA proceeds, the Pettits have two much larger sources of funds that will reduce their need to save for their nest egg. Matt expects an inheritance conservatively estimated at $200,000; and Lisa expects to sell her dental practice estimated—again, very conservatively—at $100,000. These two numbers are, like all numbers in this analysis, based on current values.

These three sources of funds reduce the Funding Target by $318,000 to $489,000. This last number is the number—in current dollars—that Matt and Lisa should try to accumulate via long-range funding. It is essentially no different from the funding they would do for any long-range funding purchase, except that the funding target is likely to be the largest in their funding program and the period over which they are funding is likely to be longer than most others.

You most likely will want—as Matt and Lisa did—to calculate the precise monthly funding contribution on the Retirement Planning Alternatives Worksheet. But before we follow the Pettits' planning process, let's calculate how much money *you're* trying to build upon for your years of financial independence.

Exercise: Capitalization of Monthly Retirement Income Requirement

1. Using a format like Figure 23-2 or a blank form from Appendix B, start with the Total Monthly Pretax Income Requirement of Figure 23-1.

2. Next subtract any anticipated sources of income. These might include social security (see below my discussion of this dubious benefit) and monthly pension benefits from defined benefit pension plans. (Pension plans that distribute funds to you in a lump sum should be entered in the Current Value of Tax-Advantaged Retirement Plans box below in the Assets Already Devoted to Retirement section.)

3. This will get you to the net Monthly Income to Be Generated by Retirement Funds. This net income must come from the earnings on your retirement nest egg. How big a nest egg? The Capitalization Factor will help you calculate this.

4. To use the Capitalization Factor, you first must estimate what rate of return you expect to get from your retirement assets at the time of your retirement. The rate of return I'm having you use in this case is the *nominal* rate of return, not the *real* rate of return we have been using in our long-range funding calculations. While 4 percent might be considered quite conservative, 15 percent is probably wishful thinking. (A return of 15 percent might also reflect a level of inflation that will make your retirement income needs rise each year.) Using a Capitalization Factor associated with a 6 percent or 8 percent return is probably safer. If your return on invested assets does turn out to be 15 percent, your conservatism will help pay for the increased requirements due to inflation.

After selecting your Capitalization Factor, multiply it by the Monthly Income to Be Generated by Retirement Funds.

5. Of course, your lump-sum retirement fund must include enough money to handle onetime costs associated with retirement, such as moving. If you have calculated your retirement income needs based on the fact that your mortgage will be paid off, you generally will be using the Retirement Planning Alternatives Worksheet to calculate what it will take to pay off your mortgage by the time you retire. But if your mortgage is a relatively small number or you are in a hurry and don't plan to analyze multiple retirement age possibilities, you may include the mortgage payoff here. This will technically result in some overfunding as you use long-range funding (which assumes there will be inflation) on a future expenditure (the mortgage payoff) that, in fact, will not be affected by inflation. Instructions for determining how much will be left owing on your mortgage when you retire are included in the instructions for the Alternatives Worksheet.

6. Finally, subtract what you already have in assets devoted to retirement. (The dollars you have set aside for retirement in your funding account are usually subtracted out in the Funding to Date box of the Long-Range Funding Recalculation Worksheet of Figure 19-3, but you may subtract them out here, if you desire. Just don't subtract them twice.) Typical entries for this section would include the amount of money in IRAs, 401(k)s, SEPs, Keoghs and your account in your employer's retirement plan. Employer retirement plans typically feature vesting schedules, limiting the amount of benefits to which you are entitled until you've put in a certain amount of service with the employer. If you're 20 percent vested, for instance, you would receive 20 percent of the amount of funds in your account. It's probably safe to include retirement plan assets at the rate of vesting that you expect to achieve at the time of your retirement or termination of employment with this particular employer.

Enter the amount in such plans in the Current Value of Tax-Advantaged Retirement Plans box.

Since you'll be taxed on your withdrawal of retirement assets, you might best subtract those taxes from the value of the retirement account. Use the rate of tax calculated in your Tax Multiplier Worksheet.

7. There are other assets that will be available to you. These might include the sale of your home, if that is your plan. (Up to $125,000 of the gain is nontaxable if you are over fifty-five when you sell, according to current tax law.) You might be expecting some sort of inheritance by that time (nontaxable, except for the estate taxes on estates of about half a million dollars or more). You might have some investment real estate that you intend to sell (you'll pay taxes on the gain). Any assets similarly available to devote to generating retirement income can be listed here and thereby reduce the demands for monthly funding to build up your retirement nest egg.

8. The bottom line of the Capitalization of Monthly Retirement Income Requirement is your long-term Funding Target. Use it just as it is, using the long-range funding techniques we discussed in Chapter 19, or use the Retirement Planning Alternatives Worksheet to test the feasibility of different retirement ages and to account for retiring your mortgage.

How Fast Can You Achieve Financial Independence?

How long will it take you to reach the point where you can retire comfortably? This is an important question to a generation that is late in starting to build up financial assets for retirement. And although I talk to few people who talk about retirement at all, those who do often speak of retiring early.

How soon you can reach financial independence is primarily a simple product of how fast you squirrel away money right now. A financial planner I knew by reputation had a phenomenal record for helping his clients achieve financial independence in just seven to fifteen years. When I examined his formula, it largely consisted of having his clients—mostly doctors, dentists and lawyers—simply put about one third of their ample six-figure incomes into qualified retirement plans.

You may not be able to cough up a cool $30,000 to $60,000 a year and retire within a decade. But the next analysis will tell you what you *can* accomplish with what you can contribute to funding each month.

Matt and Lisa, both in their late thirties, have ambitious plans to retire in their early fifties. They have therefore planned for a fifteen-year funding project. But, realistically guarding against the possibility that they may not be able to afford the monthly funding to retire that early, they also sketch out fallback Plans B and C for twenty and twenty-five years. Their three scenarios are presented in Figure 23-3.

The top half of the Retirement Planning Alternatives Worksheet deals with analyzing the payoff of the Pettits' mortgage. Their thirty-year mortgage is 84 months old at the time of this analysis, meaning it has 276 more months to run.

		Plan A	Plan B	Plan C
Years Until Retirement		15	20	25

Mortgage Payoff Funding:

		Plan A	Plan B	Plan C
Original Life of Mortgage in Months	+	360	360	360
Age of Mortgage Right Now (in Months)	-	84	84	84
Remaining Life of Mortgage (in Months)	=	276	276	276
Months Until Retirement (Multiply Years Until Retirement from Above Times 12 Months)	-	180	240	300
Remaining Life of Mortgage at Retirement	=	96	36	N/A
Monthly Mortgage Payment		1,100	1,100	1,100
Payment as % of Debt Interest Rate on Loan [12%]	+	1.625%	3.25%	+
Mortgage Balance at Time of Retirement	=	67,700	33,800	×
Payment Required to Fund $1,000* from Long-Range Funding Table (Fig. 19-2) for the number of Months Until Retirement	×	2.87	1.69	
		+ 1,000	+ 1,000	+ 1,000
Interest Rate (not Real Interest) Used* [8%]	=	194	57	

from Long-Term Payoff Planning and Prediction Table (Fig. 11-2)
or Short-Term Payoff Planning and Prediction Table (Fig. 11-1)

Retirement Funding:

		Plan A	Plan B	Plan C
Total Retirement Funding Target in Current Dollars from Capitalization of Monthly Retirement Income Requirement		529,000	529,000	529,000
Payment Required to Fund $1,000 from Long-Range Funding Table (Fig. 19-2) for the number of Months Until Retirement	×	4.05	2.72	1.94
		+ 1,000	+ 1,000	+ 1,000
Real Interest Rate Used [4%]	=	2,142	1,439	1,026

	Plan A	Plan B	Plan C
Total Both Retirement and Mortgage Payoff Funding Requirements	2,336	1,496	1,026

Use nominal (stated) interest rates, rather than real interest rates. Unlike other long-term funding targets, the amount you now estimate to be due on your mortgage at retirement will not change. It will not go up with inflation.

Figure 23-3

In Plan A, which calls for retirement in fifteen years, there would be 180 more mortgage payments before retirement, leaving a scheduled 96 payments due at the time they retired. This number—Remaining Life of Mortgage at Retirement—is used to calculate the balance due on the mortgage at the time of retirement.

Normally, this would require a financial calculator or an amortization schedule, but the Long-Term and Short-Term Payoff Planning and Prediction Tables in Figures 11-2 and 11-1 allow Matt and Lisa to calculate the approximate remaining balances without using any fancy machinery.

The Pettits' mortgage carries a 12 percent interest rate. Using the Long-Term Payoff Planning and Prediction Table in Figure 11-2, Matt finds the closest numbers to 96 months in the 12 percent column. Reading left to the Payment as % of Debt column, he determines that the percentage associated with 96 months is between two numbers, 1.60% and 1.65%, so he averages them and uses 1.625%.

Matt enters that number on his Alternatives Worksheet and divides the mortgage monthly payment of $1,100 by the percentage. The result—approximately $67,700—is the balance that will be due on the mortgage fifteen years from now.

To fund for this targeted amount, Matt uses the Long-Range Funding Table in Figure 19-2, but he uses a higher interest rate than he might normally for Long-Range Funding. That's because he knows that the mortgage payment will not rise with inflation, so his funded dollars will earn interest (relative to this targeted use) at the stated rate of earnings. Matt decides he can expect an average of 8 percent on his money for the next fifteen years. The appropriate table factor (monthly funding allocation per $1,000 of targeted expenditure) is $2.87, which Matt multiplies by the $67,700 target, then divides by $1,000 to yield a monthly payment of $194. This means that by funding $194 every month for fifteen years, invested at 8 percent, Matt will have $67,700 with which to pay off the remaining balance on his mortgage.

Next, Matt and Lisa want to determine the larger component of their financial independence funding—the lump sum required to produce the necessary income. Their requirement, based on their calculations in Figure 23-2, is $529,000. Again using the Long-Range Funding Table (Figure 19-2), Matt selects an interest rate of 4 percent (this time he's using real interest—to counteract the effects of inflation), which, for 180 months, yields a payment-per-$1,000 of $4.05. Applied to the $529,000 target, this factor yields a monthly indicated funding contribution of $2,142, which, added to the $194 mortgage payoff fund, means that it will take the Pettits $2,336 a month to reach their goal in fifteen years.

Matt and Lisa can't afford $2,336 a month out of their $4,000 of take-home earnings, so they are exploring Plans B and C, which stretch out the funding period, allowing for lower monthly funding costs.

As their incomes rise, they can recalculate their funding requirements and perhaps accelerate their planned retirement. In any case, they are now armed with a realistic, if somewhat sobering, estimate of what it will take for them to retire at various ages.

Exercise: Retirement Planning Alternatives Worksheet

1. Using a format similar to Figure 23-3 (or a photocopy of the blank form in Appendix B), select up to four periods over which you might fund for financial independence.

2. If you plan to pay off your mortgage at retirement, complete Steps 3 through 7. Otherwise, skip to Step 8. If you merely included payoff of your mortgage in your Capitalization calculation, skip to Step 8.

3. Write in the original term of the mortgage, in months, and determine how many months you've been paying on it, again in months. The difference between the two numbers is the Remaining Life of Mortgage.

4. Subtract the number of Months Until Retirement (multiply the Years Until Retirement by 12) from the Remaining Life of Mortgage. If the number is positive, enter it on the line that reads Remaining Life of Mortgage at Retirement.

5. Enter the Monthly Mortgage Payment and the Interest Rate on Loan, then use that information, together with the Long- or Short-Term Payoff Planning and Prediction Tables (Figures 11-2 and 11-1). Reading down the column representing the loan's interest rate, find the number or numbers closest to the number of months on the Remaining Life of Mortgage at Retirement line. Read left on the chart to determine the Payment as % of Debt and divide the mortgage payment by it. The result is the Mortgage Balance at Time of Retirement.

6. Apply the Long-Range Funding technique (using the Long-Range Funding Table in Figure 19-2) to determine a Payment Required to Fund $1,000 and apply it to the Mortgage Balance at Time of Retirement. However, as you do so, use an interest rate that you think you will actually earn on your invested funding money—not a real interest rate, as you normally would with long-range funding.

7. The resulting number is the amount needed to fund monthly to pay off the mortgage early. By adding it together with the monthly contribution required to build up the retirement nest egg—discussed in the following steps—you will know the amount of funding required to make your goal a reality.

8. Enter the Total Retirement Funding Target in Current Dollars from the Capitalization Worksheet. Use the Long-Range Funding Table (this time use real interest rates) to calculate the monthly funding per $1,000, then multiply that times the number of $1,000s in the total funding target. The product is the monthly funding amount required to build up your retirement fund sufficient to provide the monthly income you need after you stop working.

9. Add the result of Step 8 to the result of Step 7, if any. This is the total amount of monthly funding required to have you retire on the targeted date.

10. If the required funding is not affordable, consider a longer time frame in which to accumulate the funding, as well, of course, as other adjustments you can make in your budget to accommodate the large funding requirement.

Investing Your Retirement Funds

Retirement funding is likely to be the largest single fund in your funding system. It is also likely to be the most diversified. After a few years of making large monthly contributions, you will have a sizable amount of cash available, which you may begin diversifying into equities, bonds, real estate and so forth.

Of course, some of your retirement funds (although not likely all, due to federal contribution limits) will be in IRA, Keogh, SEP, 401(k) and company-sponsored "qualified" retirement plans. A qualified plan has been approved by the IRS for tax-free treatment—the earnings in the account are not taxed and, in most cases, the contributions to the account are made with pretax dollars.

When you make part of your retirement funding contribution to a qualified plan (and get a tax deduction for the contribution), you should increase your retirement funding by the amount of tax savings from the deduction you got. The monthly funding contribution you calculate using regular long-term funding or using the Retirement Planning Alternatives Worksheet assumes that the contributions are made with after-tax dollars—and that the contributions made now won't be taxed when they are withdrawn after retirement. But contributions made to an IRA or other qualified plan are made with pretax dollars. Less pretax money needs to be devoted to making the targeted funding contribution if some of the contribution is returned in the form of tax savings. And less money than planned will be available for retirement if some of it is taxed when it's withdrawn from the IRA and put in with the rest of your retirement assets to generate monthly retirement income.

To solve this potentially dangerous problem, divide your contributions to a qualified plan by your Tax Multiplier and pretend that you contributed only the resulting smaller amount.

For example, if you had a tax multiplier of 1.5 and made a $2,000 contribution to an IRA, and had a goal of funding $12,000 toward your retirement that year, your calculation would look like this:

Targeted Funding Contribution for Year		$12,000
IRA Contribution	$2,000	
Tax Multiplier	÷ 1.5	
After-Tax Equivalent		1,333
Net Still to Be Contributed to Funding		$10,667

What About Social Security?

What *about* social security? Will it be there when you retire? More to the point, will it be there *for you* when you retire?

My personal prediction (which is no more valid or reliable than your plumber's or dentist's opinion, so you should also consult these people) is that social security will exist but that it won't help the rich—and that if you follow the principles of this book you may be rich enough to be eliminated from the social security program.

Social security pays out benefits to recipients not with the money that the recipients contributed but with the social security taxes those of us who are still working pay. It is therefore not an insurance program, as its charter implies, but a welfare program, making transfer payments from one segment of the population to another.

The social security system inadvertently became a government-sponsored Ponzi scheme, paying off people who entered the program early not with a combination of investment profits and a return of contributed capital but by turning around and paying off the older participants with the contributions of the new entrants.

Unless you're self-employed, you probably don't have a very clear picture of just how large the social security tax is. In 1988, if you earned $45,000 or more, both you and your employer each paid social security tax (it's legally a tax—not a contribution to the fund) of $3,379.50. Furthermore, your portion (although not your employer's) was paid with after-tax dollars. You paid taxes on the money you never got (and perhaps never will get). If you and your employer did not have to make this contribution, together you could have made a contribution to a qualified plan (such as a 401(k) plan) of over $7,700. A retirement contribution of that magnitude, made every year for thirty years, would ensure an extremely comfortable retirement for you.

But social security taxes aren't all for your retirement; they're also for the people who have already retired and are collecting benefits now.

Although cutting social security benefits is something few politicians have the guts to propose, there is, understandably, growing sentiment against a welfare system that taxes the working and pays benefits to the elderly poor *and* rich alike. There is no "means test" (evaluation of neediness) associated with social security benefits.

As one commentator puts it, "We have created a system of transfer payments that shifts funds not from the rich to the poor, but mainly from the young to the old."*

We're paying now because we are, comparatively speaking, "the young." But don't forget that we're the baby boom generation. There are colossal numbers of us contributing to a program that's staying afloat because so very many of us pay into it. What happens when this population bulge decides it's lawn chair and crossword puzzle time? How much of our children's paychecks will have to go toward our retirement income?

The pressure on this retirement system—together with the other forms of intergenerational borrowing, such as the national debt—will make social security reform, according to my crystal ball, inevitable. And one of the more likely reforms, in my view, would be to abridge or eliminate benefits payments to people who had the means to fund their own retirement.†

On the other hand, changes were made in the social security system in 1983 that were designed to get us through the baby boomer crunch. If the actuaries who work for the Social Security Administration know what they're doing—and if assumptions about inflation and the state of the economy for the next several decades hold up—social security benefits will be available to the baby boomers throughout our retirement (although the outlook will be grim for our children getting any benefits).

How much should you count on receiving from social security when you're retired? The safest answer is: Don't *count* on anything. Do your planning as if you'll get not a penny. Then, comfortable in your retirement, if the Social Security Administration should elect to send

---

*Alfred L. Malabre, Jr., *Beyond Our Means: How Reckless Borrowing Now Threatens to Overwhelm Us* (New York, Vintage Books/Random House, 1988), p. 12.

†The law is already moving in that direction by making social security benefits partially taxable when recipients receive more than a threshold amount of income.

you a check each month, you can just send it to your kids. They'll need it.

In 1988 the Social Security Administration instituted a program that, for the first time, allows you to find out how much your retirement benefits might be at retirement. (Previously, this information was available only to people nearing retirement.) The form to request this information is available by calling your local Social Security office. Mail your completed Request for Earnings and Benefit Estimate Statement to the Social Security Administration, Albuquerque Data Operations Center, P.O. Box 4429, Albuquerque, NM 87196.

Getting Your Mortgage to Retire When You Do

As you can see by the worksheets in Figures 23-1 through 23-3, the question of whether or not your mortgage is still around is crucial to your retirement planning. You may be resigned to the fact that your mortgage will be a fact of life—well, for life. In this case, no adjustment should be made on your Retirement Planning Alternatives Worksheet for the disappearance of mortgage payments.

But for many people, paying off their home mortgages is a fundamental part of their retirement planning. Having your occupancy costs reduced to merely utilities and taxes is a major boon to your postretirement budget. And there are a number of schemes (not the least of which is simply acquiring another mortgage) by which you can take advantage of the equity buildup in your home to help finance retirement.

Even if you intend to keep making payments on your mortgage past your date of retirement, you may want, for analysis purposes, to assume that your mortgage has disappeared. You may not actually elect to pay off the mortgage at that time, but your planning will have left you with the money to do it.

Another way to guarantee a mortgage-less retirement is to prepay your loan. You can use the Long-Term Payoff Planning and Prediction Table in Figure 11-2 to calculate the amount of the extra payment you should make to retire your mortgage ahead of time. Some writers are great advocates of paying off the home mortgage as a method for saving. It is, however, more appropriate in some situations than in others. Accelerated debt retirement often has the advantage of offering a higher return on your invested dollar than you can get elsewhere. Very simply, paying down a loan at 12 percent will generate more interest expense savings than investing at 8 percent will generate interest income. However, accelerated loan payoffs, as an investment, lack liquidity. Once you've made extra payments, there is no way to get them back. You cannot switch to some other "investment" that is now offering a higher return than your mortgage. And you can't use the money for emergencies, interfund borrowing, collateral for loans and so forth.

Plan for the repayment of your *existing* home loan, notwithstanding the fact that you expect to buy and sell new residences between now and the time you retire. The point of retirement funding—or any funding, for that matter—is not to precisely predict what will actually happen, but to fund appropriately for the circumstances you're in right now. If circumstances change—and they almost always do—you can replan your funding based on the changed circumstances. But you'll be "standing on the shoulders" of your previous funding efforts, and you can be confident that the funding that you are doing now will be enough—that you won't be having to catch up later because you're underfunding now.

Living with Uncertainty

The analyses in this chapter appear more precise than they actually are—or could ever possibly be. The intent here is not to be exact but to develop a ballpark sense of what kind of monthly funding contribution is required to provide you with approximately the funds you need when you retire. We aren't interested in knowing that you need to put aside $543.62 per month to reach your retirement goals, but we do want to know whether the monthly funding contribution is approximately $500—as opposed to $100 or $2,000.

As you worked through these numbers, you may have also come across another rather grim realization: Retirement funding is a very costly proposition. If you are in your mid-thirties and have done virtually nothing in this area, you may discover that the amount of money you need to set aside is astronomically large.

It's not much comfort, but you're not likely to be alone. Among the clients who come to me for budgetary consultation, virtually none have done any serious retirement saving or funding. More telling, perhaps, is that these clients—usually well-compensated professionals in their late twenties to their early forties—are not even concerned yet about retirement. Their planning centers on more immediate issues: working their consumer debt down, funding for nonretirement expenditures and bringing their spending in line with their income.

It is a generational time bomb of potentially disastrous proportions. It is very possible that a great number of us will not be able to retire when we want, nor as comfortably as we want.

On the other hand, don't despair of the task at hand. If you feel behind the eight ball, please don't just throw up your hands and give up. Ease into retirement funding. Do what you can now, trying to get "up to speed" (using the calculations in this chapter) over the next couple of years.

Years from now, if we should meet at the tennis club, it is my hope that your retirement planning—indeed, all your financial management and control—will have made you prosperous enough to be able to buy me a beer.

True wealth is not a static thing. It is a living thing made out of the disposition of men to create and distribute the good things of life.
—*Franklin D. Roosevelt*

24

Financing Your Dreams

In some ways, it's too bad that there isn't one standard number that we could all calculate and use to impress each other at cocktail parties. Come to think of it, maybe it's not such a bad thing after all.

The problem of not knowing where we stand—the problem our generation faced all along—is not destined to go away. As homogeneous as this huge population of baby boomers has seemed at times, our aspirations are still too diverse for any demographer to assess by income or wealth statistics whether we, as a generation, are successful.

We are a generation without a bottom line.

How do you define *personal* financial success? It can't merely be how much money you have left at the end of the year. We've already decided that mere aimless accumulation of wealth is meaningless.

Nonetheless, after designing a budget that's both balanced and achievable, you'll become interested in keeping track of how well you're doing.

Watching Your Wealth Grow

One of the advantages that business has over personal finance is that there are only two or three ways to define business financial success.

The bottom line in business doesn't vary much from one business to another: It's net income before or after taxes and, in small businesses, before or after the owner's salary.

How, then, do any of us chart our financial success? We can't just watch our savings account grow—we abolished savings in Chapter 2. We can watch our debt shrink, but after a couple of years that sport will disappear from under our feet as we retire the last of our consumer debt. We can watch our net worth rise, but do we include in that our rising personal assets—like those expensive skis we bought last winter—or the inflationary increase in the value of our home? Using the Financial Sanity system, we will probably experience more financial success than we've experienced in years—but how do we measure it?

Not only will the definition of financial success differ from one of us to the next; it is likely to differ for each of us from one period of time to the next. For that reason, I have designed a very flexible format to define what you consider to be the important elements of financial success—and then to track them. Figure 24-1 is an example of that format.

The first section offers a number of blank lines for you to list which among your funding accounts you feel constitute wealth-building. For instance, funding for semiannual property tax payments can hardly be called wealth-building. Nor is what you're putting away to buy backpacking gear next spring. Funds like that are clearly here-today, gone-tomorrow types of accounts. They help keep you sane, but they can't really be said to increase wealth.

Include funds for retirement, on the other hand, as well as funding for starting a new business or investment program. But other funds might not be so clear-cut. Funding to buy a new car two years from now—is that wealth-building or merely a normalization of the otherwise erratic costs of buying and paying off the capital equipment necessary to transport you and your family? I don't know—you'll have to decide. I would suggest, however, that if it's the first time you've ever accumulated funds to buy a car, it might represent wealth-building.

Go through your list of funding accounts. Those that you will enjoy watching build over many years are likely to be the prime candidates for your Wealth-Building Tracker. This worksheet, remember, is very flexible and individualistic—whatever you want to include is okay.

Debt reduction is more obviously a component of wealth-building,

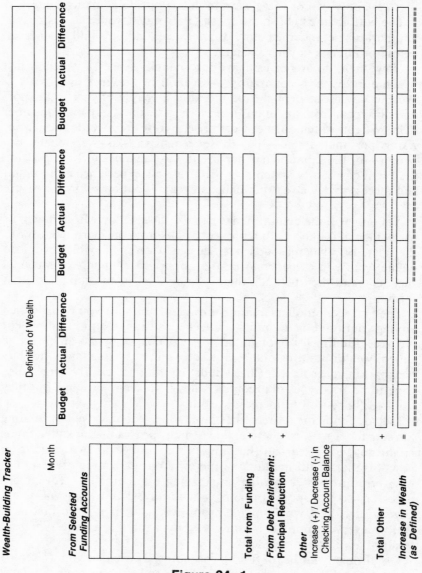

Figure 24-1

although it is often ignored. Paying off debt is one of the more profitable "investments" you can make. (Where else can you earn a guaranteed 18 to 21 percent return with no risk?) This number comes from the Principal Reduction line of your Debt Reduction Plan (see Figure 11-8), which specifically produces this number for transfer to this worksheet.

The next category is also hard to argue with: An increase in your checking account balance can reliably be considered an increase in wealth. This number comes from the Master Budget Summary or your Cash Flow Planner (see Figures 20-2 and 20-3). If it's a decrease in the checking account balance, count the number as a negative.

Exercise: Wealth-Building Tracker

1. First you must select the funding accounts whose growth you feel contributes to your wealth. There is no universal answer here; you may even want to have more than one Wealth-Building Tracker, with different criteria for each.

Accounts that normally would not be considered for inclusion in the Wealth-Building Tracker include most Annual Control expenses, like

- wardrobe
- insurance premiums
- property taxes
- gifts
- Christmas expenses
- auto repairs

and other expenses which are merely being "monthly-ized" through funding.

Accounts that almost assuredly would be included in your wealth-building calculation would include

- retirement funding
- education funding
- funding for making an investment or starting a business
- funding for the purchase of a new house
- major contingencies fund

You will have to apply more judgment and take into consideration where you already are financially when considering these funds:

- funding for purchase of your next car
- home improvements
- furniture purchases

If you've done without some of these things in the past, because you didn't have the money, funding for them now represents a major increase in your financial well-being and should perhaps be included in your wealth calculation. On the other hand, if funding for these expenses is merely lending some cash-flow sanity to the situation— you've always managed, somehow, to buy a new car of this caliber in the past—then I'd suggest excluding them from your wealth calculation.

2. The debt reduction number comes from your Debt Reduction Plan, Figure 11-8. Take the amount of the Principal Reduction line in the Total—All Debts section.

3. There may be other factors contributing to your wealth that are outside your budget, *per se.* The increase in your checking account balance is certainly one of them. (Conversely, a decrease is a negative factor in building wealth.) Get this number from your Master Budget Summary.

Other factors you may want to include might be:

- increase in the market value of your home(s) (again, I suggest using Net Realizable Value, as we discussed in Chapter 5)
- some measure of the increasing value of company-sponsored pension plans
- increase in value of various off-budget accounts and investments, such as brokerage accounts and investment portfolios
- increase in the value of your business
- increase in the cash value of life insurance policies

Again, the criteria for inclusion in the equation will be determined by you. If you feel wealthier for it, include it.

4. Total your increase in wealth. You can play other congratulatory games, too, like graphing your progress over a period of time. Getting all excited about your financial progress may seem shallow and silly, but we mustn't underestimate the value of celebration in motivating us to keep our goals and for maintaining our self-esteem. A mathematical tracking of the increase in our wealth will also help us keep a better finger on the pulse of reality: We will be less likely (than the rest of the population) to be swayed by outward signs of wealth or financial solidity when we have the "real" numbers in front of us.

5. Although the Wealth-Building Tracker as presented in Figure 24-1 with columns offers Budget, Actual and Difference columns, you most likely will start out just tracking the Actual. It is, perhaps, the ultimate in budget planning to plan the accumulation of wealth. This worksheet can work hand-in-glove with the projected Balance Sheets you created in Chapter 8.

6. Final Step: Celebrate! Celebrate all your accomplishments, even if they're less than you had hoped for. Celebration is a key factor in developing the habit of achievement. Furthermore, there is nothing like a small celebration to launch you and your partner right back into planning for the *next* milestone.

Forgotten Dreams

At this point in the Financial Sanity process, you have been supplied with a superior technology for managing your money. You are in control. If control were all you wanted, you'd be feeling eminently successful. But you wanted just a little more than that: You wanted what this book promised at the beginning. You wanted your dreams.

It's very likely that, even after all the work you've done, you still can't look at your Goals Planning Timeline and say, "All my dreams will come true." (Of course, you may never be able to say that. The person who can't dream the next dream—no matter what he's accomplished so far—suffers a poverty money can never cure.)

So, granted, not *all* of your dreams are going to come true. But will *enough* of them? Sure, you have control of your money, but do you have mastery of your dreams?

In this final chapter, we will explore the ethereal zone beyond control. We will give you a taste of a life of financial mastery, where you'll be less concerned with getting rid of problems than with making dreams come true. You'll

- plan for dreams that you've had to temporarily put aside
- watch your wealth grow and celebrate your accomplishments
- manipulate your budget to make even more dreams available to you

As you begin to plan funding in detail over longer periods of time, you have the opportunity—and the challenge—of managing what I call *funding streams.*

You find yourself dealing with changes in your funding stream when one of your funding objectives is accomplished and you no longer have to put money aside for it.

Let's say, for instance, that you have been funding $500 a month for a number of years for a very special and very expensive vacation. Your funding program was successful, you went on the vacation, you had a great time and got a great tan—now what?

All of a sudden, you've got $500 every month that you don't know what to do with. Granted, it's a pleasant enough "problem" to have, but as you advance your planning skills, you will want to have the capability of planning for these funding requirements that suddenly disappear, leaving you with the problem and opportunity of assigning those monthly funds to another need that has heretofore received less attention.

Some funding streams automatically take care of themselves—especially if you apply just a small amount of planning.

This is the source of my advice to a friend who had just made the last payment on her three-year car loan.

"Boy, it feels good not to have to make that payment anymore," Jessica said.

"What are you going to do with that extra $300 a month?" I asked her. I knew that she had not yet been indoctrinated into the Financial Sanity system.

"I don't know," she said happily, "but whatever it is, it will sure beat making car payments."

"I think you should continue to make car payments."

Jessica looked at me quizzically.

"Make the car payments to yourself," I explained. "You're going to buy a new car sooner or later, right?"

"Sure," she said. "In a year or two."

"Okay. For the next year or two, save the $300 a month in a special account just for making the down payment on your car. By the time you buy your next car you'll have a nice $6,000 in cash to make a down payment—plus whatever you can get for the car you're driving now."

"Maybe $3,000?" Jessica suggested.

"Great," I said. "So you'll have about $9,000 to put down on your new car."

"So, I can buy a $9,000 car?"

"Well, you still have $300 a month available for buying cars, right?" I continued. "On a three-year loan at, say, 12 percent, you could borrow about $8,500 with that."

"So I could buy a $17,500 car!"

"Right!" I said. "And all without skipping a beat. Just pay $300 a month whether you're paying off a car loan or not—and the down payment *and* the monthly payments will be easy for you when it comes time to buy again."

Jessica has the opportunity to level out her car ownership costs. If she didn't follow the program I had suggested, she would have an extra $300 a month to spend right now. That monthly amount of money would most likely find its way into her Baseline Cost of Living. One or two years from now, when she tried to buy a new car, she would be faced with two problems:

· She wouldn't really have much ability to make any kind of car loan payment, because she had gotten used to spending her $300 on other things throughout the month.

· She wouldn't have saved any down payment, other than what she can sell her old car for. To buy the same $17,500 car with no cash for the down payment, her monthly payments would be over $550, not $300.

Instead, with the suggestion I gave her, Jessica can now permanently stabilize her car ownership costs at $300 a month. She has, in effect, set up a mini-funding program that, if nothing else, brings some sanity and stability to her car ownership costs.

Like Jessica's car, some of your funding streams have a way of automatically allocating themselves after they have met their funding goal. You might fund diligently for years to buy a small sailboat, then continue to devote that same amount after the purchase for slip rental, maintenance, insurance and possibly a boat loan.

Pam and Todd—Planning Future Funding

Not every funding project ends so neatly. If you've successfully created your first Funding Crash Analysis and Debt Planner, you may find it useful to make use of the Future Funding Planner demonstrated in Figure 24-2.

In this example, Pam and Todd, a couple with a combined net after-tax monthly income of around $4,600, divided their budget into $200 increments and described what each $200 "block" on the grid was devoted to. For instance, the first $1,400 was budgeted for expenses, the next $600 was for debt reduction, and the rest was for various funding projects. Many funding projects were not listed separately and assigned to blocks, either because they were small or because they weren't going to be changing during the period covered by the Future Funding Planner.

As you can see, blank spaces appeared when

· additional income was generated through raises (in both September and February);
· funding projects were successfully completed (Furniture in November, New Car in February).

These blank spaces represented blocks of monthly money—each approximately $200—which have become available to devote to other funding, those unfulfilled dreams from your Goals Planning Timeline. The Future Funding Planner will help Pam and Todd see what streams of income are coming available and when, so that they can assign that income to other objectives.

Future Funding Planner

	June	July	Aug	Sept	Oct	Nov	Dec	Jan	Feb	Mar
5000	n/a	n/a	n/a	n/a	n/a	n/a	n/a	n/a		
4800	n/a	n/a	n/a							
4600	Retirement	Retirement	Retirement	Retirement	Retirement	Retirement	Retirement	Retirement	Retirement	Retirement
4400	Retirement	Retirement	Retirement	Retirement	Retirement	Retirement	Retirement	Retirement	Retirement	Retirement
4200	Retirement	Retirement	Retirement	Retirement	Retirement	Retirement	Retirement	Retirement	Retirement	Retirement
4000	Vacation	Vacation	Vacation	Vacation	Vacation	Vacation	Vacation	Vacation	Vacation	Vacation
3800	Vacation	Vacation	Vacation	Vacation	Vacation	Vacation	Vacation	Vacation	Vacation	Vacation
3600	Othr Fundg	Othr Fundg	Othr Fundg	Othr Fundg	Othr Fundg	Othr Fundg	Othr Fundg	Othr Fundg	Othr Fundg	Othr Fundg
3400	Othr Fundg	Othr Fundg	Othr Fundg	Othr Fundg	Othr Fundg	Othr Fundg	Othr Fundg	Othr Fundg	Othr Fundg	Othr Fundg
3200	Othr Fundg	Othr Fundg	Othr Fundg	Othr Fundg	Othr Fundg	Othr Fundg	Othr Fundg	Othr Fundg	Othr Fundg	Othr Fundg
3000	Othr Fundg	Othr Fundg	Othr Fundg	Othr Fundg	Othr Fundg	Othr Fundg	Othr Fundg	Othr Fundg	Othr Fundg	Othr Fundg
2800	New Car	New Car	New Car	New Car	New Car	New Car	New Car	New Car		
2600	New Car	New Car	New Car	New Car	New Car	New Car	New Car	New Car		
2400	Furniture	Furniture	Furniture	Furniture	Furniture					
2200	Furniture	Furniture	Furniture	Furniture	Furniture					
2000				Debt Payments						
1800								Debt	Debt	Debt
1600								Debt	Debt	Debt
1400										
1200										
1000					Expenses					
800										
600										
400										
200										

Figure 24–2

Exercise: Future Funding Planner

1. Make a timeline similar to the one in Figure 24-2 (or see Appendix B for a blank form). The dollar amounts down the left-hand side should be arranged in such a way that:

- They are in small enough increments that they cover the smallest significant funding stream you'll want to plan for.
- The top of the sheet includes room for the highest total income you'll earn in any month covered by the timeline.
- Everything you consider changeable during the period covered by the timeline fits on the timeline.

In other words, make your increments small enough to be useful. They can be so small, in fact, that there isn't enough room to cover all your monthly income. That's okay, as long as the parts of your monthly income that don't show on the chart are fixed (like Baseline Cost of Living expenses) anyway.

2. Using your Master Budget Summary as a source of numbers, assign labels to blocks of money on the timeline to expenses at the bottom of the timeline. If expenses are budgeted to rise during the period, reflect that rise in the blocks you assign.

3. Next, assign blocks to debt reduction, using your Debt Reduction Planner. Some of the monthly debt service may stop or decrease, which may cause you to reduce the number of boxes devoted to debt reduction on some later months of your timeline.

4. Then assign blocks to various items of funding, including a funding category that includes all "other" funding that is not specifically listed on this timeline. This information will come from your Funding Crash Analysis, which will tell you how long you will be funding for each item. This will help you know how far out on your timeline to label a particular line of boxes.

5. At this point, you will have a timeline that is mostly assigned to various items of expense, debt, and various funding projects. Where you have unassigned income, you will have a blank box, and this is where you have an opportunity to plan how you want to apply that money. This is the fun part, of course. Reviving plans you previously thought threatened is a lot more fun than budget slashing.

Scribble in your plans for making use of the available funds, then go back to your Funding Crash Analysis, Debt Reduction Planner and Master Budget Summary to reflect those plans into the formal schedules.

Advanced Choice-Making—Creative Alternatives

A working couple is able to free up one parent to spend full time raising their children, all because they moved their family from their tiny little house to a larger one with a pool.

Another family gets its dream house when Dad turns the problem of providing private-school education into an opportunity.

A successful business owner and harried mother finds islands of peace and tranquility when she "buys" hours of calm for her hectic life.

Each of the people in these examples is different from the others. Perhaps none could employ any of the devices any of the others used to improve their lives.

As you read these stories of Creative Alternatives, you will most likely say, "That's wonderful for him (or her). But I could never do what they did. They had an opportunity that I don't have."

And you'd be right. Most people who employ creative alternatives are taking advantage of special—sometimes unique—opportunities in their lives. But that's part of what makes creative alternatives fun: They're uniquely yours. They represent the fact that you looked at your life and said, "What's special about me; what's special about our family?" And you took that uniqueness and made your lives better for it in some way.

Sometimes You Just Need More Money

In the foregoing paragraphs we talked about the enviable position of choosing among your temporarily postponed dreams. Suppose, though, you don't find acceptable the picture of the future painted by the exercise you just did. What if your Future Funding Planner shows that you won't be able to afford your new ski boat until you're eighty?

You may be face-to-face with a terrible reality: You don't have enough money. You are, after all, trying to reverse a trend. You're probably trying to reverse the trend of overspending and undersaving.

You have a choice. You can work through the Financial Sanity system—staying in control and postponing purchases until you can afford them. Or you can make radical changes—large or small—in your spending or earning patterns in order to speed up the attainment of your dreams.

My preferred way to balance a budget is not to reduce expenditures but to increase income. Some of us have more ability to increase our earnings than we have talent to reduce expenditures. But others have incomes that cannot be substantially increased and, for this majority, reducing expenditures is the more available way of freeing up funds.

I'm going to give you a little exercise designed to unclog your brain to come up with creative ways to decrease your expenses.

Exercise: Generating Creative Alternatives

1. Make a list of all the expenditures you have—anything you spend your money on.

2. Next to each item on the list write down at least one thing you could do to eliminate or substantially reduce that expense.

Your ideas do not have to be reasonable, moral, legal or nonfattening. They don't even have to be particularly possible. They don't have to be anything that you would ever actually *do*. We just want to get the creative juices flowing here.

For example, when you come to rent, you could say, "Well, we could move in with my mother-in-law." It might be last on the list of things that you would ever actually do, but it qualifies as a possibility that would eliminate or substantially reduce this expense.

What I'm having you look for here are opportunities to reduce expenditures, in a structural way, in favor of other goals that you consider to be more important—things like your debt reduction goals or your funding plans.

Structural Economies

The kinds of expense reduction that I like are "structural economies." They are a permanent or onetime reduction in expenditures. They only require you to make a decision to economize once. For example, if you make a decision to move from your current apartment to a smaller and cheaper apartment, you only have to agonize over that decision once, whereas if you decide to reduce your lunch expenses by $4 a day, you will have to remake that decision about twenty to twenty-five times a month. Of course, you won't succeed every day, so your actual savings will be less than the $80 or $90 you had hoped for.

But after you move into a less-expensive apartment, I can almost guarantee that you will not be tempted to send your new landlord another couple of hundred dollars one month because you lack self-discipline.

A structural change, therefore, in your spending pattern is much more effective than economizing on an expense that requires a daily or weekly decision.

Shirley and Ned Move Up and Cash Out

Shirley and Ned bought their small two-bedroom, one-bath bungalow seven years ago. Like many people, they couldn't afford to buy even their modest home today. Prices had escalated so greatly that the equity in their home looked extremely attractive to them, but they really didn't know how to get at it. They had already borrowed on a second mortgage and spent the money, but that just added now to their monthly payment burden. They couldn't sell the property to realize their gain, because they would only be forced to buy a still more expensive home in the same metropolitan market.

Shirley was eager to stop working full time and devote more time to raising and enjoying their two young children, but the burden of monthly payments was too high for that. It wasn't as if Shirley and Ned were big spenders. They were, in fact, very frugal, nursing their two old cars along well past 100,000 miles. Their budget couldn't be cut any more than it already was.

Then Shirley and Ned got their Creative Alternative idea: They would move out of the area, to a less-expensive community. They discovered that they could buy a new, larger house (with a pool) free and clear in their new town for just what they had in equity in their old. They had discovered something different and special about themselves that distinguished them from their neighbors: They didn't need to live in the town they lived in. They discovered something special about their situation, then capitalized on it.

Another Moving Experience

Jerry lives with his wife and three children in a suburban area of California. He makes a reasonably good income from his own business, but the largest part of his budget goes toward the education of his kids. Two are in private schools because Jerry doesn't think much of the public-school district he lives in. And the third is in a private-school program for the learning-disabled.

"'Learning-disabled' doesn't mean dumb," Jerry points out. "Students with learning disabilities usually need more attention because it's usually something in the communication chain that's impaired." But it was clear to Jerry that the school district he lived in couldn't handle mainstream students well, much less any student who needed extra classroom attention.

Jerry currently spends a hefty $12,000 per year on his kids' education—$6,000 for private school for two of his children and another $6,000 for special school and tutors for his oldest boy. At the same time, his house payments on a thirteen-year-old mortgage are just $550—modest by local standards.

Financial Sanity emphasizes the notion of taking what appears to be a fixed expense—tuition, in Jerry's case—and considering, at least for a moment, the possibility of reducing or doing without that expense altogether. Creative ideas, after all, come from people who are willing to say "What if . . ."

Jerry did not begrudge the burden of hefty tuition payments—after all, it was for his kids. But he was courageous enough to challenge his own belief that there was no other way to meet his responsibilities.

Jerry moved about ten miles away to one of the finest school districts in the state. Homes there are significantly more expensive than in his community, partly because of the schools, but Jerry determined that, with his kids in that district, all three of them— including his learning-disabled son—could attend public schools. Of all the excess educational costs, only $2,000 each year for tutoring remained. Jerry's children are now enjoying a first-class education, and the whole family is enjoying a beautiful new home that was previously out of their reach.

Reminding the Business About Who Works for Whom

Many a business owner starts a business for personal purposes, only to find himself spending all day doing what's best for the business. Janet, the successful owner of a small advertising agency, was just such a person.

Janet had built her award-winning agency to a staff of fourteen. She had an expensive car and a beautiful house in an exclusive suburb. Her business kept her busy and wealthy enough to have a nannie for her son and maid for the house. She was thus freed to spend virtually all her time on her business.

For years, Janet thrived on her business and her workaholic schedule. Then suddenly, seemingly out of the blue, the hectic pace no longer satisfied her. She felt burned out and frustrated. She felt as if she was the employee and her staff, gardener and son's nannie were the bosses. She resolved to make some changes.

In just over a year, Janet shrunk the size of her agency to five people. She works a lot less and makes a little less money, but her added leisure time allows her to spend time with her son and to let the nannie go. And she has precious time to just be alone with herself—time she never felt she could take before.

Janet discovered that merely getting bigger was not invariably getting better, and that it was her responsibility to creatively get her business to support her goals and aspirations—not just her wallet.

Creative Alternatives for You

Creative Alternatives involve taking advantage of the parts of you that are unique and profiting—or economizing—from them. They can be very rewarding because they not only provide more financial opportunity, but they do so in a way that expresses you and what's unique about you.

But Creative Alternatives are not available to the mentally rigid. You'll need to unclog your thinking before taking advantage of this, perhaps the most powerful financial tool available to you.

Financial Sanity

If you've applied the Financial Sanity system, you have some rare and wonderful things:

- You have tamed the financial ups and downs of your life.
- You have brought debt under your complete control.
- You have stabilized your cash flow.
- You are confident you have provided for the necessities of your life.
- You are enjoying at least some of the luxuries on your list of dreams.

Financial Sanity was designed so that you could be unique—so that you could follow your own dreams and, for the most part, do so your own way. Financial Sanity puts your life first, ahead of money.

You now can know what your aspirations are, when you will attain them and how. This alone is a tremendously enlightening accomplishment. But you have even more. You have the ability to mold and shape your own future.

Have a place for everything and keep the thing somewhere else.
This is not advice, it is merely custom.
—*Mark Twain*

Appendix A

Accounting for the Way You Live

Like the budget planning techniques in the Financial Sanity system, the personal accounting system I have developed doesn't saddle you with unnecessary bookkeeping but still accommodates the sophisticated and sometimes quite complicated financial fabric of our lives.

The first priority is to capture elusive information "from the field." Let me explain.

The basic transactions that encompass most of our financial dealings consist of the following activities, repeated over and over:

- writing checks (or making withdrawals from Automated Teller Machines)
- charging on credit cards
- depositing checks
- spending cash.

Information from each of these activities must be captured by the accounting system and then sent to an appropriate place so that it's available when you want to retrieve it. The rest of the time, your accounting system should be as small a nuisance as possible.

Let's talk about "capturing" information. Jennifer and Joey are two bright young professionals. Early in their marriage, Jennifer decides to "get on top of their finances."

"Okay," Jennifer asks Joey. "You had $120 at the beginning of the week and you have $10 now. What did you spend the $110 on?"

Jennifer's pencil is poised above her notepad while Joey drops his newspaper in his lap and calmly searches his memory. "Let's see," he finally offers. "I bought lunch every day this week—about $6 a pop, that makes $30." Joey ponders a few more seconds and says, "Yep, I think that's about it." Joey rewraps himself in the sports section and Jennifer tries to figure out what happened to the other $80 Joey had.

This is the classic failure to capture information. While Jennifer may be able to fill in some of the blanks in Joey's recollection of the week past, she might very well end her bookkeeping session with $40 in the "unaccounted-for" account.

It's a familiar problem to just about all of us, and it can lead us—sometimes properly—to decide that keeping track of some expenditures is just more work than it's worth. I will try to steer you in the direction of creating more "automatic" capturing of information, rather than merely giving you the (bad) advice to write more things down each day.

Information can be captured in a variety of ways. The old-fashioned way is to write things down in a journal. Very old-fashioned. In fact, if you're an avid reader of those exhaustive thousand-page biographies by scholastic zealots, you'll find blow-by-blow descriptions of what the ancient famous spent, ate and sent to the laundry. Witness this illuminating entry, from the well-known composer's memorandum book of 1792, as reported in Thayer's exhaustive *Life of Beethoven:*

> House-rent, 14 florins; pianoforte, 6 florins, 40 kreutzers; eating, each time 12 kreutzers; meals with wine, 16½ florins; 3 kreutzers for B. and H.; it is not necessary to give the housekeeper more than 7 florins, the rooms are so close to the ground.*

In this day and age, we still write things down as we go through the day, but mostly we tend to restrict such activity to recording the checks we write and keeping track of expenses for reimbursement by our employer. We can also capture information in the field, not by keeping a journal but by collecting little slips of paper that tell the whole story. Because it's faster (and requires less discipline) to collect slips of paper

---

*Elliot Forbes, ed., Thayer's *Life of Beethoven* (Princeton University Press, 1967), p. 135.

while on the run, I will encourage you to eliminate in-the-field journal-keeping and rely solely on doing your detailed bookkeeping at home, in an organized environment.

Duplicate Checks

One of the better inventions for keeping track of your daily financial affairs is the no-carbon-required (NCR) duplicate check, which creates a faithful, if somewhat flimsy, reproduction of every check you write. Ask for these checks at your bank. You order them just the same way you order your regular checks, although you might be offered less in the way of cute check designs.

The NCR duplicate check is especially appropriate in the credit card and Automatic Teller Machine (ATM) era in which we live. You already are (or should be) saving the credit card soft copies and the ATM slips you generate during the day; adding the burden of slipping soft copies of checks into your wallet to record later doesn't add much inconvenience.

Especially compared to its benefit: All but the most disorganized of us can safely forget about making detailed entries in our checkbook at the sales desk while nagging, impatient shoppers in line behind us intimidate us into rushing and forgetting to write in something crucial—like the amount.

Instead, we can slip our duplicate checks into our wallets, dump them into the top desk drawer at home and, about once a week or so, enter them calmly—and neatly—into our check registers. In my humble opinion, no adult should carry checks that aren't duplicate checks.

After using the information on the soft copy of your check to make an entry into your checkbook, you're still not through with this useful slip of paper. Staple the soft copy to the front of all the documentation that goes with this purchase: sales receipt, statement, invoice, guarantee, salesman's business card, brochure, etc. (I usually do this stapling right at the store so the documents don't get separated. The sales clerk who just got enough information on you to start an FBI dossier will be happy to loan you a stapler.)

The final resting place for this informative piece of tissue, together with all its appended documentation, is your Paid Bills File, which I discuss below.

One-Write Checks

Many of us, however, write very few checks "on the road." (I write practically none; I get annoyed at the time it takes to riffle through my wallet for driver's license and credit cards. It seems to take as many pieces of identification to write a $20 check at a department store as it does to cross the border of a Communist country. So I just use a credit card, and the stores seem more than happy to pay the 3 percent commission the credit card company charges.)

For those of us who write checks mostly to pay bills, there is yet another nifty invention to make our lives easier: the one-write check system. One-write checks have carbon stripes on the back, so that, as you write the check, the essential information (date, payee, amount, check number) gets transferred onto a piece of paper below the check. The paper, of course, becomes the check register, with each entry written in the checkbook exactly as it was written on the check. The checks are lined up to the paper precisely by mounting both checks and journal on a hard board with pegs down one side; hence these systems are sometimes called pegboard systems.

One-write or pegboard systems, which have been in use for decades, are very popular in small businesses whose volume of checks doesn't warrant running them on a computer.

At about $60 to start, pegboard systems aren't cheap, but for busy people they're more than worth it. If you find yourself neglecting to keep good records some of the time, the one-write concept is a must. Pegboard systems can also successfully delay your having to plunge into the world of computerized checking.

Paid Bills File

There are, perhaps, just three reasonable ways to keep your original records of transactions, along with a whole host of inventive, lazy or idiotic ways, including keeping no records at all.

What do I mean by original records of transactions? Basically, I'm talking about the bill that you paid. Whether it's called an invoice or a statement or receipt, somewhere along the line the vendor (the person or company you're paying) has usually given you some piece of paper that says you're supposed to pay. That piece of paper—the bill—is what you should have in your Paid Bills File.

In a personal system, such as the one you're building now, about the only other piece of paper that I would always want to see in the Paid Bills File is the soft voucher copy of the check you wrote. This should be stapled to the front of the bill. Other pieces of paper that might find themselves stapled behind the bill would be copies of correspondence you might have had with the vendor or other miscellaneous documents that look important enough to keep. The key element of the Paid Bills File, however, is the bill, with the check copy stapled to its front.

Now that you have your bill with the check copy stapled to the front, where do you put it? The three acceptable alternatives are

- alphabetically by vendor
- by type of expense
- by month

My strong preference is the alphabetical vendor file. Aside from being the standard most often found in business, the alphabetical vendor file allows for easy access to your history of payments with any one vendor. "I paid your bill with my check number 429 on the fifth of October" is only seconds away with a well-maintained alphabetical vendor file. Information categorized the other two ways mentioned (by date and by expense type) is readily accessible through the journals you keep. The checks you wrote in May, for instance, are easily found in your May checkbook. And all the money you spent on Gifts is easily tracked by looking at the Gifts column in each month's Check Journal, which I'll describe shortly.

Setting up an alphabetical vendor file can be as simple as buying one of those expanding-pocket envelopes with alphabetical dividers. If you write more than ten or fifteen checks a month, however, you may want separate file folders in a filing cabinet. Make one folder for each of your major vendors, then one folder for each letter of the alphabet, which can hold paid bills by vendors for whom you haven't made a separate folder. Start a new set at the beginning of each year.

When working with an alphabetical vendor file, the name that appears in your checkbook (or Check Journal, as I discuss later in this chapter) is the key to both filing and retrieving. So, for instance, if you reimbursed Jane Fairchild for opera tickets she bought on your behalf, you would file documentation under F for Fairchild, rather than under M for Metropolitan Opera.

Similarly, the lunch you charged on your Visa card at Coffee Bistro will be found not under C but stapled to your Visa statement and filed under "First Bank Visa," because that's what appears on the check that finally paid it.

Filing by type of expense is a good alternative for those people who choose not to use the Check Journal system I describe below. If, for instance, your bookkeeping is limited to filling out one of these little check registers the bank gives you, filing paid bills by expense allows you to find out how much you've paid in various categories at any time.

Filing Paid Bills by month has practically no analytical value. Its advantage lies in the fact that it doesn't really require any filing. All you have to do is keep the paid bills in a drawer and remember to sweep them into a file or envelope at the end of the month. But in terms of retrieving information, it is the least useful of the three.

The Check Journal—a Glorified Checkbook

The bookkeeping problem most of us share is that our accounting system doesn't "send" information anywhere useful so that we can retrieve it quickly when we want it. For the average American— keeping nothing more than a simple checkbook—analyzing what was spent in any particular category by repetitively leafing through a simple check register is an inefficient and inaccurate chore. That's what makes tax time such a pain for those of us who have business and personal deductions to total up at the end of the year. Our tax-deductible expenses are mixed in with all our other transactions. The same is true for any other question we might put to our financial records. In researching how much you spent on clothes last year, you are likely to become intimately familiar with not only your clothes expenditures, but *all* your expenses—every blessed one of them—while trying to locate the forty or fifty that have to do with clothes.

Without an effective journal system, what we're looking for doesn't stand out, and what we're *not* looking for won't get out of the way. With the journal system I will show you, you'll be able to retrieve information on any expense quickly and accurately.

Very simply, the accounting journal asks that you "spread" each item to one of several columns, each labeled with an expense (or income) category. Each column, consisting only of amounts spent in that category, can be added up, for a total of all spent in that category. Further, any time you want a listing of all the items spent in any category, you need only look down the column and take note of the items that appear in it. All the other items in the journal that do not appear in that column are effectively out of the way.

To start your own Check Journal, I recommend you buy long (11-by-17-inch) accounting paper with holes punched on the short side to fit, folded, into a standard three-ring binder. Put headings similar to the ones in Figure A-1, using, of course, the categories appropriate to the way you do your spending. Alternatively, all the forms mentioned in this book—including those in Appendix A—are reproduced in Appendix B, from which you may photocopy the forms you need. Figure A-1 is an example of a Check Journal.

This new journal now replaces your check register altogether. If you use a paper-based system (such as duplicate checks) to collect information from the field, you won't have to write in your checkbook every

Date	Check No.	Payee	Check Amount	(Memo) Balance	Deposit Amount	Income Accounts		Expense Accounts:			Gas		Repair		Enter-tainment
						Salary	Interest	Visa	Interest	Clothes	Honda	Fiat	Honda	Fiat	

Figure A-1

time you write a check. Instead, at home, you will write the entry in your Check Journal, "spreading" the expense to the appropriate category and creating your accounting retrieval system at the same time.

Categories

We've talked, so far, about spreading amounts in journals to various "categories." What are these categories and how do they work?

Categories (or accounts) are merely a list of ways your money can be spent or where it comes from. Categories fall into one of five types:

- Assets
- Liabilities (Debts)
- Net Worth (Equity)
- Income
- Expenses

The first three types—Assets, Liabilities and Net Worth—you will recognize from your work with Balance Sheets in Chapter 5. The second two types—Income and the ever-familiar Expenses—correspond to the inflow and outflow categories we worked with in Chapter 6. And the work you did in each of those chapters is a good place to find candidates for categories in your journals.

Everyone should have an official list of categories that can be used. (Accountants call this list the Chart of Accounts.) The list will help you avoid inconsistencies between your journals. You don't, for instance, want your Cash Journal for one month to have a category for "Utilities" and for all other months separate categories for "Water," "Garbage" and "Gas and Electric."

On the Balance Sheet side, anything that appeared on your Balance Sheet or one of its supporting schedules should be on your category list. On the Income and Expenses side, lump different expenses together only when you're not interested in the totals as separate amounts. For instance, before the 1986 Tax Act, you might very well have lumped all your interest expense of all types together in one account called "Interest Expense." Beginning in 1987, however, different kinds of interest had different degrees of deductibility. You might, beginning in that year, have separated out "Mortgage Interest" as a separate category from all other kinds of interest expense, labeled "Other Interest."

To give you a better idea of what a Category List might look like, I have reproduced for you in Figure A-2 Sam and Wendy's Category List.

Figure A-2: Sam and Wendy's Category List

Assets
Checking
Credit Union
Money Market Fund
Traveler's Checks
Savings
Stocks
Investment in Royal Arms Apartments
Residence
Honda
VW
Other Personal Assets
IRA
Company Pension Plan

Liabilities
Visa
MasterCard
American Express
Student Loan
Car Loan
Furniture Loan
Mortgage

Net Worth

Income
Sam's Salary
Wendy's Salary
Draw from Business
Interest and Dividends
Gifts from Relatives

Expenses
Home Mortgage Interest
Other Interest
Entertainment
Groceries
Utilities
Gifts

(Figure A–2: con't)

Property Taxes
Federal Income Taxes
State Income Taxes
FICA Tax
Other State Taxes
Christmas Gifts
Home Repairs
Home Improvements
Auto Repairs
Charitable Contributions
Vacation
Education

Accounting for Credit Cards—Simplified Method

There are two ways you can account for your credit card purchases. The first and simplest way is to wait until each charge appears on your bill before entering it into your accounting books. As an example, if you bought $300 worth of gifts on your credit card in December but they didn't appear on your bill until January, you would enter them as January expenses as you paid your credit card bill from your checking account.

This simplified system works only if you pay off all of your new charges on your credit card every month (which, as we saw in Chapter 11, is what I recommend you do anyway). To protect yourself against being charged for purchases that you never made (and if you don't believe this happens—and often—ask the people who check their statements every month), take the soft copies of the charges you make out of your wallet and the bottoms of shopping bags. Collect them in a box or a file or a drawer until your charge card bill comes each month. Then match up the charges on the bill with soft copies from your collection. Staple the matched copies to the bill, and put the unmatched copies back in your drawer. This system also has the advantage of letting you know how much you'll owe on your next charge card statement: Just add up the unmatched soft copies in the drawer.

Under this simplified system, when you do pay your charge card bill each month, the amount you write the check for will have to be spread to several different accounts. As an example, consider Allison's charge account statement:

Figure A-3: Credit Card Statement—Simplified System

LAST MONTH'S BALANCE	$ 892.26	
AMOUNT PAID—THANK YOU	215.88	
NEW CHARGES	436.00	
FINANCE CHARGES	15.50	*interest*
NEW BALANCE	$ 1,127.88	
MINIMUM PAYMENT DUE	$ 34.00	

DETAIL OF NEW CHARGES

ESPRIT	04-15-89	$ 53.40 ⎤	*clothes*
THE LIMITED	04-15-89	112.86 ⎬	*clothes* 186.26
DON'S DRY CLEANING	03-27-89	20.00 ⎦	*clothes*
TOWER RECORDS	04-17-89	13.24	*records*
KEPLER'S BOOKS	04-04-89	22.05	*books*
TONY'S FIAT & ALFA SVC	04-04-89	120.00	*Fiat repair*
40TH STREET CHEVRON	04-01-89	13.50	*Honda gas*
COFFEE BISTRO	04-22-89	21.44	*entertainment*
ROBIN'S NEST	04-22-89	59.51	*gifts*
TOTAL NEW CHARGES		$ 436.00	

Allison has matched up each of the charges and stapled the soft copies to the back of the statement. She has also annotated the statement, indicating which charges will go into which accounts on her chart of accounts.

As part of her debt reduction program, Allison had previously committed to paying $75 each month against this charge card balance, including interest but in addition to any new charges. In this way, she knows that she will have her entire balance paid off by a particular date that she calculated using the charts in Chapter 11.

Accordingly, Allison writes a check for $511.00:

Debt Reduction Amount	$ 75.00
New Charges	436.00
Total Payment	$ 511.00

As she writes her check, she must be ready to spread that $511.00 to the appropriate different expense accounts. She knows how much goes to each of the expense accounts, and how much goes to interest. She only needs to do this simple subtraction to determine how much will go toward debt reduction of her Visa balance:

Debt Reduction Amount	$ 75.00
Interest Portion	15.50
Debt-Reduction Portion	$ 59.50

Here's how Allison spread her check:

The simplified method will reflect all your purchases accurately, although not necessarily in the right month. You could, for instance, knowing that you were pressing your entertainment budget for the month already, charge your end-of-the-month dinner out, confident that it would appear on next month's statement and therefore in next month's budget.

Accounting for Credit Cards—Sophisticated Method

If you crave a more accurate system, you should use the sophisticated method, which the accountants among you will recognize as a standard Purchase Journal system.

The key concept involved in the sophisticated method is actually quite simple: just keep a "checkbook" for your charges, in addition to the checkbook you keep for your checks. The only difference is that the "Check Amount" column becomes the "Charge Amount." Instead of subtracting the Check Amount from your checking account balance, you will be adding the Charge Amount to your credit card balance.

The expense account headings for the various columns will be substantially similar to the ones you used for your checkbook:

The "OK" beneath the total of the Visa Charge column indicates that the totals were checked: The total of all the column totals to the right of Charge Amount equal the Charge Amount total. This indicates that every item was spread to one column or another.

There is nothing to prevent you from using just one Charge Journal for all your charge accounts. Just make one Charge Amount column for each of your credit cards.†

Whether you use the Multiple Charge Journal or a Journal for each charge card, when you pay, for example, that $511.00 to First Bank Visa, you don't spread it to the various expense accounts as you do in the Charge Journal. You've already spread them in your Charge

---

†You could combine your Check Journal and your Charge Journal all into one journal. Just take your Charge Journal, with its separate columns for each credit card, and add one more column called "Check Amount." Add columns for Check Number and, if you like, for deposits and running checkbook balance. Although this would be very efficient, it may be confusing, especially to the accounting novice.

Date	Check No.	Payee	Amount	Visa	Interest	Clothes	Gas Honda	Gas Fiat	Repair Honda	Repair Fiat	Entertainment	Records	Books	Gifts
5/2	754	STEVE'S AUTO	650.00						650.00					
5/6	755	FIRST BANK VISA	511.00	59.50	15.50	186.26	13.50			120.00	21.44	13.24	22.05	59.51
5/6	756	VIDEO EXPRESS	650.00											

Figure A–4: Spreading Charge Card Payments—Simplified System

Date	Payee	Charge Amount	Expense Accounts		Gas		Repair		Enter-tainmant	Records	Books	Gifts
			Interest	Clothes	Honda	Fiat	Honda	Fiat				
4/1	40TH ST. CHEVRON	13.50			13.50							
4/4	KEPLER'S BOOKS	22.05									22.05	
4/4	TONY'S FIAT SVC	120.00						120.00				
4/15	ESPRIT	53.40		53.40								
4/15	THE LIMITED	112.86		112.86								
4/17	TOWER RECORDS	13.24								13.24		
4/22	COFFEE BISTRO	21.44							21.44			
4/22	ROBIN'S NEST	59.51										59.51
4/27	40TH ST. CHEVRON	14.00			14.00							
4/27	MAC'S TIRE & WHEEL	124.80					124.80					
4/30	S.F. OPERA	32.00							32.00			
	FIRST BANK VISA	16.60	16.60									
		603.40	16.60	166.26	27.50	0.00	124.80	120.00	53.44	13.24	22.05	59.51
		ok										

Figure A-5: Charge Journal Format

FIGURE A-6: Multiple Charge Journal

Date	Payee	Visa Charge	Master-Card	American Express	Interest
4/1	40TH ST. CHEVRON	13.50			
4/4	KEPLER'S BOOKS	22.05			
4/4	TONY'S FIAT SVC	120.00			
4/6	AMERICAN AIRLINES			420.00	
4/6	PALM GRILL		42.58		
4/7	PRESTON'S CANDY		13.56		
4/15	ESPRIT	53.40			
4/15	THE LIMITED	112.86			
4/17	TOWER RECORDS	13.24			

Journal. Instead, when you use this sophisticated method, just spread the $511.00 to a single column in your Check Journal labeled "Visa."

Accounting for Cash Expenditures

Perhaps the easiest way to account for cash expenditures is the method I use—spend as little cash as possible and spread it all to a category called "Miscellaneous Cash Expenditures."

But many people don't want to give up spending cash. Some people don't feel they can control themselves writing checks or, especially, using credit cards. Many people I have worked with don't even carry their credit cards, or have cut them up (a radical, demonstrative move that I feel is unnecessary if you're using the Financial Sanity approach). Some people can't even trust themselves to carry their checkbooks.

If you withdraw a predetermined amount of cash each month or week, spending cash can be a very visible way to keep track of how much you've spent so far—when the cash is gone, the spending stops.

So, for those people who insist on spending significant amounts of cash, here are some suggestions for keeping up with what you're spending it on.

One method is to annotate your ATM receipts (or the duplicate copy of your check, if you write checks for cash). If you get new, fairly small infusions of cash fairly often, you might remember what you spent the last withdrawal on. Every time you go to get more cash, pull out last time's ATM receipt and write down estimates of what you spent that money on. Then, when you bring that receipt home to enter in your Check Journal, you can spread the expense to the various categories, based on what you wrote on the receipt.

Another method involves saving the receipts you get for all your cash purchases. Of course, you won't always get a receipt for every purchase, so you should carry a small notepad to make up your own receipt when none is offered. Whenever you go to the bank to get more cash, take the previous ATM receipt and all your collected receipts and drop them into a bank deposit envelope from the ATM. Then, when you get home and sit down to your accounting, the receipts will let you know how to categorize the amount you withdrew. Staple the receipts to your ATM slip before filling it in your Paid Bills File.

Of course, in both of the above methods you are likely to have money that you can't account for; that's why you'll still need a miscellaneous account, like "Unidentified Cash Expenditures," in your Category List.

The compulsive recordkeepers among you might want to keep a full-blown Cash Journal. It can be maintained just like a Check Journal, with cash withdrawals being treated like deposits and disbursements being entered and spread like checks. You may want to keep this journal not at home, with the rest of your accounting records, but in your diary, wallet or organizer—whatever you carry with you—or a portable separate notebook, so you can make entries in the field. I've seen people use the booklet-style check registers supplied by banks for this purpose, but you'll need something that allows you to spread expenses to the appropriate category columns.

If you receive cash without writing a check or visiting an ATM—if you receive tip income, for instance—you are almost bound to keep a journal to enter both the ins and the outs of your wallet.

Any time you're dealing with cash jingling around in your pocket, you're going to have to settle for a lower level of accuracy and completeness than you do elsewhere in your accounting system. Once you've understood and accepted this, whatever system you use to capture your cash transactions should be designed around your personal style, spending habits and the value of the information you're trying to collect.

If You Have Your Own Business

If you have your own small business, here are a couple of special rules that will cut away a great deal of the initial accounting confusion you might otherwise experience.

First and foremost, get a separate checking account. The separate business checking account becomes the focal point for your business accounting. It avoids the Herculean task of having to sift through a year's worth of vaguely familiar checks, receipts and charge slips, trying to figure out which were business and which personal.

Similar in concept to the separate business checking account—but not nearly so essential—is the separate business charge card. This is very popular with small business owners, and even employees on expense accounts, because it lumps all business charges in one place for easy accounting. (The charge card does not have to be in the name of your business, even if your business is a corporation. In fact, it's something of a pain to get a business credit card, whereas most people have more than enough personal charge cards in their wallet to be able to allocate one or two for business use only.)

Since you have a separate business checking account, and perhaps a separate business charge card, you will have separate business journals: a Check Journal at minimum, and perhaps a Charge Journal. And, too, you will have separate Trial Balance summaries and special reports. Businesses do tend to require more accounting than personal systems, of course.

Even though you will have a completely separate set of books for your small business, you can still keep your books the same way I suggested you keep your personal books. The reason is simple: The system I suggested you use for your personal finances is basically a standard small-business system. After years of trying different personal systems of my own design and of others, I finally had to realize that the tried-and-true systems devised to keep business books were the most efficient and reliable. If it isn't broke, don't fix it.

Conversely, I think you'll also come to recognize what I saw, quite by accident: The Financial Sanity system is ideal for the financial planning, management and control of a small business as well as personal finances.

Appendix B

Financial Sanity Blank Forms

The worksheets in this book form a comprehensive financial management system. Each of the forms works with the others to become the Financial Sanity system.

A blank form is included for virtually every exercise except those that can be completed on plain paper. The forms in this appendix may be photocopied for your personal use, preferably on a copier that enlarges. You'll want to make several copies of some of the forms in order to provide enough room for detail or because you'll be filling out several separate versions.

If you want to make just one efficient trip to the copy shop, here are suggested quantities:

    8 Goals Planning Timeline
    6 Balance Sheet
    4 Inflow-Outflow Information Sheet

3 Information Needed List
6 Spending Power Analysis
6 Debt Reduction Planner
6 Funding Tracking Ledger
6 Funding Crash Analysis
8 Long-Range Funding Recalculation Worksheet
6 Budget Monitoring Analysis
4 Master Budget Summary
18 Cash Flow Planner
3 Tax Multiplier Worksheet
3 Mortgage Affordability Worksheet for First-Time Buyers
3 Mortgage Affordability Worksheet for Second-Time Buyers
3 Monthly Payment Required to Fund Down Payment in Inflationary Real Estate Market
3 Calculation of Retirement Income Requirement
3 Capitalization of Monthly Retirement Income Requirement
3 Retirement Planning Alternatives Worksheet
6 Wealth-Building Tracker
4 Future Funding Planner

I advise you to put the work you've done in a three-ring binder that will become your permanent Financial Sanity workbook. When completed, your workbook will be a self-contained planning and analysis unit and have the following components, each of which might be separated by tabbed dividers in your binder:

Information Needed List (Chapter 6)
Inflow-Outflow Information Sheet (Chapter 6)
Goals Planning Timeline (Chapter 3)
Balance Sheet(s) (Chapter 5)
 · Supporting Schedules
Spending Power Analysis (including forward projections) (Chapter 7)
Debt Reduction Planner (Chapter 10)
Funding Crash Analysis (Chapter 17)
 · Major Purchases List (Chapter 14)
 · Unscheduled Contingencies List (Chapter 16)
 · Annual Control Expenditures List (Chapter 15)
Funding Tracking Ledger (Chapter 13)
Master Budget Summary (Chapter 20)
Wealth-Building Tracker (Chapter 24)
Yellow-Pad Mini-Budgets (Chapter 21)

You may want to include a final section for miscellaneous information.

The accounting system described in Appendix A can also be housed neatly in a binder, either separately or combined with the Financial Sanity planning binder. Its components include:

Check Journal (Appendix A)
Charge Journal (Appendix A)

or merely the combined journal for checks and charges (Appendix A).

Combining all your Financial Sanity exercises makes for an incredibly portable planning tool. Once you have completed the Inflow-Outflow Information Sheet, you can simply take your workbook to the beach and do your financial planning there.

Goals Planning Timeline

Preparation
Date [ ]

Period Covered [ ] through [ ]

(Label boxes below with time periods to be covered, e.g., months, quarters, years, etc.)

(For each line item, enter the expected dollar amount, if known, or "X" if unknown)

Goal

(List events, income and expenditures)

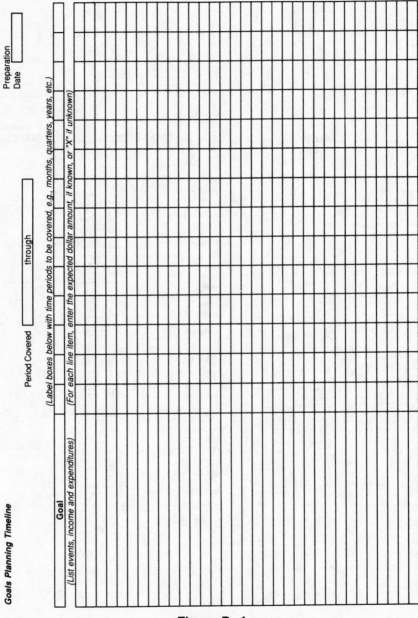

Figure B–1

Balance Sheet

As of (Date): [   ]

Assets	**Liabilities & Net Worth**	**Net Worth Analysis**

Assets

Ref.

Short-Term:

Cash [   ] $[   ]

Other Liquid Assets [   ] [   ]

Total Short-Term Assets [   ]

Longer-Term:

Investments [   ] [   ]

Personal Residence [   ] [   ]

Personal Assets [   ] [   ]

Retirement Funds [   ] [   ]

Total All Assets $[   ]
========

Liabilities & Net Worth

Ref.

Short-Term:

Credit Card Debt [   ] $[   ]

Lines of Credit [   ] [   ]

Tax Liability [   ] [   ]

Other Debts [   ] [   ]

Total Short-Term Liabilities [   ]

Longer-Term:

Term Loans [   ] [   ]

Mortgage(s) [   ] [   ]

Other Debts [   ] [   ]

Total All Liabilities [   ]

Net Worth (Assets minus Total Liabilities) [   ]

Total Liabilities Plus Net Worth (Must equal Total Assets) $[   ]
========

Net Worth Analysis

Short-Term Net Worth [   ]

Long-Term Net Worth [   ]

= $[   ]
========
Net Worth

Figure B-2

Inflow-Outflow Analysis

Description	Code	Amount	Frequency	Nonmonthly When Next Payment Falls Due	Debt Repayments		
					Debt Owed	Interest Rate	Minimum Payment

Figure B-3

Information Needed List

	Information Needed	Source(s)	Answer

Figure B–4

Spending Power Analysis

Major Events During Period ☐

	Balance Sheet			**Difference**
	Earlier Date	Later Date	√	Period Covered
	/ /	/ /		___ mos.

ASSETS

Short-Term

Cash ☐ ☐ ☐ + ___

Other Liquid Assets ☐ ☐ + ___

Longer-Term

Investments ☐ ☐ ☐ + ___

Personal Residence ☐ ☐ + ___

Personal Assets ☐ ☐ + ___

Retirement Funds ☐ ☐ + ___

Total Assets ☐ ☐

LIABILITIES

Short-Term

Credit Card Debt ☐ ☐ ☐ − ___

Lines of Credit ☐ ☐ − ___

Tax Liabilities ☐ ☐ − ___

Other Debts ☐ ☐ − ___

Longer-Term

Term Loans ☐ ☐ ☐ − ___

Mortgage(s) ☐ ☐ − ___

Other Debts ☐ ☐ − ___

Total Liabilities ☐ ☐

NET WORTH ☐ ☐

Extraordinary Expenditures/Adjustments

Normal New Personal Assets + ___

+ ___

+ ___

+ ___

Spending Power for This Period ☐

Adjustments to Calculate Spending Power for Next Period

+ ___

+ ___

+ ___

+ ___

Projected Spending Power for Next Period ☐

Monthly* Spending Power for Next Period ☐

(* Divide Spending Power by number of months in period covered.)

Figure B–5

Debt Reduction Planner

Month: [   ]   [   ]

		Planned	Actual	Difference	Planned	Actual	Difference
Debt:	Balance Forward						
[ ]	Interest						
Interest Rate:	Payment						
Annual: __%	New Charges						
Monthly: __%	New Balance						
Min.Pmt.: $	Principal Reduction						
Debt:	Balance Forward						
[ ]	Interest						
Interest Rate:	Payment						
Annual: __%	New Charges						
Monthly: __%	New Balance						
Min.Pmt.: $	Principal Reduction						
Debt:	Balance Forward						
[ ]	Interest						
Interest Rate:	Payment						
Annual: __%	New Charges						
Monthly: __%	New Balance						
Min.Pmt.: $	Principal Reduction						
Debt:	Balance Forward						
[ ]	Interest						
Interest Rate:	Payment						
Annual: __%	New Charges						
Monthly: __%	New Balance						
Min.Pmt.: $	Principal Reduction						
Debt:	Balance Forward						
[ ]	Interest						
Interest Rate:	Payment						
Annual: __%	New Charges						
Monthly: __%	New Balance						
Min.Pmt.: $	Principal Reduction						
	Balance Forward						
Total — All Debts	Interest						
	Payment						
	New Charges						
	New Balance						
	Principal Reduction						

Figure B-6

Planned	Actual	Difference	Planned	Actual	Difference	Planned	Actual	Difference

Funding Tracking Ledger

Month	Fund					
Fund						

Balance Forward					
Allocation					
Expenditure					
Adjustments +/-					
New Balance					

Balance Forward					
Allocation					
Expenditure					
Adjustments +/-					
New Balance					

Balance Forward					
Allocation					
Expenditure					
Adjustments +/-					
New Balance					

Balance Forward					
Allocation					
Expenditure					
Adjustments +/-					
New Balance					

Balance Forward					
Allocation					
Expenditure					
Adjustments +/-					
New Balance					

Balance Forward					
Allocation					
Expenditure					
Adjustments +/-					
New Balance					

Total - All Funds					
Balance Forward					
Allocation					
Expenditure					
Adjustments +/-					
New Balance					

Figure B-7

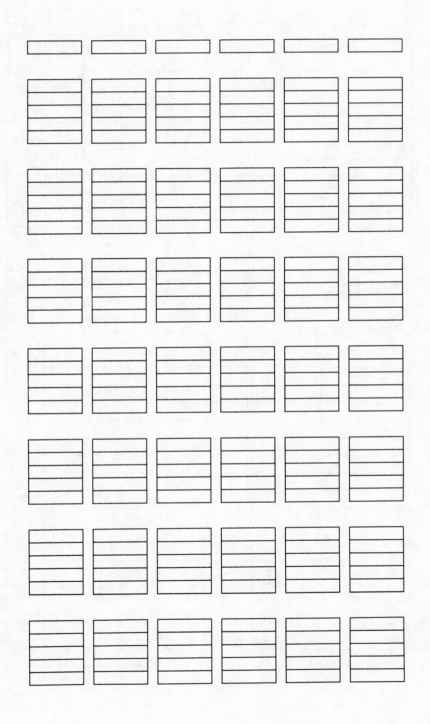

Funding Crash Analysis

Description	Monthly Allocation	Timeline Mos.	Timeline Total	Funding To Date				
Total Allocation — Timeline Expenditures					A			
Cumulative Timeline Expenditures (Add Total from Line A to Prior Month's Line B.)					B			

Description Control & Contingency	Monthly Allocation	Period Mos.	Period Total	Funding To Date	Period Description

Control & Contingency Monthly Allocation		Cumulative Allocation — Avg. Control & Contingency	C	1	2	3	4
Monthly Allocation — All Expenditures		Cum. Allocation — All Exps. Plus Total Funding To Date	D				
First Degree Funding Surplus/(Shortfall) (Subtract Line B from Line D) Total Funding To Date »»»			E				
Second Degree Funding Surplus/(Shortfall) (Subtract Line C from Line E)			F				

Figure B-8

Timeline

5	6	7	8	9	10	11	12	13	14	15

Long-Range Funding Recalculation Worksheet

Description of Funding Objective

Estimated (or earliest) anticipated date of expenditure (Month-Year)

Current Date (Month-Year)	Currrent Cost	Funded to Date	Needed to Fund	Time Left to Fund	Real Rate	Table Payment	New Monthly Allocation
-				mos.	%		
-				mos.	%		
-				mos.	%		
-				mos.	%		
-				mos.	%		
-				mos.	%		
-				mos.	%		
-				mos.	%		
-				mos.	%		
-				mos.	%		
-				mos.	%		
-				mos.	%		
-				mos.	%		
-				mos.	%		
-				mos.	%		
-				mos.	%		
-				mos.	%		
-				mos.	%		

Figure B-9

Budget Monitoring Analysis

		Month	Budget	Actual	Difference	Budget	Actual	Difference

Income

Total Income

Fixed & Variable Expenses

Total Fixed & Variable Expenses

Better Than / <Worse Than> Budget

Figure B-10

Budget Monitoring Analysis

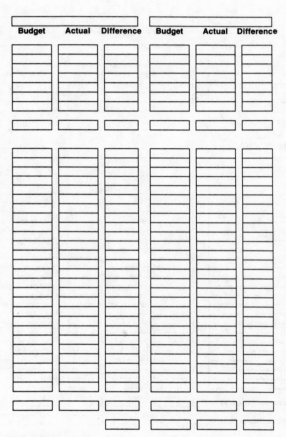

Figure B–11

Master Budget Summary

Month

Income
(Total from Budget Monitoring Analysis) +

Funding
(Monthly Allocation — All Expenditures from Funding Crash Analysis) −

Debt
(Payment for Total — All Debts from Debt Reduction Planner) −

Fixed & Variable Expenses
(Total from Budget Monitoring Analysis) −

Budgeted Increase/<Decrease> in Checking Account Balance =

Figure B–12

Cash Flow Planner

Cash Flow Budget   *Month of* [   ]

Checking Account Balance at Beginning   + [   ]

Budgeted Increase/<Decrease> in Checking Account Balance
(From Master Budget Summary)   + [   ]

Projected Ending Checking Account Balance   = [   ]
                                                           ========

Actual Cash Flow Summary

Projected Ending Checking Account Balance   + [   ]

Better Than / <Worse Than> Budget
(From Master Budget Summary)   + [   ]

Funding:
Budgeted Monthly Funding Allocation
(From Funding Crash Analysis)   + [   ]
Direct Spending
(From Funding Tracking Ledger)   - [   ]
Due To / <Due From> Funding Account   ----------------
(This amount should be deposited in the Funding Account.) +/- [   ]

Deposits Actually Made to Funding Account   - [   ]

Withdrawals from Funding Account   + [   ]

Debt Reduction:
Purchases Charged to Credit Cards   + [   ]
Payments:
Payments Budgeted
(From Debt Reduction Planner)   + [   ]
Payments Made
(From Debt Reduction Planner)   - [   ]

                                                       +/- [   ]

Checking Account Balance at End   = [   ]
                                                           ========

Figure B–13

Tax Multiplier Worksheet

Tax Bracket

| Gross Income | | Tax Rates | | Combined Tax |
Single	Married	Federal	2/3 of State	Bracket
up to $20,000	$35,000	15% +	% =	%
up to $45,000	$80,000	28% +	% =	%
over $45,000	$80,000	33% +	% =	%

Tax Multiplier

	+ 100 %	100 %
Combined Tax Bracket (from above)	−	%
After-Tax Net on Gross Income	= % ÷	%
Tax Multiplier		1.

Figure B–14

Mortgage Affordability Worksheet — for First-Time Buyers

Sources of Funds:

Monthly Rent
Monthly Amount You Currently Spend on Rent   + [＿＿＿＿]

Other Housing Costs
Include Any Associated Costs, Such as Garage Rental   + [＿＿＿＿]

Monthly Savings
How Much You've Been Able to Save Each Month
  That You Can Apply to Monthly Housing Costs
  (Do not include savings that you intend to continue
  setting aside for other purposes.)   + [＿＿＿＿]

Avoided Costs
Any Monthly Costs You Will No Longer Incur as a Result of Moving
  (An example might be a net reduction in commuting costs.)   + [＿＿＿＿]

Other Available Funds
(This might include income from a rental unit on the purchased property
  or any expected funds inflow as a result of the move.)   + [＿＿＿＿]

Total available cash   = [＿＿＿＿] +

Nondeductible Costs:
                                        New   Old
Insurance   + [＿＿＿] − [＿＿＿] = [＿＿＿] +

Utilities   + [＿＿＿] − [＿＿＿] = [＿＿＿] +

Other Increased Costs
(Include increased commuting costs,
  gardening, cable TV, etc.)   + [＿＿＿] − [＿＿＿] = [＿＿＿ ₃] +

Total Nondeductible Increased Costs   = [＿＿＿＿] −

Net Available for Mortgage and Taxes   [＿＿＿＿] =

Tax Multiplier   *(From Tax Multiplier Worksheet)*   [1•] ×

Maximum Justifiable Monthly Payment for Mortgage and Taxes   [＿＿＿＿] =
                                                                  =========

Figure B–15

Mortgage Affordability Worksheet — for Second-Time Buyers

Tax-Deductible Expenses:

	New	Old	
Monthly Mortgage Payment	+ [____]	- [____]	= [____] +

Annual Property Taxes
Monthly Property Taxes   + [____] - [____] = [____]
÷ 12 = [____] +

Add Any Additonal Monthly Tax-Deductible Expenses   [____] +

Subtract Any Decreases in Monthly Tax-Deductible Expenses   [____] -

Net Increase in Tax Deductible Extra Monthly Costs   [____] =

Combined (Federal and State) Tax Bracket   100%   x
(From Tax Multiplier Worksheet)   - [____] % = [____] %

Net Increase in Monthly Costs Converted to After-Tax Dollars   [____] +

Nondeductible Expenses:

Change in   New   Old
Annual Insurance Premiums   + [____] - [____] [____]
÷ 12 = [____] +

Change in
Other Annual Nondeductible Costs   + [____] - [____] = [____]
÷ 12 = [____] +

Change in Utilities (Monthly Average) + [____] - [____] = [____] +

Change in Other Monthly Nondeductible Costs
(including Homeowner Association   + [____] - [____] = [____] +
  Dues and Condominium Fees)

All Other Nondeductible Additional Monthly Expenses   [____] +

Less Any Decrease in Nondeductible Monthly Expenses   [____] -

Extra Money Needed per Month   + [____] =

Sources:
Monthly Savings Available to Be Applied to Housing Costs   + [____]

Monthly Funding Allocations Available to Be Converted to Housing Cos + [____]

Voluntary Budget Changes to Accommodate Increased Housing Costs + [____]

Total Planned Sources of Extra Money for Increased Housing Costs - [____]

Shortfall / <Excess> of Funds Available   = [____]

Figure B–16

Monthly Payment Required to Fund Down Payment
in Inflationary Real Estate Market

Current Purchase Price of Desired House $ _____

Down Payment Percentage for Conventional Loan *(usually 20%)*   + ____ %
Typical Closing Costs in Your Area   *(Use 3-5% if you don't know.)*   + ____ %
                                                                              x
Percentage of Purchase Price Needed in Up-Front Cash   ____ %

Total Down Payment Requirement for Conventional Mortgage   + $ _____

If Some Funding Money Has Already Been Accumulated:

Less Amount Funded to Date $ _____   - $ _____
Estimated Annual:
    Appreciation Rate of Housing   + ____ %
    Less Interest Rate on Invested Funds - ____ %   x
                                           = ____ %

Annual Inflation Differential $ _____
                                                    ÷ 12

Monthly Funding to Make up for Inflation Differential $ _____

Amount Needed to Fund for Down Payment   = $ _____
                                                       ÷ $1,000

                                                         $ _____
                                                              x
Multiplier   *(from table below)*   _____

                                                       + $ _____

Monthly Funding to Make up for Inflation Differential   *(from Above)*   + $ _____

Monthly Funding Required to Reach Down Payment Goal   = $ _____
(Note: Unlike regular long-range funding calculations,
this amount should be increased annually to reflect normal inflation.)

Monthly Payment Required to Accumulate a $1,000 Down Payment
(in Current Dollars)   **in a Highly Inflationary Real Estate Market**

		Time To Build up Down Payment			
		2 Years	3 Years	4 Years	5 Years
Expected	10 %	44.18	29.69	22.44	18.09
Rate of					
Appreciation	15 %	48.13	33.81	26.71	22.51
in Cost					
of House	20 %	52.25	38.29	31.57	27.77

Figure B–17

Calculation of Retirement Income Requirement

Current Monthly Income   *(after withholding)*   + ☐

Subtract:
   Eliminated Funding
   Items currently being funded that won't need to be funded after retirement

Income Taxes	*(Taxes after retirement will be added in below.)*
Retirement Funding	

                          Total Eliminated Funding   - ☐

   Eliminated Expenses

Commuting	
Mortgage Payments	*(if your house will be paid off by then)*

                          Total Eliminated Expenses   - ☐

Add:
   New Funding

Travel	
Sports/Leisure	
Medical	

                          Total New Funding   + ☐

   New Monthly Expenses

Medical Insurance	*(increase over current costs paid by you)*
(Use today's rates for a person of your planned age of retirement.)	
Rent	*(if selling residence)*

                          Total New Monthly Expenses   + ☐

Total Monthly After-Tax Requirement   = ☐

Tax Factor *(Use Tax Multiplier Worksheet.)*   x ☐

Monthly Pretax Income Requirement   ☐

Figure B–18

Capitalization of Monthly Retirement Income Requirement

Monthly Pretax Income Requirement   *(from Calculation of Retirement Income Requirement)*   + ☐

Less:
  Anticipated Other Sources of Income

Social Security	*(if you are comfortable relying on its availability)*	

                                                      Total Other Income   - ☐

Monthly Income to be Generated by Retirement Funds

Capitalization Factor:

If you expect to earn investment returns of this:	*Multiply your monthly requirement by this:*
4%	300
6%	200
8%	150
10%	120
15%	80

                                                                              x ☐

Lump Sum Needed to Generate Retirement Income   ☐

Add:
  One-time Costs Associated with Retiring

Moving		
Pay Off Mortgage	*(This is an analytical shortcut. For a more accurate answer, leave this box blank and complete the Retirement Planning Alternatives Worksheet.)*	

                                                      Total One-Time Costs   + ☐

Subtract:
  Assets Already Devoted to Retirement

Current value of tax-advantaged retirement plans   ☐
Less taxes on withdrawal   ☐

Current value of non-tax-advantaged retirement assets		
Home	*(Count only if home is to be sold. Use current value less selling costs. Make sure mortgage is paid off. Use Retirement Planning Alternatives Worksheet.)*	

                                                      Total Other Assets   ☐

Total Retirement Funding Target in Current Dollars $ ☐
(Fund with rest of long-range funding or use Retirement Planning Alternatives Worksheet.)

Figure B–19

Retirement Planning Alternatives Worksheet

	Plan A	Plan B	Plan C
Years Until Retirement			

Mortgage Payoff Funding:

Original Life of Mortgage in Months

Age of Mortgage Right Now (in Months)   −

Remaining Life of Mortgage (in Months)   =

Months Until Retirement   −
(Multiply Years Until Retirement from Above Times 12 Months)

Remaining Life of Mortgage at Retirement   =

Monthly Mortgage Payment   Interest Rate on Loan [ ] %   + %   + %   + %

Payment as % of Debt
from Long-Term Payoff Planning and Prediction Table (Fig. 11-2)
or Short-Term Payoff Planning and Prediction Table (Fig. 11-1)

Mortgage Balance at Time of Retirement   =   ×   ×   ×

Payment Required to Fund $1,000*   ÷ 1,000   ÷ 1,000   ÷ 1,000
from Long-Range Funding Table (Fig. 19-2)
for the number of Months Until Retirement
Interest Rate (not Real Interest) Used*   [ ] % =

Retirement Funding:

Total Retirement Funding Target in Current Dollars
from Capitalization of Monthly Retirement Income Requirement

×   ×   ×

Payment Required to Fund $1,000   ÷ 1,000   ÷ 1,000   ÷ 1,000
from Long-Range Funding Table (Fig. 19-2)
for the number of Months Until Retirement
Real Interest Rate Used   [ ] % =

Total Both Retirement and
Mortgage Payoff Funding Requirements

* *Use nominal (stated) interest rates, rather than real interest rates. Unlike other long-term funding targets, the amount you now estimate to be due on your mortgage at retirement will not change. It will not go up with inflation.*

Figure B–20

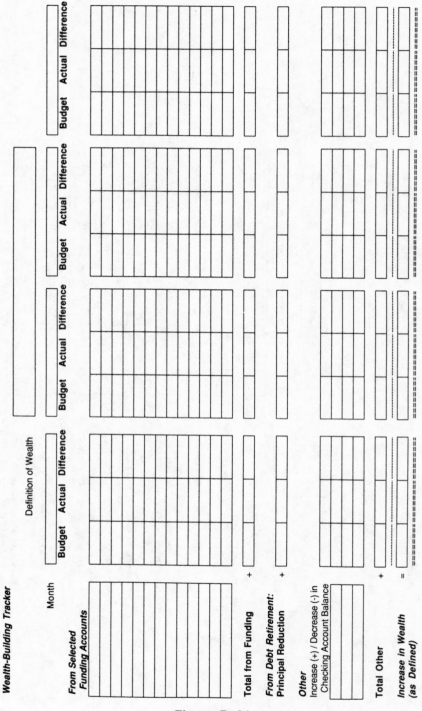

Figure B-21

Budget   Actual   Difference

Budget   Actual   Difference

Budget   Actual   Difference

Budget   Actual   Difference

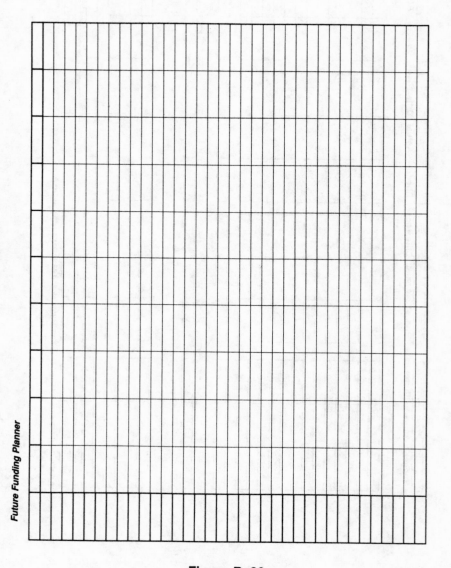

Future Funding Planner

Figure B–22

Charge Journal

Date	Payee	Charge Amount		Expense Accounts	*Interest*									

Figure B–23

Check Journal

Date	Check No.	Payee	Check Amount	(Memo) Balance	Deposit Amount	Income Accounts		

Figure B-24

Expense Accounts

Expense Accounts

Multiple Charge Account Journal

Date	Payee	Charge Amount	Charge Accounts			

Figure B–25

Expense Accounts									
Interest									

Index